THE PEN Y GWRYD HOTEL
TALES FROM THE SMOKE ROOM

THE PEN Y GWRYD HOTEL
TALES FROM THE SMOKE ROOM

With an introduction by
Jan Morris

Compiled and edited by Rob Goodfellow, Jonathan Copeland and Peter O'Neill

Gomer

Published in 2016 by
Gomer Press, Llandysul, Ceredigion, SA44 4JL

ISBN 978 1 78562 149 9

A CIP record for this title is available from the British Library.
© Copyright Robert Goodfellow, Jonathan Copeland, Peter O'Neill and
Gomer Press 2016

This book is published with the financial support of the
Welsh Books Council.

Printed and bound in Wales at
Gomer Press, Llandysul, Ceredigion

For Dorothy, Bessie (Bess) and Joyce (Jo).

And for Paul Newby.

CONTENTS

page

Rupert Pullee   xi
Acknowledgements

Jan Morris   xv
Introduction

Geoffrey Pocock   1
Walks from the Pen y Gwryd Hotel

Neeraj Rana   5
World mountaineering's 'holy grail'

Chris Bonington   7
PyG – long may it never change

Rosemary Hocking   9
Keep on a path

Desmond Hall   12
A barman's tale

Michael Ward   16
There was an aura

John Blackmore   19
The hotel on the corner

Ken Jones   22
Blodwen of Pen y Gwryd

Kay Mitchell   26
Going to extremes to understand critical illness – Xtreme Everest

Peter Hillary   29
You will just have to read Ed's book

Katharine Anne Lerman   31
Peter Spencer Coppock – the man behind the camera

Ffion White   35
Climbers, walkers and …

Tony Astill   37
'Grandly present are their memories still'

Rebecca Stephens   41
And there we stayed

page

Paul Newby   44
Throne of the Gods

Eliza Winkler   50
A lace-trimmed apron and a feather duster

Rosie Lloyd   53
Arthur Lockwood and the Pen y Gwryd

Neil Robertson   58
The Pen y Gwryd Hotel – functional antiquity

Jim Perrin   60
PyG – Reflections from Raggedass Road

Betty Humphreys   64
The Pen y Gwryd Hotel – girls and boys and bicycles

Alice Burton   67
The Snowdon Club

Joe Brown   69
'I'll phone Joe Brown, he'll know what to do'

Anna Lawford   73
The Alpine Club and the Pen y Gwryd Hotel

Dane Tobias   77
PyG … Rick Stein … Jamie Oliver

Rob Collister   80
Pen y Gwryd memories

Ed Webster   85
Chasing after giants

Elaine Travis   89
Wartime Pen y Gwryd

William 'Bill' Roache   93
Where great memories are always present

Caradoc 'Crag' Jones   95
'Hats *orff* in the house!'

Ben Reedy   98
Wetter inside than out

page

Doug Scott 102
The PyG, undeniably the centre of British climbing life

John Neill 105
In memory of Chris Briggs

Ann Verity 108
Pen y Gwryd days

Mike Dent 111
The Rucksack Club – *Concerning inns*

Andy Harbach 116
Walking Snowdonia

Chuck Evans 119
'Whatever Mr Briggs says is true'

Joseph Blackburn 121
Pen y Gwryd recollections

John Disley 125
In memory of Jo Briggs

Chris Warren 128
All you need is love, love … and a television set

David Matthews 130
PyG anecdotes

Nick Longland 133
A Longland family affair

Nicola Maysmor 136
The PyG has … gone to the dogs

Harvey Lloyd 138
The PyG site – from Legio XX Valeria Victrix to the Luftwaffe

Harvey Lloyd 144
Dipping into the *Locked Book*, 1884–1953

H.P.S. Ahluwalia 150
Reach higher and seek the strength within

Gwyn Berry 154
People are talking

Gordon Lindsay Jones 156
The Welsh 3000s challenge

Norbu Tenzing Norgay 162
Flying in to the PyG

page

Margaret Clennett 164
Reminiscences of a PyG maid – a fictional account of the
founding of the Pinnacle Club in 1921

Chris Lloyd 169
'Put up a flare … the people will come from the mountains'

Hugh Brasher 172
Chris Brasher

Paul Carling 174
The man upon the stair

Miryam MacPherson 177
The PyG-Andalusian sherry connection

Piers J. Hale 181
Charles Kingsley and the Pen y Gwryd

Julian Freeman-Attwood 191
Remember to take abseil gear to the bedroom

Christine Birch 194
The Everest Room

Ken Smith 240
The smallest churches in Snowdonia

Michael Smith 243
The Yorkshire Ramblers' Club and the Pen y Gwryd

Jim Milledge 248
Moulam's rules

Mike Conlon 252
On conducting essential mountaineering background research

Emily Pitts 256
The PyG – a home for *all* climbers

About the Compilers and Editors 259

To Bob
with best
wishes

Rupert Pullee

ACKNOWLEDGEMENTS

EVERY BOOK has a beginning – the point at which the seed of an idea was planted. It was in 2010 during the bicentennial celebrations of the founding of the Pen y Gwryd, or 'PyG', that Rob Goodfellow, Jonathan Copeland and Peter O'Neill suggested that we begin to compile stories about the hotel. Of course, we had Vernon Hall's *A Scrapbook of Snowdonia* (1982) to guide us. (The work is still available through Amazon Books UK.)

It bears a special mention that the very first contributor to *The Pen y Gwryd Hotel: Tales from the Smoke Room,* in the form of a wonderful introduction, is also an author (of many books), none other than the distinguished travel writer and *The Times* embedded journalist accompanying the 1953 British Everest Expedition, Jan Morris.

The curious thing about the hotel – 'A venerable, modest and celebrated inn' – as Jan Morris so eloquently describes it, is that the premises are not nearly as important as its remarkable patrons. And so, this book is not about the hotel as much as it is about everything around (and inside) the Gwryd, stories about people, their observations and adventures, achievements and celebrations.

Following Jan's introduction, you will discover that the opening contribution is by Geoffrey Pocock, the author of *Walks from the Pen y Gwryd Hotel* (2009). Geoffrey is one of many people (too long to list here) who watered the seed planted in 2010, some 200 years after the founding of the original remote mountain farmhouse (soon to be coach house) at the headwaters of a small river, both affectionately known as 'the Gwryd'.

At this point, I want to thank Paul Newby for his extraordinary editorial assistance – a true labour of love, Harvey Lloyd for sharing his research on both the history of the PyG site and the hotel's *Locked Book* archive and Tony Astill for his many invaluable suggestions (as well as for his unrivalled contribution to the art and literature of the mountains and mountaineering.)

In particular, I want to thank Ken Jones for his scrutiny of Welsh-language words, place names and terms, as well as his generosity in sharing his considerable local knowledge, network of friends and professional contacts. *Diolch o galon am bob cymorth.*

For the design of the Everest Room ceiling signatures key, I want to acknowledge Terrease McComb from the New Zealand-based creative firm Ginger Milkshake. For assistance on individual contributor portraits I wish to also acknowledge Isaac Smith of Melbourne-based Isaac Smith Design.

Significantly, this book has received pleasing support from many of Britain's most illustrious climbing and walking clubs, and this is reflected in the contributors you will soon encounter: Anna Lawford, the Honorary Secretary of the Alpine Club; Michael Smith, the past-President of the Yorkshire Ramblers' Club; Margaret Clennett, the Pinnacle Club's former Honorary Secretary and President, and current Club Archivist; Mike Dent, the Rucksack Club's former Secretary and Vice President and current Archivist; and Emily Pitts, Founder and Editor in Chief, of Womenclimb UK. This depth of interest in the PyG was gratefully recognised and supported by Ceri Wyn Jones of Gomer Press, Wales's largest independent publisher and, for that, I make a special mention of thanks.

My brother Nicolas and I now manage the Pen y Gwryd Hotel, the third generation of family proprietors after my grandparents, Chris and Jo Briggs, and my parents, Brian and Jane Pullee, and it is to them that I extend my final and most heartfelt gratitude.

Rupert Pullee is the co-proprietor of the Pen y Gwryd Hotel – one of the most famous hotels in the world and 'The Home of British Mountaineering'. Before going into 'the family businesses' he studied hotel management in Manchester and worked and travelled in the United States, Australia and Indonesia.

www.pyg.co.uk

Jan Morris

INTRODUCTION

A⊤ 53°05'N, 4°00'W, in the mountainous north west of Wales, there stands a venerable, modest and celebrated inn called Pen y Gwryd – or PyG in the vernacular. The Welsh name signifies that the building stands at the headwaters of the little river Gwryd and it is also close to the junction of the two main roads around Snowdon, the highest mountain in Wales, higher also than any mountain in England, and an immemorial site of legend and adventure.

In the first century AD, the Romans recognised the strategic importance of this isolated place and established a marching camp close by. In the 20th century, the British Army built fortified strong-points there (in case the Germans invaded Britain from the west). The Roman camp has long vanished, the Royal Artillery's abandoned pill-boxes remain and the inn, among its cluster of outbuildings, now has rather an oasis air – alone among the bare mountains, while the traffic of the 21st century intermittently passes by, sparse in winter, sometimes overwhelming in the tourist season.

In another sense, though, the location is still strategic. When the Pen y Gwryd was founded, in 1810, it was doubtless a consoling halt for travellers and their horses reaching this haven out of such dauntingly lonely landscapes. Over the generations, its presence in the very lee of Snowdon has made it not just a tourist destination, but above all a kind of base camp for mountaineers, a comfortable, club-like establishment impregnated with the values and traditions of Alpinism. Plenty of non-climbers stay there too: but when they arrive at the Pen y Gwryd Hotel with its logo of crossed ice axes they must very soon realise that they are entering one of the great climbers' inns of Europe.

The style of PyG is staunchly idiosyncratic, a homely jumble of rooms and corridors. It is characterised in many visitors' minds by one marvellous Victorian bathroom, a prodigy of enamels and brass piping, and it is lovingly maintained by the family proprietors – themselves inspired by their forebear – the legendary hotelier Chris Briggs, who was not only a stalwart of the Snowdon Mountain Rescue team but also High Sheriff of the County of Caernarfonshire.

Generations of mountaineers have contributed to the ambience, coming to Pen y Gwryd not only to climb the neighbouring heights, but to celebrate anniversaries, birthdays, friendships, first ascents or heroic failures; it was here that the idea of the egalitarian Climbers' Club, now one of the most influential of sporting institutions, was hatched in December 1897. Hardly a well-known British climber of our time and hardly a famous foreign Alpinist either, has not checked in at one time or another over the bar counter of PyG (there being nothing as formal as a reception desk).

Those champions are inescapable still, because the PyG is full of their mementoes, old and new, all over the place. There are ropes and climbing boots and oxygen containers and crampons and commemorative mugs. There are smilingly posed groups of celebrants. Here is a photograph, identified as '1897', taken, we are told, 'When the Abraham brothers were secretly planning their attempt on Lliwedd's Slanting Gully'; King George VI of England and his Queen Elizabeth survey the plans for the future Snowdonia National Park from the Pen y Gwryd, July 1947; and here a triumphant group of adventurers home from their first ascent of Kangchenjunga in 1955; and above the fireplace, Chris Briggs the High Sheriff innkeeper looks benignly down at his guests in full regalia.

It is not at all a mausoleum. It feels as though all those worthies up there are still around, still sharing with us their high memories and their pleasures. Some still are, of course, some have only recently said goodbye to the inn, and, in particular, Pen y Gwryd is frequented by the shades of the climbers who first reached the ultimate peak, the highest place on the earth's surface, in 1953.

Mount Everest has been climbed a thousand times since then, but in history that first ascent must always remain a mountaineering climax. For PyG it was a sort of climax too, because it was there that the members of the successful expedition trained themselves for the adventure. Grandly present are their memories still. There on these walls are the heroes in their prime – John Hunt the stalwart British leader, cheerful Ed Hillary the New Zealander, Tenzing Norgay the Sherpa of Sherpas – and here too we see them and their colleagues ageing and greying at their annual merry reunions in the hotel.

One by one they have left us now but, like a thousand other climbers, they live on here, and year by year visitors from around the world try to decipher their fading signatures on the bar-room ceiling and, perhaps, sense something of their happiness in this place. Everest 1953 was only one great moment in the history of Pen y Gwryd; but I suspect that for generations to come people will still respond from the heart to a little piece of rock that stands above the fireplace in PyG's 'Smoke Room'. It is a fragment from the very summit of Everest, picked up on 29 May, 1953, the day mankind first stood there, and presented to the PyG itself by Sir Edmund Hillary, Knight of the Garter, (1919-2008), 'In memory of a long friendship'.

Jan Morris is a Fellow of the Royal Society of Literature and the author of some 40 books of history, travel, biography, memoir and fiction, and was the only newspaper correspondent embedded with the successful 1953 British Everest Expedition.

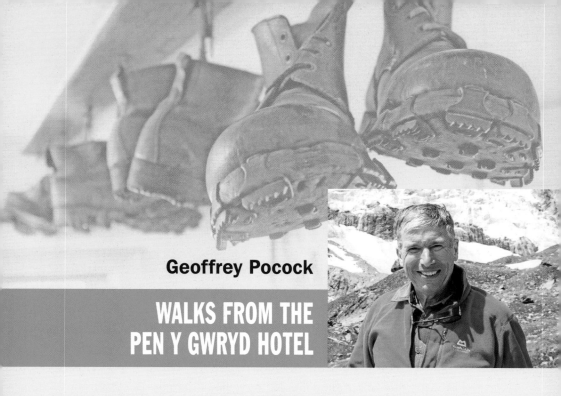

Geoffrey Pocock

WALKS FROM THE PEN Y GWRYD HOTEL

I CROSSED THE SLATE threshold of the Pen y Gwryd Hotel for the first time one evening in the early 1970s. It was rather like entering a rugby scrum in a mountaineering museum. The bar was heaving with climbers and walkers, celebrating the day's successes or planning their next day's epic on the nearby peaks and crags. I was nonplussed by the apparent absence of a bar until, having worked through the first and second rows of persistent thirsty patrons, a small hatched window appeared through which drinks were dispensed.

On the other side I could see a relative oasis of calm – 'the residents' smoking room' (the Smoke Room). After a couple of local ales, I returned to the Youth Hostel at Pen y Pass with a vivid impression of the 'The Home of British Mountaineering', complete with the photographs and climbing artefacts that generously covered the walls. And I thought how nice it would be to one day find myself on the other side of that small window.

When that day came and I entered the Smoke Room for the first time, I sat quietly and listened to the conversations around me. It was much the same convivial atmosphere as the public bar, with the exception of the presence of a powerful conductor, and a most lively host. Our host teased the obvious exaggerator, rebuked (in the most diplomatic fashion) anyone making an impolite comment and gently ridiculed guests who attempted to go to bed before midnight. I had met Jane Pullee.

Chris Briggs's daughter Jane, just like her father, came to symbolise the spirit and ambience of the PyG. While Jane was attending to her many duties in the evening, Chris would stand with his back to the wall in the Smoke Room, with his signature half-pint pewter tankard of ale in hand, and engage his guests in the art of pleasant conversation (it is still possible to see the patch he polished with his navy blue blazer). Chris was an accomplished hotelier and did everything to make his guests feel at home. But, despite his efforts, the old heating system had a mind of its own. Impossible as it might seem now, in those times residents were used to waiting for hot bathwater. One winter's night (and they were real winters back then) leaking ancient pipes brought down the ceiling of room 19. Fortunately, it was not occupied. Nowadays a modernised system provides more than ample hot water, although the PyG's other endearing eccentricities remain – but you will just have to discover these for yourself.

In his younger days Chris Briggs was an active member of the Snowdon Mountain Rescue team but, by the time I met him, he mostly limited himself to good advice (as I well know). One day in late September my group set off to Lliwedd to climb Craig yr Aderyn. It is not a difficult route but three on a rope is always slow going and rarely visited ascents on Lliwedd are characterised by a patina of slippery growth. It was approaching the time for the hotel dinner gong to sound and we were only half way up the crag. And it was well after dark before we were ready for the final pitch. During our slow progress, telephone calls were going back and forth between the hotel and concerned relatives. Jane knew we were competent climbers and was reluctant to call Mountain Rescue but, in the end, Chris's advice prevailed, 'We had better call the rescue team; it looks bad at the inquest if we don't'.

As the years went by, the type of people staying at the hotel slowly changed. The public bar became less riotous and the residents tended more to walkers than climbers. It seemed that many people who are attracted by the hotel's excellent reviews and wonderful reputation had little actual experience of the mountains. To assist them, I produced a simple leaflet describing a few walks from the hotel. One of these walks, the Snowdon Horseshoe, is included below. At the same time (having taken early retirement) I wrote a couple of alpine walking guides. I was taught the art of guidebook writing by the late Robin Collomb, so I found myself in a good position to take on something more ambitious. *Walks from the Pen y Gwryd Hotel* was commissioned by Rupert and Nicolas, Brian and Jane Pullee's sons (and Chris Briggs's grandsons) who had just taken over the running of the hotel.

The emphasis on walks from the hotel and back again, without recourse to a motor vehicle, was not in the slightest influenced by any environmental concerns. It was a reflection of the fact that many people who came to the hotel to enjoy its relaxed atmosphere spent much of their time during the week driving, parking, commuting, and being herded with other people. The idea of having a hearty breakfast and strolling out of the front door of the hotel to spend a day on the hills before returning to a deep hot bath and a beer in the Smoke Room, with the minimum of hassle, is perhaps the greatest attraction of staying at the Pen y Gwryd, and one that, like countless patrons from all over the world, keeps me coming back year after year after year.

THE SNOWDON HORSESHOE

Walk up the road to the Youth Hostel and car park at Pen y Pass, 30 minutes. From the upper car park the Pyg Track (pronounced 'pig' and sometimes also spelt 'Pig Track') is obvious; follow it westwards, gaining height steadily to Bwlch y Moch, one hour 15 minutes. The Pyg Track carries straight on but for Crib Goch turn up right (signpost) on a good path that leads to the East Ridge of Crib Goch.

As you gain height, the route becomes less well-defined and you will have to make your own way. Work up several little pitches following the scratches and polish on the rock until you reach the final rocky staircase which leads directly to the first, false, summit two metres lower than the true summit, which lies on the long ridge that stretches out before you, two hours 15 minutes.

Make your way along the ridge. Bold walkers in calm conditions will teeter along the very top; more cautious people will walk just to the left of the ridge using the top as a handrail. After about 400 metres you will arrive at the first pinnacle. Skirt this on the left to a small dip then scramble steeply up to continue working over and around more pinnacles keeping close to the apex of the ridge.

At last, easier ground is reached at Bwlch Coch. Ahead lies Crib y Ddysgl, which is nicely reached by following the ridge avoiding any temptation to lose height to the right over the cliffs of Clogwyn y Person. From the trig point on Crib y Ddysgl, three hours 15 minutes, an easy descent leads to Bwlch Glas where the Llanberis path is taken to the summit, three hours 45 minutes. If you feel you have had enough go back to Bwlch Glas and go down via the Pyg and Miners' Tracks.

To continue on the Horseshoe, descend the South Ridge for about 200 metres distance to reach a finger stone. Turn left down a loose slope until easier ground leads to a junction where the Watkin path descends, four hours 15 minutes. Ahead, the ground rises to the West Peak of Lliwedd which is reached by an amusing scramble over large, stable blocks, four hours 45 minutes.

Once on the summit, follow the ridge over the East Peak to Lliwedd Bach before descending more steeply to Llyn Llydaw, five hours 15 minutes. Do not cross the causeway but turn right on the jeep track to Pen y Pass where a signed path runs parallel with the road to the hotel, six hours.

Geoffrey Pocock has been climbing and walking in the UK and the Alps for the best part of 45 years. During his working life, he was a senior civil servant in the Ministry of Defence working in aerospace materials and structures and high energy physics. He managed to make himself dispensable and retired when he was 50. Since then, he has spent even more time indulging his passion for hill walking and long-distance alpine tours.

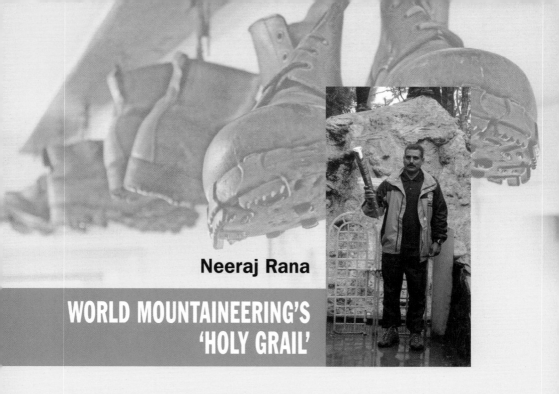

Neeraj Rana

WORLD MOUNTAINEERING'S 'HOLY GRAIL'

IN THE RUGGED mountains of North Wales, the Pen y Gwryd Hotel is conserving a most important piece of rock-climbing history: a simple length of climbers' rope and steel karabiner that forever links 'The Home of British Mountaineering' with the first successful ascent of Everest. This rope symbolises and commemorates past glories but also acknowledges rock climbing's continued appeal to a new generation of young adventurers.

The Himalayan Mountaineering Institute, of which I am a former Principal, is surrounded by the sculptured tea estates for which this northern Indian region is universally famous. Known by its abbreviation 'HMI', the Institute commands a breathtaking panorama of Kangchenjunga, the world's third highest peak, after Everest and K2. Kangchenjunga means 'The Five Treasures of Snows', which, according to local belief, represents the five repositories of God, namely gold, silver, gems, grain, and holy books. Kangchenjunga was first climbed on 25 May, 1955, by Joe Brown and George Band as part of a British expedition which, like the 1953 British Everest Expedition, also trained in the mountains of North Wales and were based at the Pen y Gwryd.

5

The 'holy grail' of mountaineering history can, in fact, be found at PyG in a special cabinet display called 'The Hotel's reliquary of items used by the Everest team'. It is the very rope that linked New Zealander Edmund Hillary and Nepali Sherpa Tenzing Norgay on 29 May, 1953, during the last stage of the first successful ascent of the world's highest mountain. The summit rope, and other items such as Tom Stobart's enamelled mug (pictured in the Royal Geographical Society's famous photo of Hillary and Tenzing immediately after their descent from the Everest peak), George Band's straw hat, Lord Hunt's string vest and the 1953 Expedition pay book (featuring Sherpa porters signing for their wages with thumb prints) are such an important part of climbing history that the PyG is, in a sense, conserving these irreplaceable artefacts for future generations of climbers, adventures and walkers, not just in the UK but all over the world.

Neeraj Rana is the former Principal of the Himalayan Mountaineering Institute. He was the first Indian national to scale the world's fifth highest mountain, Mount Makalu in the Nepal Himalayas. (He was also the first man to fly a paraglider to an altitude of 6,850 metres without oxygen.) In 2013, Rana led the first Indian schoolboys expedition to Everest on behalf of The Lawrence School, Sanawar (founded by Henry Lawrence and his wife Honoria in 1847). He currently operates an adventure company based in the mountains of Himachal Pradesh. www.oceantosky.in

Chris Bonington

PYG – LONG MAY IT NEVER CHANGE

I FIRST ENTERED the Pen y Gwryd Hotel as a 16-year-old in 1951. It was my first visit to Snowdonia and my first climbing trip. I think I penetrated the inner sanctum of the Smoke Room a couple of years later when I was beginning to climb hard. I remember that I was old enough to order a pint (even when I was 18 I barely looked 15!) And through the Pen y Gwryd I got to know quite a few members of the Cambridge University Mountaineering Club and the Climbers' Club.

By this time I had, of course, met Chris and Jo Briggs – but I got to know them a lot better in 1953 when I spent a wonderful summer living in the road menders' hut by the Cromlech Boulders between leaving the Royal Air Force (having failed pilot training at Cranwell) and transferring to the Royal Military Academy Sandhurst. I incurred the wrath of Jo Briggs when I took Janet, one of their trainees, up Kaisergebirge Wall – rated 'Extreme', and at that time one of the hardest climbs in the Llanberis Pass. I was summarily banned from the Pen y Gwryd for being 'so irresponsible' – especially with one of the young ladies in the Briggs's care. As I recall it was at least a year before I was forgiven.

I've had so many good and memorable times in North Wales and at the PyG since. I can't remember exactly when I was invited to sign the ceiling of the Everest Room, but it was an honour to join that illustrious band, most of whom over the years had become good friends.

The last time I was in the Pen y Gwryd was to celebrate the 60th anniversary of 1953 British Everest Expedition ascent in May 2013 – sad but very sweet – so many old friends having passed away but so good to reminisce with Jan Morris, the then embedded Welsh correspondent for *The Times,* together with the some 80-odd members of the 'Everest family', as John Hunt once described them – relatives and friends of expedition members now passed on.

I will always hold the Pen y Gwryd so very dear; and long may it never change.

Chris Bonington is a British mountaineer, writer, photographer and lecturer. He made the first British ascent of the North Wall of the Eiger and led the expedition that made the first ascent of the South Face of Annapurna. He went on to lead the successful first ascent of the South West Face of Everest in 1975 and then reached the summit of Everest himself in 1985 with a Norwegian expedition. In 1974, Bonington received the Founder's Medal of the Royal Geographical Society and, in 1985, the Lawrence of Arabia Memorial Medal of the Royal Society for Asian Affairs. He has written 17 books, fronted numerous television programmes and has lectured to public and corporate audiences all over the world. He received a knighthood in 1996 for services to mountaineering.

Rosemary Hocking

KEEP ON A PATH

I AM A British beef producer. My 'boys' are all light brown South Devon steers. They are a very large, quiet, slow, docile breed which suits me well.

Yearlings are brought the 31 miles back from market to our farm on a cattle lorry. I then keep them in an area where I can talk to them until they get to know me. They have a reliable supply of fresh water and there is as much hay as they can eat. I have a small bucket that I use to give them extra food, one at a time, so they soon get used to being fed by hand. I get great enjoyment from meeting them several times a day so, when they are turned out into the fields, they still come to me as soon as I rattle the old metal pail, which is nice.

West Cornwall has very mild winters and, with our small fields, it's fine for the boys to be outside all the year round. I arrange my holidays at the PyG at times when they don't need to be fed hay, which works out very well indeed.

PyG and I met really by coincidence. My hairdresser, Mr Hicks, said,

> I know where you would love to go for a holiday – to the PyG.
> Just go up the M5 to Worcester, turn left, go to Capel Curig,

turn left and you will see a hotel in the middle of nowhere. In the evenings, you will not have to say a thing; just sit in the Smoke Room and listen; you will find the company charming and the stories interesting.

I took Mr Hicks's advice and, the next day, telephoned to book a room for Saturday, 16 September, 1978. And, for 17 wonderful years, I took my son Christopher who so enjoyed every minute of his time in the mountains.

Mostly we drove. It is 400 miles by road door-to-door (or an eight-hour journey with two hours stopping time), but it was well worth it. I have kept a diary all these years and I recently re-read my entry of that day: 'We arrived at the lovely hotel at 4.15pm. Very friendly welcome. We had dinner at 7.30pm.'

Christopher passed away suddenly in November 1995. My first thought was that I would never go back to the PyG again. But I did the following October and, this time, it was on the train. I now leave the farm at 5.45am and, if I'm lucky, I reach Bangor station and then travel on by private car arriving at the PyG by 5pm.

Over the past ten years, I have stayed twice a year, often walking up Snowdon, which I never seem to tire of.

When one walks out of the front door of the PyG, one is standing in the middle of the most extraordinary scenery and, with the rise and fall of the mist, every hour can be different. One of my favourite 'front door' walks is to go north up the Miners' Track to Llyn Caseg Fraith east of Glyder Fach. It is very steep and stony, but that is to be expected. One day in mid-October, when I was walking on my own, deep in thought, a grouse suddenly flew up and frightened the life out of me but, gaining my breath and strength, I carried on again.

Another walk I like to recall is Gelli to Capel Curig. Again it was in mid-October and again I was walking on my own. Snow was lying in deep pockets. When I arrived on the plateau I knew that I had to keep north until I arrived at my reference point. On that particular day I couldn't see my hand in front of my face with the mist being thick as it was. (At least I could read my compass, which I always keep with me.) I knew that when I reached the small *llyn* I had to go east and then keep heading east. (I was not on a path and Mr Briggs had always told me to keep on a path). Anyway, I was still going up and I came across a flock of wild goats. The billy had a good long look at me but, thank goodness, he stayed on his rock.

After a while I realised that I was descending, which is what I was expecting (well, at least hoping) and so I persisted onwards. Suddenly, I could see the stone fence line and the distinctive wooden stile. I had dropped below the mist. I continued on to Capel Curig and there I caught the Sherpa bus back to the PyG where I was met with a roaring fire and a very warm welcome back … as usual.

Rosemary Hocking was born in Penzance into a farming family with ancient connections to the land. By her own admission, she 'doesn't see the need to leave West Cornwall too often'. As a younger woman, she won the Taunton Jumping Festival Sash of Honour and qualified for the Horse and Rider of the Year show at Wembley, London. These days, her passions are raising beef cattle and walking in Snowdonia.

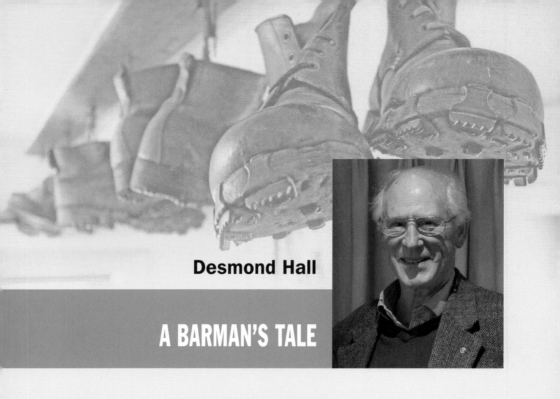

Desmond Hall

A BARMAN'S TALE

Ale man, ale's the stuff to drink,
For fellows whom it hurts to think;
Look into the pewter pot
To see the world as the world's not.

A. E. Housman, from *A Shropshire Lad*

Fᴀʀ ʙᴇ ɪᴛ from me to suggest that climbers think less than your average person but I am able, from experience, to attest that they are first-class drinkers.

I was first introduced to PyG by my parents, in 1948 at the age of 11, enjoying a half-term break from the splendid local educational establishment at Heronwater, Betws-yn-Rhos. We relished an early supper before my return to school, the only other occupant of the dining room being Jo Briggs. She made a great impression, though her parting shot was rather fierce: 'If that boy wants to come again for heaven's sake get his hair cut.'

Evidently I must have followed instructions because when, in 1955, I asked to come again as barman, it was allowed. I had already cut my teeth behind the bar at the Surrey Tavern outside The Oval cricket ground and, whilst the clientele there was fairly upmarket at lunchtime, the same could not be said about the evenings. Indeed, the only similarity between the two places was the density of the cigarette fumes.

Drinks at PyG were served from the same position as they are now, with the aperture through which this was done no more than three feet square. Furthermore, at busy times, the entire Smoke Room was thronged with residents and it was necessary to probe around at knee level to serve drinks or collect empty glasses. Worthington 'E', Chris Briggs's speciality, was kept across the corridor behind the still room, so each pint meant a journey and a balancing act to get it back to the consumer reasonably full.

My main fellow bartenders were Chris himself and Miss Crutwell, or 'Crutty' to her friends. On a busy evening and working flat out, we might take £85, which won't impress you but that was a good sum in those far-off days. In later years, I also worked with Doug Verity who was the regular full-time employee, as opposed to the holiday relief.

My job was something of a cushy number compared with the girls, of whom there were many. They had to rise at 7am but I was allowed a long lie-in until 8.15 and in the evenings Chris would usually send me off to bed about 11pm; he had to stay up until the last guest felt inclined to retire, often being obliged to linger until the small hours whilst one or two punters swapped climbing tales (most of which he had heard before). The only downside for me was having to sleep in the bunk house. Now don't get me wrong, the bunk house was a splendid haven for a night or two for the impecunious young climber and I spent many a peaceful night there. However, by the time you had groped your way round to it in the dark for the 50th time, and picked your way round the piles of wet and smelly clothes on the floor, its attractions did begin to pall and the deep, deep comfort of a room in the inn would have been luxury indeed.

Both Chris and Jo Briggs were a delight to work for and I remember being given an unexpected day off to go to play golf with Doug and regular superb lunches cooked by Jo and taken in the small staff room adjacent to the kitchen. On fine afternoons, and especially in that glorious summer of 1959, we would all pile into 'PYG 1', which I think was a Morris Estate in those days, and be driven by Chris to Black Rock Sands for a swim. No seat belts and no worries about overcrowding in those days. The car must have had at least eight people in it at times (including one in the luggage compartment.)

In the evenings, we sometimes had the locals in. You could tell they were locals by their lovely Welsh lilt but also by the order of 'a pint of beer, a large whisky and a Babycham for the wife please'. The large whisky would be downed at the bar unbeknown to the wife and the beer supped in innocent companionship with the lady.

The biggest bone of contention was the price of soft drinks and, in particular, orange squash. Picture the scene as this thirsty climber arrives, just off the mountain …

Climber: 'A pint of orange squash please.'

Chris Briggs: 'Certainly sir, that will be one shilling and sixpence.'

Climber: 'We don't pay that sort of money where I come from.' (Probably Yorkshire.)

Chris Briggs: 'Better go back there then.'

Sundays could be challenging, as in some Welsh counties including Caernarfonshire, only residents were allowed alcohol on Sundays. Chris had the answer in the form of Cydrax, a non-alcoholic fizzy apple drink. Did we have any of that rubbish? Of course we didn't. It was cider, and both we and the regulars knew it. I did, however, have to be pulled up by the management in the early days for not concealing the label under my hand while serving.

> And Noah he often said to his wife when he sat down to dine,
> 'I don't care where the water goes if it doesn't get into the wine.'
>
> G. K. Chesterton, from *Wine and Water*

The one thing that may be said with certainty about the PyG is that water never got turned into wine, nor indeed beer, though it did get into many strange places, and temperature variations could be, to say the least, unpredictable. This was despite Chris spending many happy hours up aloft with his mole wrench and his plumber's mate, a duty later gallantly taken on by Brian Pullee.

There was a longish spell when there were only two temperatures, very hot and scalding. A gentleman who was a few minutes late for dinner was visited by Miss Crutwell who banged on the bathroom door asking him what he meant by it; this elicited the response that he was waiting for his bathwater to cool. There was another considerable period when the whole side of the boiler house was left open for several weeks, contributing to early global warming on the Glyderau.

An even stranger episode occurred when there was a special routine to achieve a satisfactory bath-time experience. This involved turning on the cold water tap first and, once it had given forth a small offering, gently easing the hot water tap open. If performed in the correct sequence, this worked well, but failure to follow the routine would cause the hot water tap to go into a sulk and produce only a few millilitres of dark sludge and a cloud of steam. However, one must not complain. Lashings of hot water always seemed to reach the right place in the end and, in the rare event of total failure, one could always sit in the Victorian bath and admire the architecture. Nowadays, if one gets in early, one may even book an ensuite; it is almost like staying in a hotel!

They were wonderfully happy days and the summer work times were much missed after my medical training was complete. However, it is in keeping with the family spirit of PyG that, following my work under Chris and Jo, my son Mick was subsequently a barman under Jane and Brian Pullee, and now, my grandson Angus has started down the same route with their sons Rupert and Nicolas.

Desmond Hall was born in Paddington and educated at Heronwater, Marlborough, Guy's Hospital and at the PyG. He was 42 years in General Practice in Buckinghamshire. He is married to Ann, also a GP, and has three children and seven grandchildren. In retirement, his interests are golf, travel and picture framing. He is still a regular visitor to the PyG. His father, the eminent anaesthetist Vernon Hall, was the author of *A Scrapbook of Snowdonia*.

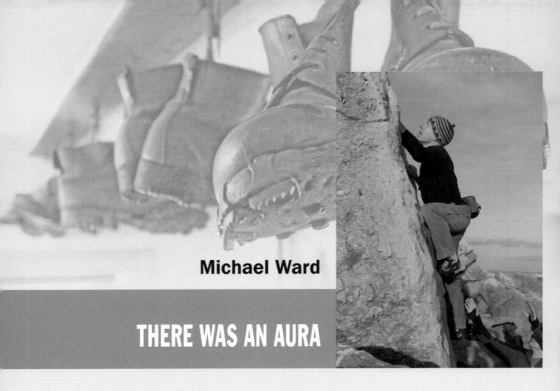

Michael Ward

THERE WAS AN AURA

I STARTED CLIMBING in the mid-1960s, when I was about 14 years old.
Back then, with hardly any indoor climbing walls, most people began
as I did, with hillwalking. Climbing was viewed as a logical progression.
You did everything in big, clumpy mountaineering boots. Outcrops were
practice for British mountain routes. Then you went to the Alps. Maybe,
if you became very good, you reached the Himalayas. The greatest goal
imaginable was the summit of Everest.

The centre of British climbing was Snowdonia. The Climbers' Club
huts at Helyg and Ynys Ettws had hosted many famous climbers. But even
they couldn't compete with the Pen y Gwryd. That's where the Everest
team had trained. That's where they'd left their signatures scrawled on
the ceiling of the famous Everest Room.

I first visited Snowdonia with my girlfriend Maggie in 1971. I was 18,
no longer a beginner but still with much to learn. Back then, E grades
didn't exist. VS (Very Severe) was the 'gold standard'. If you could climb
VS consistently, you were a good climber. XS (Extremely Severe) was for
'gods', not mortals. By 1971, although I'd done a few VSs, I was still only
leading V Diff/Severe consistently. With no wires or cams, even these were
challenging. If you fell off, chances were you'd be badly hurt, maybe killed.

We spent our first night in Snowdonia in Humphreys' Barn in Nant Peris. I gave Maggie my sleeping bag and dossed on the stone floor. Next day, we decided to move into the Climbers' Club hut at Cwm Glas Mawr. Back then, it was the only Climbers' Club hut that allowed women. I was a member of the Irish Mountaineering Club; we had reciprocal rights with the Climbers' Club. For a pound sterling deposit, you could get the key to Cwm Glas Mawr from the Pen y Gwryd.

As Maggie and I started walking up the Llanberis Pass, the heavens opened up. Before we'd reached the Grochan we were soaked. By the time we'd got to the Cromlech boulders we were shivering spasmodically. Grimly, we carried on through sheets of rain and a bitter wind that contemptuously cut through layers of clothing. Dinas Mot disappeared into the mist. Up and up we went, over the top of Pen y Pass and back down again.

Eventually, we staggered through the door of the Pen y Gwryd like proverbial drowned rats. This was hallowed ground where so many great mountaineers had been before us. There was such an aura to the place. I tried to take it in but, in my dazed, exhausted state, I couldn't. We asked for Chris Briggs and a genial, kindly man appeared. God knows what he thought of our bedraggled state. He took our deposit and gave us the key to Cwm Glas Mawr. With very little money, there was no question of us staying to eat or drink. We had to get back across the Pass as quickly as possible, into Cwm Glas Mawr and somehow light a fire before the onset of hypothermia.

(There is a wonderful 1959 British Pathé newsreel of Chris Briggs during the zenith of his time as team leader of the Snowdonia Mountain Rescue Committee. See www.britishpathe.com/video/mountain-rescue/query/Chris+Briggs.)

Reluctantly, we exchanged the comforting warmth of the Gwryd for the gusts of wind and rain outside. Numbed fingers fumbled with zips. As we stood there summoning the resolve to leave our temporary sanctuary, two corpulent, expense-account types, much the worse for wear, barged through the door behind us. 'Well, what did you think of that lunch?' one enquired in gratingly plummy tones. 'About as rough as you could possibly get!' the other one drawled. The pair of them dashed through the sleeting rain to a top-of-the-range Mercedes, jumped in and roared off. Maggie and I stared mutely at each other. About as rough as you could possibly get? What on earth were they talking about?

There are moments in your life which are pure epiphanies; you learn lessons that remain with you. Even at age 18, I could walk through the door of a business and know instantly whether it was well run. Although I'd failed to fully comprehend the full historical significance of the Pen y Gwryd at the time, it was obvious that Chris Briggs ran a tight ship. And these over-fed, over-pampered ninnies were so jaded they just couldn't appreciate it. I decided, then and there, that I never wanted to be like them.

Over the following decades, I came to appreciate the Pen y Gwryd more fully. I've been there in the first light of dawn and at the last rays of the setting sun. I've seen it through eerie tendrils of mist and on crisp, winter mornings. There's something primeval, even totemic, about its position. There's an aura. And, on that first visit, there was also a lesson.

Michael 'Mick' Ward started climbing in the mid-1960s, while barely in his teens. Professionally, he has worked as a psychologist, management consultant and writer (including many climbing articles). In his 50s, he got into 'serious new routing'. According to Ward, 'I couldn't be bothered before. I must have done about 150 now'. Now in his early 60s, he still trains hard to improve as a climber.

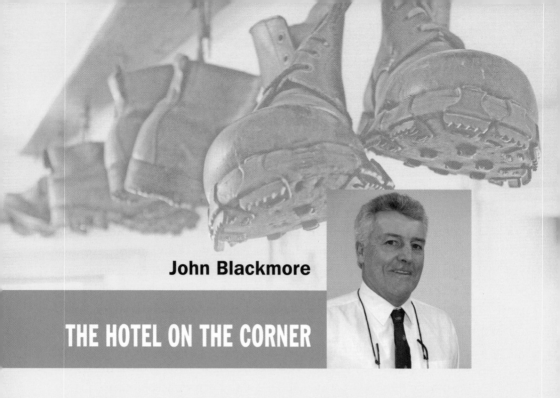

John Blackmore

THE HOTEL ON THE CORNER

I N 1988 I began working as a distance education teacher with Broken Hill School of the Air. Part of this job involved visiting children on large sheep stations that covered vast areas of 'outback' New South Wales on land so arid it could only carry, on average, one sheep for every ten acres. Our school, in fact, boasted a playground covering over a million square kilometres.

At the end of that school year, I headed off on my first overseas trip as a member of a party of Australian cricketers touring the UK. We were staying in historic Shrewsbury, and we had some free time, so I managed to persuade two of my teammates to take a day trip to the north-western corner of Wales. They took some convincing to go for an evening drive with me to a hotel 'on the corner of a road in the middle of remote Snowdonia'.

After we arrived, but before we could quench our thirsts with a customary local ale, mine host Jane Pullee informed us that she wasn't quite ready for us for dinner and sent us over the Llanberis Pass for a drive.

My two companions were from sheep stations and both had been students of Broken Hill School of the Air. It didn't take them long to figure out that, in the next valley, there were some shearing sheds. Bligh Ridge, who came from a station 'out the Back o' Bourke' and Justin McLure, who hailed from tiny Tilpa (a hamlet on the banks of the Darling River), remarkably found a lot of grazing lingo they could exchange with these Welsh shearers, one of whom had worked in Australia. Keeping their animals warm and out of the snow was, of course, a foreign concept to my companions.

Three years later I made it back to the Pen y Gwryd Hotel. On my first visit, Jane's family had only just hosted a reunion for Edmund Hillary and the rest of the Everest Expeditioners, as they had done on a five-year cycle since 1953. For me, this visit was my reunion with Jane, her husband Brian, their sons Rupert and Nicolas, along with Jane's father Chris Briggs.

Things were different for me on this visit as I came with Donna, my wife of less than 12 months. We were driving from one end of the UK to the other – John O'Groats to Land's End – which we accomplished in less than two weeks. To cover this amount of territory in such quick time, I am sure locals thought us madder than March hares.

We did take in some of the finer points of the hotel, however, such as being given our own set place at the dinner table for meals, along with taking one's ablutions in the stand-alone Victorian bath which showed off magnificently the blue purity of the local snow-melted water, heated for the edification of visitors. When the mist rolled in across the adjacent lake and shrouded the ivy-covered walls of the hotel at day's end, retreating to the fireside inside the bar at PyG became the evening's treat. And this was where we found Jane most hospitable.

In 2004 I returned once more to PyG. This time I travelled from Australia on my own but brought with me to the hotel two friends who hailed from the well-known rugby town of Neath in South Wales where, in the 1870s, the meeting to form the Welsh Rugby Union was held. In the week before travelling up through the valleys of mid Wales and over the Brecons, my friend Bernard Pike, his wife Ann and I had warmed up by visiting the seaside village of Laugharne. We were given directions by a bemused local man to Dylan Thomas's boathouse, where *Under Milk Wood* was written. He told us in his broadest brogue to 'Go back, turn right into the car park, head to the castle … and … mind the tide!'

By the time we had headed through the Llangollen Valley, past Betws y Coed, Capel Curig and up the pass to Pen y Gwryd, my friend Bernard had regaled us with a complete rendition of the Welsh national anthem *Hen Wlad fy Nhadau* ('Land of my Fathers'). This set the tone for a special few days of wining, dining and taking the trip on the Snowdon Railway, which, at its sharpest points of relief, edges its way along a ridge that has ravines and precipices on either side of the tracks that take your breath away.

More evenings by the fireside were to come but, by now, another generational change had become imminent at the PyG. With the old ways of Jane's father, established by others long before him, echoing down the hallways of the upstairs and downstairs of this quaint but significant hotel, the Pen y Gwryd continues to stand sentinel on its isolated countryside corner.

John Blackmore has worked as a teacher in the New South Wales public education system since 1980. Every month, for the last ten years, Blackmore has written a feature article for the magazine *About* in the Shoalhaven District where he lives. He has held two exhibitions of his writing, in 2008 and 2014, in the Bay and Basin area. Centred on the stories in his feature articles, they have been included as part of the biennial 'Seechange Winter Arts Festival'. In 2009, he published *Shoalhaven's Mr Sport* for the 25th anniversary of the Bernie Regan Memorial Sporting Trust based in the town of Nowra. Over the years, he has contributed articles to numerous regional newspapers across New South Wales including the *Barrier Daily Truth* in Broken Hill, the *Illawarra Mercury* in Wollongong, the *South Coast Register* in Nowra, and various Far South Coast newspapers in the towns of Bega, Merimbula and Eden, as well as being an editor for three years of a school magazine called *Over To You,* published as an annual tradition of Broken Hill School of the Air since its establishment in 1956.

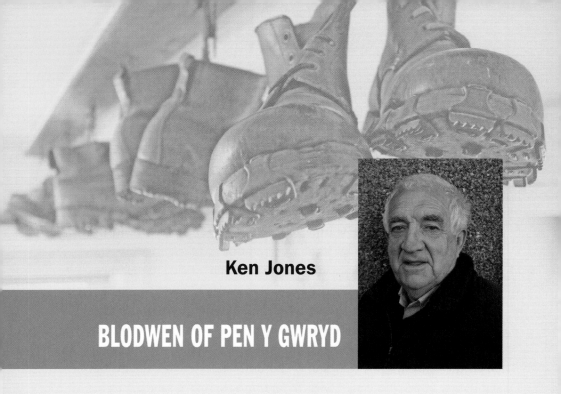

Ken Jones

BLODWEN OF PEN Y GWRYD

Blodwen Jane Griffiths was born in Llwyn Padarn, Llanberis on 2 November, 1887. She was the eldest of seven children born to Owen and Ann Griffiths. Llwyn Padarn is a small single-storey cottage situated by Church Lane in Llanberis. The 1901 census shows that there were nine adults and children living in the cottage, which is remarkable considering its small size. The cottage was built *circa* 1780 and there is evidence that the Griffiths family lived there from the beginning.

The last two decades of the 19th century were a very lively period in Llanberis – a time when the slate industry was at its peak, the chapels full and eisteddfod culture thriving. It is quite possible that Blodwen was named after a light opera of the same name composed by Dr Joseph Parry (1841-1903). The most famous song from the production was the duet 'Hywel and Blodwen', which was sung all over the world during the same period. The Llanberis Parish census for 1881 shows that Dr Joseph Parry and two of his sons stayed in the village where the opera was performed at the local concert hall.

Blodwen is a girl's name in the Welsh language and is derived from the word *blodyn* ('flower') and *gwyn* ('white') and this is the name that was given to the first born of the Llwyn Padarn family. The other children were given names that were most common at the time such as David, Mary and Elizabeth.

Although the 1901 census states that Blodwen continued to live in Llwyn Padarn, it is quite possible that she had already started work at the Pen y Gwryd Hotel. This was at the time when all in the village were monoglot Welsh speakers. She attended the local primary school but, as with all the other children of the time, the education on offer was very basic. The school, however, was probably the only place where she came into contact with the English language during her childhood.

In the Llanberis valley at the beginning of the 20th century there was only one career choice for the boys after leaving school and that was working in the Dinorwig Slate Quarry. Work prospects were also very limited for the girls, with the majority finding work as maids or servants in the local area.

One has to wonder how Blodwen found work at the Pen y Gwryd in the first instance as there is a distance of about five miles from her home to the Gwryd, including the steep climb up the Llanberis Pass. It does appear that she started there as a full-time servant in 1902, when the hotel was owned by the proprietor of the Royal Hotel, Capel Curig. The manageress at the time was Miss Ethel Florence Bloomfield and it is well known that Miss Bloomfield was extremely proficient with her work and she also took great care of her staff. It was obvious that Miss Bloomfield thought highly of Blodwen and she continued to work for her and later her husband, Arthur Lockwood, during their time as tenants and later as owners of Pen y Gwryd.

When Mr and Mrs Lockwood sold Pen y Gwryd, Blodwen continued to work for them as a maid in their nearby home, Hafod y Gwynt. When Chris and Jo Briggs took over the tenancy of Pen y Gwryd in 1947, they encountered numerous difficulties in employing experienced and reliable staff. This was mainly because of the remoteness of the hotel and the lack of public transport. It was at this time that Arthur Lockwood came to the fore and recommended that Chris and Jo employ Blodwen as she knew everything about the hotel.

Blodwen was a 'sprightly' spinster in her 60th year when she joined Chris and Jo, and continued there until her retirement. Employing

Blodwen was, no doubt, the best decision that Chris and Jo made during their long and successful tenure at Pen y Gwryd. As my own home in Llanberis is only about 100 yards from Llwyn Padarn, I can recollect some of Blodwen's visits to the cottage and, in later life, her visits to her brother David and her sister Lizzie. She was small in stature with neat white hair and was always quick and light on her feet. She never wore any make-up and always wore dark clothes without any detailed attention to the fashion or the styles of the day. Although Pen y Gwryd is now famous for its role prior to the conquest of Everest, one can easily add to this that Miss Blodwen Griffiths was one of the outstanding characters of the establishment during the past century.

At the Pen y Gwryd, visitors and staff always referred to her as 'Blodwen' but, here in Llanberis and especially to the younger generation of the day, she was always addressed as 'Miss Griffiths'. She undertook almost all the functions at the hotel, beginning with the most basic work such as cleaning the bedrooms and so on. At work she always wore a long black dress, a white cap and white starched apron, in the long tradition of those who served in more gracious times. She worked at an incredible pace and was always the first to appear in the morning and the last to finish at night. There is an excellent photo of her in her working regalia in a most prominent place in the Smoke Room at the hotel. Only a few of the older guests can still testify to her character and work habits. Everyone agrees, though, that she was absolutely dedicated to her work and that working at Pen y Gwryd was her main pleasure in life. She possessed all the graces of a maid of the time and always referred to the guests as 'sir' or 'madam' and to the owner as 'master'. In later years, and as the most senior member of staff, she always attended to the needs of Mr and Mrs Briggs and their daughter Jane and would even do so on her day off. She regarded them as her family and the respect and affection between them was mutual; the Briggs family always cared for her as one of their own.

It was a regular occurrence for her to make herself available at the desk, when the guests paid for their stay before departing on their homeward journey and Blodwen was always prompt to ask whether they had been impressed with her service. This is when everyone paid with cash and Blodwen was an expert at being in the right place at the right time for the 'tip'.

Owing to the remoteness of Pen y Gwryd, there was nowhere for Blodwen to have a break from work and to relax. There was nowhere either for her to spend her money, especially as she had been kept and fed at Pen y Gwryd and Hafod y Gwynt for over 70 years. I am sure that she must have been able to save a tidy sum of money in her lifetime. It is even mentioned today in Llanberis how she always visited the village on her day off every Wednesday – to deposit her wages in the local bank. The thought of retirement never crossed Blodwen's mind and she continued to work at Pen y Gwryd almost to the end of her days.

As a tribute to her devotion to Pen y Gwryd, Mr and Mrs Briggs posted the following in *The Times,* on the occasion of her 80th birthday on 2 November, 1967.

> **MOUNTAINEERS** all over the world will be interested to learn that Blodwen of Pen y Gwryd is 80 years old today. Still going strong.

Following the publication, she received many telegrams and cards from friends and admirers throughout the world. She was and always will be known as 'Blodwen of Pen y Gwryd'. Blodwen died on 5 March, 1973, having spent her last years in Llanberis with her aged brother and sister in the cottage where she was born. She is buried in the family grave in Nant Peris Cemetery.

(A Welsh version of this contribution is available on www.gomer.co.uk)

Ken Jones is a retired civil servant. He was born and raised in Llanberis, North Wales. He founded the international Snowdon Race in 1976 and organised the event for the first 30 years. Ken also founded the Eryri Harriers Running Club in 1977, as well as the Snowdonia Marathon in 1981. He continues to be the secretary of a committee that established a twinning link between Llanberis and the Italian town of Morbegno in Lombardy. This followed participation in the Snowdon Race by runners from that city for 25 years. Jones is a double kidney transplant recipient and is secretary of the Ysbyty Gwynedd Kidney Patients Association. He continues to take an active part in village life and is secretary of the Llanberis Community Centre. He is also a keen conservationist and historian.

Kay Mitchell

GOING TO EXTREMES TO UNDERSTAND CRITICAL ILLNESS – XTREME EVEREST AND THE PYG

XTREME EVEREST (XE) is a team of dedicated intensive care doctors, nurses and scientists. They conduct experiments on themselves and other volunteers at high altitude in order to develop novel therapies to improve the survival rates of their patients. Because it is very difficult to study patients in intensive care units, not least because they are so ill, the team volunteer themselves as subjects. In order to simulate the critical conditions of intensive care, the team went to Everest, the world's highest mountain, in 2007.

The oxygen levels on the summit are a third of those at sea level – similar to those experienced by patients in intensive care. The team even performed tests on themselves in the 'Death Zone' (at an altitude where there is barely enough oxygen to support life). In addition, 208 volunteer subjects joined the 2007 expedition, trekking to Everest Base Camp, so that they could provide invaluable data about how they adapted to the low levels of oxygen found at this altitude.

The XE Executive had spent several years planning the research expedition and putting together a crack team of healthcare professionals. Most of these individuals worked in anaesthesia or critical care and had a love of climbing and exploring the outdoors. Prior to leaving for Nepal, the majority of the team gathered at the Pen y Gwryd for a weekend in February 2007, in order to get to know each other. It gave the leaders the opportunity to lay the ground rules for how the research expedition would be managed once the group had arrived in the country.

The Pen y Gwryd was chosen because of its association with the first ascent of Everest. Our expedition leader, Professor Mike Grocott, had also spent his stag weekend at the hotel and was very fond of it. The Pen y Gwryd owners allowed the XE team to take over the hotel for the entire weekend. They agreed that we could put up extra camp beds to ensure that everyone could stay on site. It made for an amazing atmosphere. Some team members brought guitars and songbooks; the whisky flowed and so did the music. It was surprising how many people in the team could sing – or was my judgement impaired by the single malt?

On the Saturday the whole group trekked up Tryfan in a howling gale and then headed back to the hotel for hot baths and a slap-up dinner. The singing continued into the early hours of the morning. (Getting up for the breakfast gong, a Pen y Gwryd feature, was a bit of a struggle.) The team left for Nepal just over a month later to undertake the largest medical research expedition ever carried out at high altitude.

Additional questions needed to be answered, so more volunteers were investigated during a number of studies in the Himalayan Alps and also in hypoxic chambers. Intensive care represents the knife-edge between life and death. Extreme illnesses require cutting-edge research to provide solutions. The XE team continues to use the data collected to explore better ways to manage patients who are at risk of dying from such critical illness.

Xtreme Everest members have returned to the Pen y Gwryd every year since 2007, to catch up and prepare for further studies. The welcome at the foot of Snowdon has always been extremely warm and staff members have tolerated some very poor singing and some very late nights. Rupert and Nicolas Pullee's hospitality at the Pen y Gwryd has enabled Xtreme Everest to build its team and deliver our research year on year.

Xtreme Everest is a not-for-profit organisation, led by doctors and scientists from University College London, the University of Southampton and Duke University in the United States. In the UK, one in five of us will end up in intensive care at some point in our life. Of those, 20 per cent will die. Despite intensive care being one of the most sophisticated areas of hospital care, even now in the 21st century, there is still limited understanding of why some people survive and some die. Hypoxia, a lack of oxygen reaching the body's vital organs, is a common problem for patients in an intensive care unit.

www.xtreme-everest.co.uk

Kay Mitchell qualified as a Registered Nurse in 1988 and specialised in intensive care. She holds a BSc in Human Sciences from University College London and an MSc in Adult Critical Care from Imperial College London. She is currently undertaking a PhD at the University of Southampton related to epigenetics and hypoxia. Mitchell currently works in Southampton four days a week as a senior research manager, supporting the critical care and hypoxia research programs led by Professor Mike Grocott. One day a week, she works in London, leading a Centre for Nurse and Midwife-led Research. Mitchell project managed most of the research expeditions carried out by the Xtreme Everest consortium at altitude and in chambers since 2005. In her spare time, she enjoys running, rock climbing and mountaineering and has been known to do the odd sprint triathlon.

Peter Hillary

YOU WILL JUST HAVE TO READ ED'S BOOK

M Y FATHER, the late Edmund Hillary, spent only about 15 minutes at the summit of the highest point on earth, at 11.30am on 29 May, 1953, but countless days celebrating reunions and renewing old friendships at the Pen y Gwryd Hotel, in the mountains of North Wales, a modest climber's inn and a place he loved.

It was my father who took the photo of his climbing partner Tenzing Norgay posing with his ice axe and, if you look closely at the famous image, you will notice a humble length of rope wrapped around Tenzing joining the two climbers, the same one so long and lovingly preserved at the PyG.

The conquerors of Everest reconvened at the Pen y Gwryd Hotel the following October, in the autumn of 1954, and met there for dinner every 29 May thereafter, though, after a decade, the reunions were set at every five years.

In his book *View from the Summit,* my father recalled a story about the first reunion party at the Pen y Gwryd, organised by the Alpine Club. Fresh from becoming the first man to stand on top of the world, Ed Hillary arrived late at the hotel. He was informed that Lord Hunt and the rest of the Everest party had set off to climb Snowdon. My father immediately headed off after them without bothering to change into something more appropriate. On the way up he was waylaid by a distinguished old gentleman who gave him a severe dressing down about his inappropriate attire, which the man said, gave 'hill walkers and climbers a bad name'. The man turned out to be none other than the then President of the Alpine Club.

My father described their handshake when they were formally introduced in the Smoke Room of the Pen y Gwryd later that evening. For details, you are just going to have to read Ed's book.

Peter Hillary is the son of Edmund Hillary and was raised on stories of mountaineering and adventure. Like his father, Hillary has climbed Everest and established a new route across Antarctica to the South Pole. He works with foundations that support the schools and hospitals located around the foot of Mount Everest.

www.peterhillary.com

www.edhillary.com

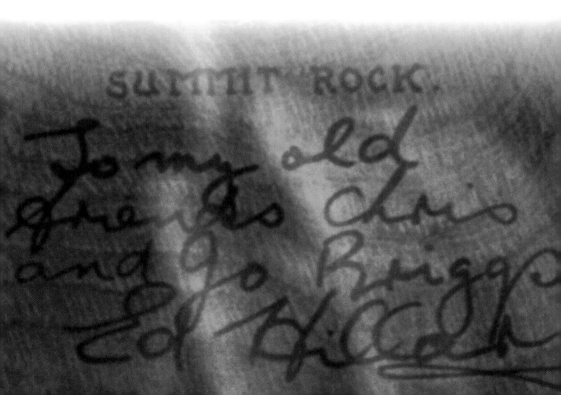

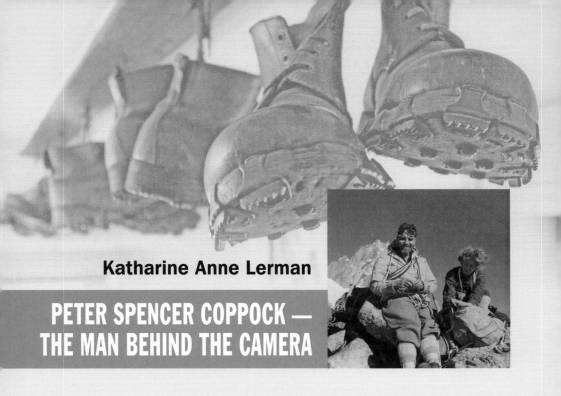

Katharine Anne Lerman

PETER SPENCER COPPOCK — THE MAN BEHIND THE CAMERA

MY FATHER, Peter Spencer Coppock (1922-2001), took a suite of black-and-white photographs of the Pen y Gwryd and its surroundings. This photographic journal constitutes an irreplaceable contribution to the archive of this most famous of British mountain inns.

The story behind the photograph of Blodwen, the PyG's 'maid of maids', goes back to a time when Peter, like many men of his generation, volunteered, at the age of 18, for war service. Peter spent three months training at HMS Collingwood at Fareham, Hampshire and then became an ordinary seaman. His first draft was to a *Dido* class cruiser which survived several torpedo hits and came to be regarded as a 'lucky ship'. After 14 months, he became a midshipman. By the age of 20 he was a sub-lieutenant and, after two-and-a-half years of active service, he became a lieutenant at the age of 22. He spent most of the Second World War in the Mediterranean, taking part in the Sicily landings of July 1943, the assault on the Italian mainland in September and the Anzio Offensive in January 1944. Six weeks after the Normandy invasion in June 1944, he landed at St Tropez in the South of France in a combined operation to pin down the German divisions there and seize the ports of Marseilles and Toulon.

31

After a long leave from August 1945, Peter returned to the Mediterranean after Christmas and became official naval photographer on the staff of the Commander-in-Chief, Mediterranean. In this role he travelled extensively, visiting Istanbul, Sevastopol, Yalta, Cyprus, Crete, Gibraltar and Malta. In Malta, he met and became engaged to Denise Wilson, a Third Officer in the WRNS and the naval librarian there. They married in Watford, Hertfordshire on 21 August, 1948 and had two daughters, Caroline and me.

After his demobilisation, Peter trained as a medical photographer. He worked at the Hospital for Sick Children in Great Ormond Street, London, for six days a week, while also attending evening classes three times a week at the Regent Street Polytechnic (now the University of Westminster). Once qualified, he was offered a job at University College Hospital but seized the opportunity to become a staff photographer on *The Field* magazine. He subsequently worked in Fleet Street as a press photographer for the *Daily Sketch*, *The Times* and the *Daily Telegraph*. Later, he worked as a medical photographer at Stoke Mandeville and Mount Vernon hospitals.

At Stoke Mandeville in the 1960s he assisted the renowned neurologist, Ludwig Guttmann, in his work with patients who had spinal cord injuries and he took photographs at the annual International Stoke Mandeville Games (now recognised as the original Paralympic Games). From 1968 to 1983, he worked for the Port of London Authority as staff photographer for the Dockers' newspaper, *The Port*. He also taught photography at Watford Technical College (now West Herts College).

Peter developed his interest in rock climbing while he was at school. He kept a diary and, in 1942 when he was training as a seaman, he noted sadly that a friend was climbing again in North Wales, 'and I am not with him'. In 1948, he attended the annual Romanes Lecture in the Sheldonian Theatre at Oxford given by Lord Schuster, Permanent Secretary to the Lord Chancellor for over 30 years, on the subject of 'Mountaineering'. As a member of a small climbing group, he made regular weekend visits to Snowdonia in the late 1940s, 1950s and early 1960s. He also went on a summer climbing expedition to Switzerland, staying at Zermatt and taking spectacular photographs of the Matterhorn and Monte Rosa.

My father loved staying at the Pen y Gwryd, where he had his own mug (an idea that started with Peter and was later to develop into the hotel's unique tradition of individual tankards for each member of the 1953 Everest and 1955 Kangchenjunga Expeditions). He probably made his first visit there in 1951. In a diary entry for Friday 11 May of that year, he wrote, 'Journey to The Pen y Gwryd Hotel, Nant Gwynant, and Caernarfon for climbing article'. (Presumably the article was for *The Field*, as he was working for this magazine at the time, moving to the *Daily Sketch* later that year.) On Saturday 12 May he noted, 'Climbed on Dinas Mot and Dinas Cromlech, then did Slape on Clogwyn y Grochan'. On Sunday 13 May, he climbed in Cwm Silyn. On Monday 14 May, he writes, 'Was a magnificent day, very warm, brilliant sun with snow on the peaks'.

Peter's diaries show that in 1959 and 1960 he visited North Wales virtually every month, sometimes for a week but mainly for weekends. He often went climbing with what he called 'the Land Rover Group' (which included David Cons, Dennis Kemp, Philip Hulatt, and Tom Andrews). He also climbed with my mother, Denise, before my sister and I were born, and with other women climbers such as Beryl Griffiths, Felicity Hurst and Betty Seifert. (Betty Seifert was one of the first two women to be elected to membership of the Alpine Club in their own right after women were allowed to join in 1975. The other was Sally Westmacott, the wife of Mike Westmacott, a member of the first team to conquer Everest in 1953.) In December 1960 my father noted, 'Worst weekend experienced in Wales. Gale force wind, almost continuous rain … tent complete with contents blown away without trace …'

It's not clear whether Peter had a favourite climb, though he did climb Crackstone Rib on Carreg Wastad in both October 1960 and June 1961. Other specific outings mentioned included Crib Goch (3 January, 1959) in snow and ice and noting, in contrast to other days in the mountains, that Sunday 4 January was, 'A glorious snow day'. In the Llanberis Pass, he also climbed Flying Buttress on Dinas Cromlech, Wrinkle on Carreg Wastad and Nea on Clogwyn y Grochan. (This route was named after Nea Morin, a renowned climber of her generation and the eventual mother-in-law of Charles Evans who had been John Hunt's deputy leader on Everest in 1953.) Further afield, he also mentioned Rowan and Canopy on Tryfan's Milestone Buttress. What is especially evident is that he and Chris Briggs were great friends, that he loved the PyG and that this is clearly reflected in the timeless quality of his photographic legacy.

Katharine Anne Lerman is a historian of modern Germany who has published widely on imperial German politics and culture. She has taught 19th and 20th-century European history for over 30 years at the University of Exeter, the University of Wales, Lampeter, and London Metropolitan University, specialising in the origins of the First World War, the collapse of the dynastic empires and the Holocaust. Photograph of Peter Coppock and climbing companion Felicity Hurst, 1962.

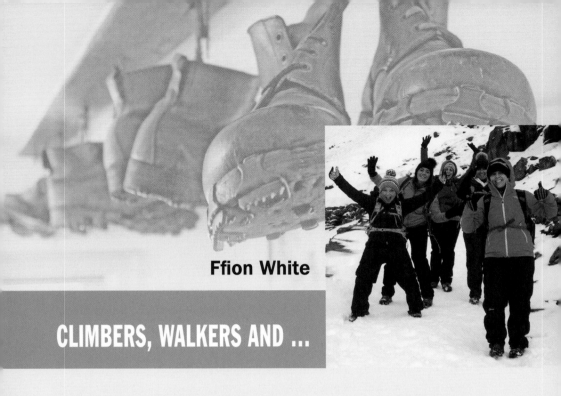

Ffion White

CLIMBERS, WALKERS AND ...

THE 14 (or 15) Welsh peaks with a height of at least 3,000 feet (914.4 metres) fall within three ranges, namely, Snowdon (Yr Wyddfa, 3,560 feet), Glyderau and Carneddau. (Interestingly, the discrepancy in the total results from the modern inclusion, in some reckonings, of an extra pimple, scarcely a mountain peak, on the main northern ridge of the Carneddau.) Since well before Roman times, these surprising mountains were already steeped in Celtic legend, the prehistory playground of giants and fairies and water monsters.

The Roman Army under Governor Gnaeus Julius Agricola had its own lifestyle retreat of sorts here too, a marching camp for over 1,000 men, including some 'equestrian activities', situated at the head of Dyffryn Mymbyr and Moel Berfedd. The northern rampart of the camp actually runs right through the current location of the Pen y Gwryd Hotel.

Although nobody could possibly suppose that the summit of Snowdon remained untrodden by human feet until the 17th century, the first *recorded* ascent of Snowdon has been attributed to the gentleman wanderer and botanist Thomas Johnson (1639). The first recorded rock climb in Britain is credited to pioneering clerical adventurers, also in search of interesting plants, Peter Bailey Williams and William Bingley,

35

who ascended the Eastern Terrace of Snowdon's Clogwyn Du'r Arddu on Bingley's vacation from Peterhouse, Cambridge in 1798. But these pioneers, and even the 1953 British Everest team, were all relative newcomers to these parts. The truth must be that, for millennia, these hills have given countless people like you and me the opportunity not only to admire some of the best views in Britain but also to enjoy the life-affirming benefits of physical exercise and mountain air in the company of like-minded friends.

The Snowdonia National Park is in fact one enormous outdoor fitness wonderland covering 823 square miles (2,132 square kilometres). The park has 1,497 miles (2,410 kilometres) of public footpaths, 164 miles (264 kilometres) of public bridleways and 46 miles (74 kilometres) of other public rights of way. In addition, over 200 activity operators in the mountains and coastal area cover a range of sea-to-summit activities as diverse as 'pole fitness' and 'Bollywood Burnout'.

And so, within a day's walk of the front door of the Pen y Gwryd Hotel, you just might be less likely these days to meet walkers and climbers than practitioners of Zumba, Pilates, Global Bokwa Beat or Yoga. In fact, retreats and organised fitness events have largely eclipsed many other mountain activities as the best ways to get fit, de-stress, lose weight and rediscover peace and tranquillity.

Ffion White studied Outdoor Leisure and Travel Tourism at Llandrillo College, North Wales. Together with Paul Edwards, who studied Sports Science at Llandrillo and Football Science and Personal Training at John Moores University Liverpool, they run the outdoor pursuits company Bespoke Fitness and Events. White and Edwards show visitors to the mountains how to both 'embrace their adventurous side' and 'enjoy the experience of getting into shape'. One aspect of the business organises adventure, fitness and weight loss retreats in various locations, including the Pen y Gwryd Hotel.

www.bespokefitnessandevents.co.uk

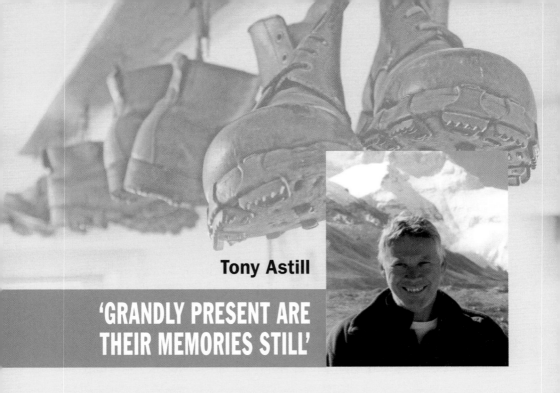

Tony Astill

'GRANDLY PRESENT ARE THEIR MEMORIES STILL'

I N THE FINAL pages of *Rock Climbing in North Wales* (1906) by the Abraham brothers, George and Ashley, there are some advertisements, including one for 'Pen y Gwryd Hotel. Under new management of the Royal Hotel, Capel Curig. The oldest and finest mountaineering hotel in Wales'. I decided to continue this tradition by including a 1935 advertisement in my own book *Mount Everest: The Reconnaissance 1935.*

PEN Y GWRYD HOTEL
NANT GWYNANT – SNOWDONIA

The Home of British Mountaineering, catering particularly for climbers. At the foot of the Glyders and close to Snowdon. All modern comforts. Hot and cold water in bedrooms. Spring mattresses. Drying Room, Boot Room and Billiard Room. Packed lunches. Electric light.

This Home of British Mountaineering is also highly recommended in *Notes and Recollections of an Angler* by John Henry Cliffe, published

Photograph of Tony Astill by George Band (using Tony's camera.)

in 1860, which is the first book mentioned in the bibliography of *Mountaineering in Britain* by Clark and Pyatt. This states, 'In the midst of this solitudinous region formerly stood a wretched roadside ale-house, known as "Pen y Gwryd Inn"'. Through the enterprise of the landlord at that time, Henry Owen transformed the PyG into 'A very comfortable inn, where not only the wayfarer meets with civility and attention, but even in the culinary department he will have no reason to complain'.

Nor did I on my first visit.

Together with two friends, we were on a 'One Green Bottle' camping adventure down the valley at the Capel Curig Training Ground. Licensing laws at the time dictated that Sunday was 'dry' in Gwynedd so we had to while away the Sunday evening elsewhere. This was the first time that I met Chris Briggs (and remember that I was a complete stranger to him). He suggested that we enjoy our day on the Glyderau, return to PyG for a shower, with warm towels provided, book a table for dinner and, as such, become 'residents' and then spend the evening there. A wonderful solution gratefully accepted! And so, my own affair with our favourite hotel started on that evening about 40 years ago. And, as chance would have it, Chris soon discovered that I could assist in providing an insurance valuation for damage to his library of mountaineering books by some leaky roof water.

On another visit, whilst my wife and I were enjoying dinner, the central table of the dining room was taken up by a large group of medical students who had just completed the 'Three Peaks'. One of their party suddenly collapsed on the floor, presumably exhausted. Brian Pullee immediately attended to him and enquired, in an almost comical retort, 'Is there a doctor in the house?'

Brian, always dapper with cravat, would dispense pre-dinner drinks from behind the bar (but what was his regular tipple?). Time for 'The Gong'. Where else is a gong struck for dinner these days? Jane Pullee, in traditional Welsh waiting maid's dress, would take our order and always made us feel at home, like a friend of the family, and that tradition has been continued by their sons.

For us, the PyG will always remain a special place for spending a night or two to meet with old friends. The hotel has also played a part in making my new friends too, whom I might not have otherwise met and, in that place, one can almost feel the presence of those who are no longer with us.

Some hotels lay claim to being haunted. The PyG has seen so much climbing history that it is in fact 'haunted' with stories and personalities, back to the earliest days of climbing. And, as Jan Morris writes in her wonderful introduction to this book, 'Grandly present are their memories still'. These wonderful reminiscences are jogged by the souvenirs that decorate the residents' bar; the row of engraved beer mugs that commemorate the climbs of great mountains; the shrunken head given by George Band and by the photographs of old climbers that adorn the walls. Long may the PyG remain untouched by the passing tourists who stop for chicken and chips in a basket and are politely sent on their way!

For those who do reside, and it occurs to me that some locals may never have enjoyed that pleasure, the idiosyncrasies of that accommodation retain a memorable charm; mattresses that leave couples very close together in the middle; and the vintage bathrooms shared. (Where else in the world would boiled eggs for breakfast be kept warm in their own woolly hats?)

My final debt to the PyG is that the 40th anniversary of the first ascent of Everest put me in touch with the 1953 British Everest team, many of whom became good friends (though no such fuss was made about the first ascent of Kangchenjunga, which also has strong ties with PyG through local mountaineers Joe Brown, Charles Evans and John Jackson.)

So it was that, in 1995, when George Band returned to Kangchenjunga on a trek to celebrate the 40th anniversary of that first ascent, he kindly invited me to join them. The expedition artist Lincoln Rowe produced a beautiful pastel of Kangchenjunga from Octang and, when some months later it was exhibited, I was fortunate enough to red dot it before anyone else and, on hearing this, Tony Streather suggested that it would make an excellent fine-art print. I was able to arrange this and the first four summiteers agreed to sign a limited edition print of 100 copies, all of which made their way to New Zealand for Norman Hardie to sign as well. I gave 12 more artist's proofs to those who were closely involved in the climb including, of course, one to the Pen y Gwryd where it can still be seen today hanging in the hotel dining room.

Tony Astill has dealt in the art and literature of mountains and mountaineering for over 40 years. The hunger for adventure and the insatiable appetite for escapades is what first drew him to start collecting rare mountaineering books. Astill is the author of *Mount Everest: The Reconnaissance 1935, The Forgotten Adventure,* which was awarded Best Book Mountaineering History at the Banff Mountain Festival 2006. Astill's list, 'The Top 100 British Mountaineering Books' can be seen at www.mountaineeringbooks.org

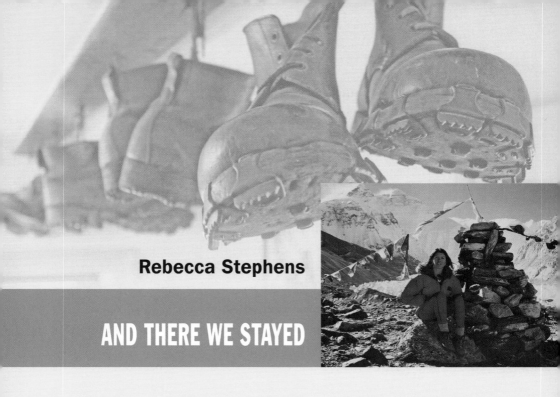

Rebecca Stephens

AND THERE WE STAYED

I HAVE STAYED at the Pen y Gwryd a handful of times; loved the Victorian baths and creaky floorboards. I always feel happier in old places than new; I like the patina, and the layers upon layers of stories that inhabit them – and the Pen y Gwryd is certainly not short on these. The hotel oozes atmosphere from every dark-beamed crevasse and slate-clad fireplace.

One weekend, a carful of us headed from London to Wales to climb the fourteen 3000s. I can't remember the name of the lady who ran the place at the time; Danish, I think. Bark worse than her bite. 'No supper after 8pm', we were told, ringing on a mobile from stationary traffic on the M4 as we and a million other people unloaded from the city on a Friday afternoon. We arrived sometime after 10pm and five suppers had been put to one side, neatly protected with cling wrap, awaiting our arrival.

Packed lunches were left out for us on the Saturday morning and we set out early and climbed up and down eight of the fourteen 3000s, Snowdon and Tryfan included. I revelled in a rare moment of isolation among a jigsaw of boulders high on Tryfan, the light fading, and the small figure of a friend far below, waiting for me on the col.

I've yet to find anything more rewarding than a long day in the hills and a hot wholesome meal of an evening. My limbs ached pleasingly as I wrapped my legs under me and curled into a large comfy chair in the Pen y Gwryd sitting room, soaking up the direct heat from the flames of the fire. Then, unravelling my legs, I walked slowly, stiffly, the length of the corridor to the dining room.

'Can't think why these Londoners come all this way to climb 14 peaks,' voiced the Danish lady, sweeping between the seated guests. 'Why, indeed?' we asked, and poured another glass of wine.

The following morning the sky was a clear blue with promises of a perfect summer's day. We lingered over breakfast, limbs stiffer even than the night before. I can't remember which of us it was who first dared suggest there might be options other than climbing the remaining six peaks. We had all heard our Danish friend's words.

There wasn't a rush to don our walking boots, or pack our sacks. We strolled lazily into the pretty garden at the back of the hotel, walked its length to a natural pool, cold as the mountain stream that fed it. We stretched out on the newly mown grass and gazed up, fascinated by the coloured arcs of paraglider wings circling overhead. And there we stayed and read the Sunday papers.

Rebecca Stephens is a British journalist, mountaineer and television presenter. On 17 May, 1993, Stephens became the first British woman to climb Everest. The following year she went on to become the first British woman to scale the Seven Summits, the highest mountain on each of the seven continents.

Stephens's early career was in journalism, working first as reporter and then Deputy Editor of one of the *Financial Times* magazines. It was while writing for the *Financial Times Weekend* that she was assigned to Everest and discovered her passion for climbing. She continues to draw on her experiences of the outdoors and business to write articles for the *Financial Times*, as well as *The Times*, *The Independent*, *The Telegraph* and *The Mail on Sunday*. She has regularly appeared on television, as a presenter on *Tomorrow's World*, *Science Zone* and *Enterprise South*, and as a guest on *Call my Bluff*, *Through the Keyhole*, *Blue Peter*, *Ridge Riders*, *The Battle of the Books*, and *Date with an Artist*. In 2003, she was one of the judges for the Man Booker Prize for contemporary literature.

Since 1995, Stephens has been actively involved with the Himalayan Trust UK, established by Edmund Hillary to help the Sherpa people help themselves.

She chaired The Himalayan Trust for three years from 2011 to 2014 and now continues her role as a trustee. Stephens is also an ambassador of the Shackleton Foundation, founded in 2007 by descendants of Ernest Shackleton's Antarctic expeditions to help disadvantaged and socially marginalised young people. A Fellow of the Royal Geographical Society, she is a member of the Alpine Club. www.himalayantrust.co.uk

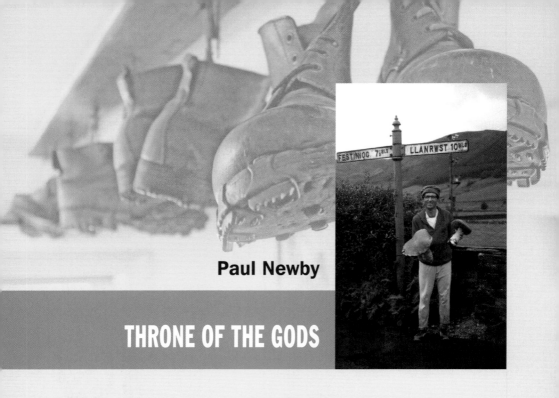

Paul Newby

THRONE OF THE GODS

L ONG, LONG AGO, when the mountains were young and we were
even younger, and silly with it, my fate decreed that I should hand
a large item of sanitary chinaware across the bar of the Pen y Gwryd
Hotel. This is how it came to pass.

One early December (1963 if I remember rightly), I was enjoying
the Cambridge University Hare and Hounds (cross country running
club) Holiday, based at Pont y Pant Youth Hostel in the Lledr valley in
Snowdonia, not too far from the Pen y Gwryd. This annual 'holiday'
consisted of a mixture of enormously long mountain and forest runs
with some quite arduous and serious walking and scrambling, as well
as a systematic survey of the pubs of the district. We soon met another
older mountaineer and fell runner, one George Rhodes, known already
to some of the senior members of our party. In a field near the hostel,
George had a caravan which he used to visit year round. On one occasion
we found him there surveying the damage after it had blown over in a
gale. When he heard that we were planning an expedition to the PyG he
said, 'Ah, that's grand, you can save me a journey'.

It transpired that George, who hailed from Stoke-on-Trent in the
Potteries district of England's Midlands, knew Chris Briggs quite well,

44

having been a faithful visitor to the hotel ever since Chris welcomed him in as a young refugee from a flooded campsite in the 1940s. On this occasion George had agreed to do Chris a favour by fetching a lavatory pan, needed for the hotel, from a factory near his home. George asked us to deliver it for him, and none-too-subtly hinted that there would surely be some free beer in it for us if we did so.

To our eternal shame, several of us also thought it would be a rather jolly jape to deliver the article ceremonially over the bar of this renowned establishment. We already knew, after all, that there was only one front door and, as Jan Morris has reminded us in her Introduction, that the bar consisted only of a serving hatch, and moreover, that the hotel boasted no other reception desk. We could hardly be expected to seek out an unobtrusive back door in the darkness of a winter's night. Other athletes discreetly melted away so it was a small party who put the gleaming white object into the boot of our captain's mother's Morris Oxford. The captain was among those who, for some reason, did not wish to be involved in the escapade. He handed me the keys and we set off through the early evening darkness, wondering only whether the remembered serving hatch would prove to be big enough.

We arrived without mishap, parked easily – an early weekday evening in December was not going to be the PyG's busiest time. I embraced the throne firmly with both arms and we all went in. I placed it on the shelf from which drinks were served, partly blocking the hatch, to the bemusement of the very few other drinkers already ensconced in one or two of the little alcoves which remain essentially unaltered today. It took a while to attract any attention, but eventually an elderly lady appeared behind the hatch (well, she must have been at least 30 years old – but perhaps this was in fact the redoubtable PyG maid, Blodwen Griffiths herself, then aged about 76). She was holding a large pitcher of beer freshly drawn from the barrel, ready to pour for her customers, as was still the way at the PyG and a few other rural hostelries in those days. While I tried to explain our mission, it rapidly became clear that she was not at all amused. Initially she was also unwilling to understand that the china was indeed destined for, and ordered by, the hotel. Eventually a young man was produced, and he came round to the public side of the hatch and took it away; I do not remember whether he thanked me.

It seemed to us that there was a complete lack of humour in the house, and certainly no free beer. We downed our paid-for pints swiftly in a corner and slunk away. Who knows whether it would have been any different if Chris Briggs himself had been present to receive the prize. Although I used occasionally to boast that I was probably the only mountaineer ever to have handed a lavatory across the bar of that famous climbers' hotel, for many a long year I felt too embarrassed to darken the door of the PyG, nor could I pass by without cringing in shame that such a jolly jape had vanished so ingloriously down the pan.

Jan Morris has also reminded us of the PyG's distinguished Victorian plumbing, and its equally distinguished clientele. I cannot help wondering occasionally about the fate of the throne which I once handled, and about the gods of the mountaineering community who still return there from time to time. Nowadays, I do always enjoy my visits to the PyG but they are infrequent because my own base in North Wales is just a little too far away for a comfortable drive after drinking or dining, and much too close to need ever to stay at the hotel overnight.

My familiarity with the spot did not, of course, begin in 1963. As a very small boy 'Penny Gerrid' was an important landmark on my mental map, between home in the West Midlands and the seaside on Cardigan Bay where my parents kept a caravan or two for several years in the early 1950s. I did not learn to try to pronounce Welsh names more accurately until a little later. One dim late afternoon, disaster struck my father's old Lea-Francis shooting brake as we ground up the interminable, winding slope from Beddgelert to Pen y Gwryd. The terrible noise was the breaking of a rear spring, an old-fashioned cart spring with overlapping steel 'leaves' intended to form an elegant inverted arc. Knowing that in those days there was a small workshop and petrol station at Pen y Gwryd, an outstation of the main local garage in Beddgelert, my father made the decision to press on upwards. Sure enough, kind Mr Pritchard, the owner of the two garages, was still at PyG when we eventually limped in. Mr Pritchard jacked up the heavily laden Lea-Francis and soon had us on our way again, with a stout chunk of timber lashed in place to keep the body of the car clear of the rear axle. As my childhood continued its slow course, I always remembered that exciting incident of the road, and I was sad when the workshop eventually became derelict, leaving only a, by now, rather incongruous petrol station just opposite the hotel.

Much later, after my wife and I joined the Snowdonia National Park Society (now the Snowdonia Society) we found that the petrol station at PyG was becoming a cause célèbre. The late great Chris Brasher, mountaineer, athlete, Olympic gold medallist and co-founder of the London Marathon, who eventually became a personal friend through our running club, the Thames Hare and Hounds, was deeply committed to the Society's objectives of preserving the landscape and heritage of Snowdonia. He was a prime mover of the Society's campaign to close the perceived eyesore of the PyG petrol station, and eventually put up the money to buy it outright in order to bulldoze it. Clearly this was an example where landscape trumped heritage. I don't think Chris ever understood my sentimental attachment to the Pen y Gwryd Garage and my sadness when his argument was won and the eyesore opposite the hotel disappeared forever.

Going back to the years just after the Second World War, this was a period when British filmmaking took off in a big way, but budgets were low and exotic foreign locations were out of the question. North Wales with its grand landscapes, still reasonably free of modern accretions, became a popular location for filming. Several great classics were made within a stone's throw of Pen y Gwryd, notably including *The Inn of the Sixth Happiness* (starring Ingrid Bergman, 1958), shot in the valleys around Beddgelert to recreate the China of the real-life missionary Gladys Aylward, and the really improbable *Carry on up the Khyber* (1968), in which a five-barred gate at the bottom of the Watkin Path up Snowdon doubled as the outer limit of the North West Frontier of British India. The hilarious and bawdy *Carry on up the Khyber* was rated among the ten best films of all time (perhaps tongue in cheek, or should we say foot in mouth?) by no less an authority than the distinguished critic Colin MacCabe, now Professor of English and Film at the University of Pittsburgh, formerly of Cambridge and Exeter Universities.

47

It seems certain that some of the stars of these films would occasionally, or perhaps even habitually, use the PyG as their watering hole to assuage the rigours of their lives on location. I know for a fact that some of them ranged more widely over North Wales. In 1968 my much younger brother Steve was still a little lad who loved to earn extra pocket money by standing at the gate of the mountain road just above our cottage and opening it for the infrequent passing motorists. The going rate was usually about twopence (two heavy old pennies) but especially kindly or generous drivers might give him as much as sixpence. Steve tells of one fine day during the filming of *Carry on up the Khyber*, when the unmistakable personage of Sid James stopped his car and waited for him to open the gate. Evidently keen to impress his female passenger, the great man handed over half a crown for services rendered (two shillings and sixpence – now just 12½p, but then a small fortune for a small boy). Our gate, long since removed, was remarkably like the now immortal barrier on the Watkin Path which represented the Khyber Pass. And that lady friend of Sid James is perhaps today an elderly but famous actress who could even be reading this right now.

To come right up to date, one of my most recent visits to the hotel was for the celebration in 2013 marking the 60th anniversary of the first ascent of Everest, when the Alpine Club hosted the few survivors and numerous descendants of the 1953 British Everest Expedition and its extended family of supporters. A splendid evening reception was laid on by the new generation of Chris Briggs's own extended family.

Even more recently, on the strength of that Everest event, I proposed the PyG for the 50th anniversary of one of my own lesser mountaineering expeditions, and went in to discuss possible arrangements. However, I was sadly outvoted by my team and we met instead in the French Alps in the summer of 2015. Ah well, the PyG will still be there for us. I really must get on the phone and book a quiet and restrained, but suitably nostalgic, dinner with my wife.

Paul Newby is Editor Emeritus of *The Photogrammetric Record* and a Fellow of the International Society for Photogrammetry and Remote Sensing. Paul's professional life involved land surveying and mapping in the UK and numerous countries overseas, as well as technical translation and editing, not least in support of parts of the present volume! He built the trig point on the summit of St Lucia's Petit Piton, iconic landmark of the Caribbean, and has provided English copy about surveying and mapping for the walls of the Swiss Parliament and for the Swiss Alpine Museum. Paul is also an amateur mountaineer and athlete and an unofficial bard, with a long-standing connection with North Wales.

As a fell runner, his fastest time up and down Snowdon (from Llanberis) was a little under 80 minutes. Without fear of contradiction, he claims to have reached the summit of Snowdon between 100 and 200 times, by a wide variety of routes and in all conceivable conditions (though rarely more than once in a day), and he still does so at least once a year. Elsewhere, Paul's mountaineering life has included 'compleating' the Munros of Scotland and Furth, as well as higher climbs in the Alps, Turkey, the Hindu Kush, Himalaya and Andes. Closer to home, his most recent bardic exploit was in Cwm Penmachno's *Strictly Cwm Laughing*.

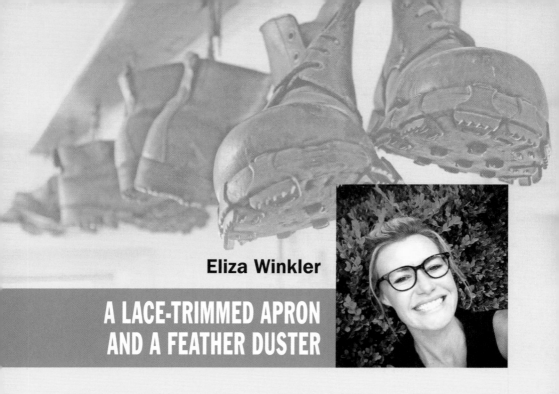

Eliza Winkler

A LACE-TRIMMED APRON AND A FEATHER DUSTER

U NLIKE THE MANY who visit the Pen y Gwryd Hotel to conquer Snowdon or contemplate life's vagaries and marvels, it was the god-awful sight of the bottom of the barrel that found me there. I needed to work and make money to continue my European travels. It was a desperate situation – but not serious. I had a job and so a means to an end; but never did I imagine that I would actually grow to love and later miss such a peculiar and wonderful place.

While the lush dewy mountains of North Wales are well known and admired, it was the characters – residents and staff alike – who graced the Pen y Gwryd that made it my home away from home.

The Pen y Gwryd is a traveller's inn. It is remote. It sits neatly and confidently on the toes of Mount Snowdon and is embraced by the seemingly boundless lichen-green-grey outcrops of the Glyderau. After my journey from London, I was greeted on the platform of Bangor railway station by the lady of the house, Jane Pullee, a no-nonsense businesswoman with soft classic tastes equally matched with a stern love of formality … and discipline. At the hotel, I was briefed on the daily tasks, handed a lace-trimmed apron … and a feather duster – and shown my room.

In my time, Jane Pullee's two sons, Rupert and Nicolas, had just started to manage the everyday running of the Gwryd. To my surprise, neither of them looked anything like the hobbit-like creatures I expected to find in a place like 'the Gwryd'. I quickly learnt that, for the next year from 7am until 7pm six days a week, I would be washing mops, drawing curtains, turning down sheets, 'hoovering' (which antipodeans call 'vacuuming'), scrubbing baths, preparing a local Welsh cheeseboard selection for after dinner and, much later, swanning with the best of them in front of a roaring open fire in the Everest Room.

With a staff comprised of two Polish girls, two Danish chefs, two British boys and two Australian travellers, it made for an interesting octo-dynamic. We all worked hard and we all worked well.

Under the watchful eyes of their mother Jane, Rupert, a somewhat eccentric gentleman dreamer and Nicolas, a well-travelled adventurer, directed us through the everyday verse and chorus of hotel work. There was something still and peaceful in the madness of the Pen y Gwryd's relentless routine, especially Friday to Sunday, mid-term break and 'bloody bank holidays'.

Somewhere in between polishing the brass doorknobs and hanging tea-towels in the drying room, and of course beeswaxing the ancient oak furniture, laying and lighting the coal fires and mopping the slate, there would be time to segue across the frost-tipped grass to the cedar sauna by the pond. And there ... 'to sleep, perchance to dream' – and soak up the ample simplicity that only comes when you ... stop. Savouring quiet moments was one of the many new skills I learnt during my Gwryd tour of duty; that and how to roll a cigarette like a champion, as well as an appreciation of old-fashioned British white bread without a trace of fibre or goodness.

The daily double-decker bus that ran to the seaside town of Llandudno was my day-off staff routine, a weekly dose of reality that reminded me that I lived in a modern time with Myspace.

No matter what way you pick up the Gwryd, and no matter what angle you look at it, when I close my eyes, at any moment, I'm back in front of the fire at the end of a long shift with the never-say-die, late-night patrons and an ample gin and tonic.

Eliza Winkler was raised on the south coast of New South Wales, Australia, the second child of Martin and Rosemary Winkler who forged a family and many friendships in a paradoxical realm of coast-meets-country. Winkler travelled to Wales and worked at the Pen y Gwryd Hotel in 2006, following in the footsteps of her elder sister Angela who worked at the hotel in 2003 and was on staff for the 50th Anniversary celebrations of the 1953 British Everest Expedition. She went on to study Communications and Media at the University of Wollongong and is now working as a journalist with Fairfax Media, Australia. Angela Winkler went on to study Law and is now a Senior Associate at Wotton & Kearney Lawyers, Sydney.

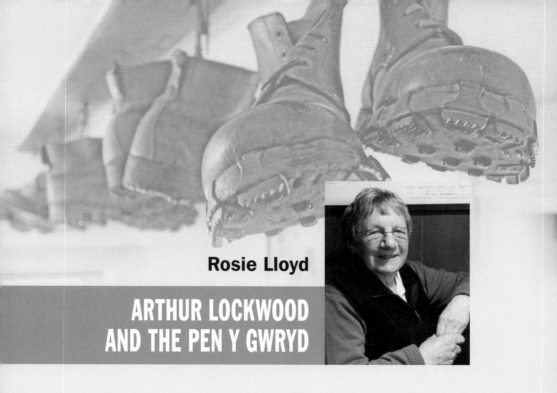

Rosie Lloyd

ARTHUR LOCKWOOD AND THE PEN Y GWRYD

ARTHUR LOCKWOOD was born near Doncaster in 1885 and attended Penistone Grammar School (founded in 1393), Barnsley, in what is now known as South Yorkshire. Lockwood chose not to go to university but rather, at age 15, secured an electrical engineering apprenticeship with Leeds City Lighting Company at a time when electricity generation and transmission was in its infancy.

Thoughts of his future career as a hotel owner must have been far from his mind at that time. Completing his apprenticeship, Lockwood set out to gain a broader experience working for the Durham Collieries Power Company and then the Newcastle-upon-Tyne Electricity Company in 1907. At the age of 24, he applied to the recently opened (August 1906) Cwm Dyli Hydro-Electric Power Station, then operated by North Wales Power and Traction Company; his knowledge and experience was clearly respected and he was appointed Engineer-in-Charge (August 1908) before later becoming Superintendent.

Moving to Snowdonia, Lockwood sought accommodation in the Pen y Gwryd Hotel, the nearest available to Cwm Dyli. In 1906, Florence Gertrude Bloomfield (born 1876) moved to North Wales to manage the

PyG on behalf of W. Hampson. Arthur married Florence on 10 May, 1909, in Beddgelert after a nine-month courtship.

Lockwood worked full-time at Cwm Dyli, presumably walking to and from work in all weathers. When he was offered accommodation in the newly built on-site bungalow, he turned it down in favour of the hotel. During this period, Lockwood gained membership of the Institute of Electrical Engineers and later became an Associate.

Lockwood obviously settled quickly in his new life. He developed a keen interest in the weather and he became involved in recording rainfall and temperature statistics, both for his own interest and for the use of the power station. A chapter in Herbert Carr's *Mountains of Snowdonia* is jointly authored by Arthur Lockwood and Professor Kennedy Orton. It is entitled 'The Weather in Snowdonia'. It illustrates Lockwood's academic knowledge of weather patterns and his growing love for the hills.

> Apart from the physical pleasures of a contest with the elements (sometimes most keenly enjoyed in retrospect), it is upon the doubtful days that the great moments happen with such distracting fleetness …

Lockwood writes about an 'absolute drought' on 11 June, 1914, after recording 21 days without rain, the result of which was that local drinking water supplies dried up. He compares this with 8 August, 1914, when there were 6.35 inches of precipitation, which was nearly as heavy as 14 October, 1909, when 7.18 inches fell in just 16 hours, a comparison that could be made with December 2015.

Soon after his arrival at Pen y Gwryd in 1909, Lockwood led a climb, on an enigmatic route, which became known as Lockwood's Chimney on Clogwyn y Bustach ('Cliff of the Bullock'), which lies partly hidden in the woods above Cwm Dyli Power Station. Who his companions were or other details are lost but it is presumed that he climbed with guests from the hotel. At the then contemporary grade of 'difficult', Lockwood's Chimney is an easy climb by modern standards requiring less style than brute force to ascend but, with the minimum of equipment and experience, it would have definitely posed a challenge at the time. This is the first evidence of Arthur Lockwood being noted as an 'expert mountaineer', words that appear in the local newspaper in 1918. After his involvement in a mountain rescue, Lockwood is recorded as recovering a body after which he 'conveyed it to Pen y Pass'. Other documentary evidence of his skills are hard to find in the records but it is said that Brigadier Charles Grenville Bruce invited Lockwood to join the 1922 British Everest Expedition; unfortunately his wife Florence would not agree to this.

Another interest that Lockwood took with him to Snowdonia from Yorkshire was fishing. Again, in the book *Mountains of Snowdonia*, Lockwood writes a chapter entitled 'Notes on Angling'. The title downplays the contents; rather, his account contains a deep knowledge about fishing the lakes and rivers that surround the Gwryd. In time, his great passion for fishing inspired him to build Lockwood's Lake, sometimes incorrectly called Llyn Pen y Gwryd. He clearly saw it as a facility for use by his guests and for himself. With very limited resources, both physical and financial, Lockwood built the dam to restrain the stream that ran past the hotel, an amazing achievement.

Despite being a Yorkshireman, Lockwood set about being involved in the local community. He was a parish councillor in Beddgelert (which at that time was a monoglot Welsh-speaking community). In September 1916, Lockwood put a scheme forward to the Parish Council to put street lighting up in the village. It was turned down on the basis of cost; the council were already heavily involved in a water and sewage scheme. In 1919, he was returned unopposed.

Lockwood's management skills must have been involved when a Territorial Army unit was formed and based at Cwm Dyli. It is assumed that he was appointed Major for his services; his work in Cwm Dyli was a reserved occupation, so he did not serve in the First World War. In 1919, Lockwood resigned from Cwm Dyli, dissatisfied with his salary, and went to Burma, initially to take up a job on the Mansam Falls, Shan State. He retained the tenancy of the hotel. Later the same year, he moved to India where he was appointed supervisor for the building of a hydro-electric plant at Simla. Whilst away, his brother-in-law managed the hotel. In 1921, Lockwood's brother-in-law telegraphed that the hotel was up for sale. Lockwood sailed home from Rangoon (then part of British India) and he and Florence bought the Pen y Gwryd in October of that year.

During the early 1920s, Lockwood set up a garage at the Pen y Gwryd that was to exist until the early 1990s. Initially, using the old coach house buildings, Lockwood expanded across the road. (The site opposite the hotel where the petrol filling station once stood has been rehabilitated and incorporated back into the Snowdon National Park.)

In 1926 Lockwood made a curious find on a plateau leading up to Glyder Fach. It was the skeleton of a man of about 50 years. Moss had grown into the cranium as the body must have been there for upwards of three years. Amongst the remains was a briar pipe, a penny dated 1898 and a watch that ticked when shaken. It is presumed that the man was taking a short cut over the Glyderau, sought shelter in a pen and died of exposure.

Mountain rescue and the Pen y Gwryd were a natural match. Arthur Lockwood, with his mountaineering skills, quickly became involved. In the 1920s, the Joint Stretcher Committee was formed. In 1933 Arthur Lockwood was asked to co-ordinate rescues in the northern area of Snowdonia, by what became known as the Mountain Rescue Committee. Accordingly, the Pen y Gwryd Hotel was designated a Mountain Rescue Post from the early 1920s although, from the first days of its establishment, people in trouble on the hills would have naturally gravitated towards the Gwryd for help. (Chris Briggs took over where Arthur Lockwood left off in 1947.)

The Mountain Rescue Committee stored a range of equipment on site in the 20th century, ready to be used in an emergency. They also appointed Lockwood as post supervisor and a Thomas stretcher and other rescue equipment were stored at Pen y Gwryd. In a booklet published in 1938, entitled *First Aid* (issued by the First Aid Committee for Mountain Clubs), the hotel, under the proprietorship of Lockwood, was noted to be responsible for the evacuation of injured climbers from Lliwedd, Snowdon, Crib Goch, Cwm Glas, Craig Yr Ysfa, and Clogwyn Du'r Arddu.

In September 1940, the Pen y Gwryd was taken over by Lakeside House Preparatory School; the children were evacuated from Bexhill-on-Sea. This involved some 35 pupils in four forms under headmaster Mr A. H. Williams. By August 1944 the Lockwoods were losing their enthusiasm for hotel work and sold the business to Mr Riddett, the son of an earlier Climbers' Club member and the Lockwoods retired to the house next door, Hafod y Gwynt.

Interestingly, on 19 July, 1946, Mr and Mrs Lockwood were introduced to King George VI and Queen Elizabeth when they visited the Pen y Gwryd, escorted by Mr Clough Williams-Ellis; their visit was based on the proposal to establish a National Park in Caernarfonshire.

After the Second World War, Lockwood became the chairman of the Conway River Board, a respected position in the management of water resources. In 1952, he was central in proposing a fish pass up the Swallow Falls, on the upper River Llugwy (a tributary of the Conwy) to allow salmon access up to the upper river, noting how important it would be for fishing in the area. Nothing came of this idea; the river board could not finance the project. In the 1950s, in the garden of Hafod y Gwynt, Lockwood built a fish hatchery, the only one in this part of Wales.

Florence Lockwood died in 1969, aged 93. By 1970 Arthur Lockwood was a semi-invalid. He was cared for by his friend Mr Pritchard who moved into Hafod y Gwynt. He went into a nursing home in Llanrwst in 1971 where he died on 15 January 1973, aged 87.

The scanty records available of Arthur Lockwood's full life, both before, during and after his 30 years at the Pen y Gwryd, clearly do not reveal even part of the story of his life, just as the PyG's *Locked Book* tells little about his time at the hotel. Lockwood kept a detailed diary but this is now lost as a reference. Arthur Lockwood did not seek personal promotion in this field; his skills were rather based on his practical education and, building on this, he became a successful businessman, contributing much to the area in which he lived and loved.

Rosie Lloyd (née Sheppard), was born and spent her early years in Essex. Whilst training to be a science schoolteacher, she attended an outdoor pursuits training course at Plas y Brenin in 1961, as a representative of the Ranger Girl Guides. On the course, she met her future husband and moved to Wales. In 1972, they were both appointed managers of the Youth Hostel at Pen y Pass, bringing about a close relationship with the Pen y Gwryd Hotel. Later in the mid-1980s, they purchased Hafod y Gwynt, the house that Arthur Lockwood had owned and lived in.

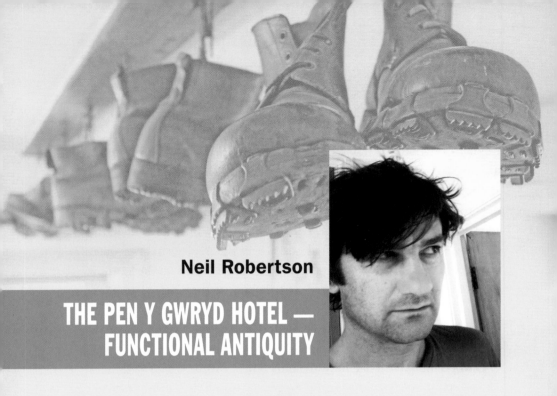

Neil Robertson

THE PEN Y GWRYD HOTEL — FUNCTIONAL ANTIQUITY

Visiting the time-worn fabric of the Pen y Gwryd Hotel rarely requires an excuse. For this remote mountain accommodation actually *is* what many others aspire to be: a genuine, unique and charming old place with real history and no gloss.

Pushing open the heavy wooden door, having just landed the contract to create their new website and printed material, was thus a double delight. This was a task that gave me the opportunity to engage with the hotel's story and to bring to life the feelings one gets of 'functional antiquity'. It was also a task to be treated sensitively, as we were being trusted with history.

During the first meeting with Rupert and Nicolas Pullee (third-generation owners), we established the scope of the project and assigned roles. We toured the hotel and grounds and were showered with old books, magazines, cuttings and general PyG-related information.

Back at our drawing boards, we assimilated this wealth of information and began to forge the general feel and tone that we wanted our designs to convey. We decided to keep print colours muted, possibly monochrome, to use a serif font, and to make good use of the photographs already taken by Nicolas's partner (and soon wife-to-be) Nicola Maysmor.

A second meeting was held to discuss these broad principles and to firm-up some of our ideas on format and layout. Further input from the owners gave direction to the documents' flow and desired copy. At the third meeting, we presented a brochure spread mock-up that was approved. We requested that further photos be taken. After all this immersion in the hotel, writing the copy suddenly became simple and the brochure was finished very quickly. Other printed work rapidly followed.

All the while, ideas for the website were stirring: we wanted to make a bold image-driven statement, rejecting both the soft-furnished visual embellishments of most hotel fare and the stark minimalism of modern hotels. As the brochure had already paved the way in terms of style, creating the site was a fairly swift business.

More-than-satisfied clients means a good feeling all around. What is more, the prospect of continued interaction with this venerable hotel ensures me a genuine source of delight for the future.

Neil Robertson was born in North Wales. He worked 'on and off' at the PyG in the 1990s, starting with the summer of 1991, which he remembers as 'great times'. He likes to recall 'nipping up Glyder Fach during the three-hour afternoon break in a split shift, and back, with a shirt and tie on for the evening meal service; Jane Pullee's hand firmly on the tiller, as the good ship PyG steamed through the late night and early morning, entertaining guests in the Smoke Room'. Robertson met his partner while she was working at the PyG in 2005 and … 'rescued her'. These days, he divides his time between website design and growing eucalyptus trees. These provide foliage for florists all over the UK and are grown just outside Llanrwst. www.uklyptus.co.uk and www.robertsondesignstudio.co.uk.

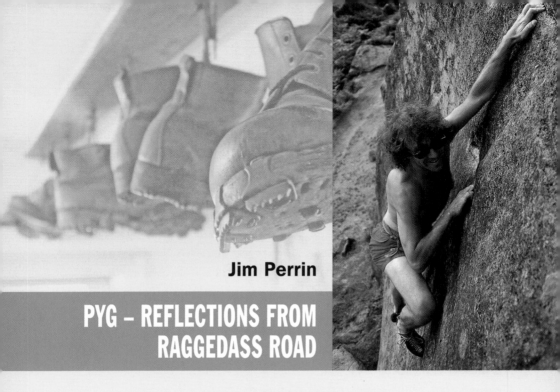

Jim Perrin

PYG – REFLECTIONS FROM RAGGEDASS ROAD

A VIVID MEMORY from the early 1960s – Dougie Baines tanked up in the Everest Room, inveigling me into taking a ride down The Pass for a quick afternoon climb on Clogwyn y Grochan. I grab my sack, perch on the back of the racing seat of his DBD34 500cc Gold Star, and we take off up the road. Those tuned BSA singles sounded like bags of rusty nails till you hit the sweet spot and they came on the cam at about 7000 rpm. Then they began to rocket. We were doing 90 by the time we got to the Magnetic Bend (know why it's called that?) and he dropped down to second, opening the throttle, our right knees inches from the tarmac and his footrest (there was just the stub of a hub for me to rest a toe on) sending up showers of sparks in required fashion. We passed Gorphwysfa at over the ton and I shut my eyes for the descent down the other side. The climbing afterwards felt easy. Can't remember what we did, but it would have been standards from the repertoire – up Brant Direct and solo down Brant, show a bit of respect to the off-balance, crux groove of Kaisergebirge Wall, race up Karwendel which was supposed to be harder but wasn't: just a right-hand reach for a hidden jug and a lurch across to good flakes, nothing to it when you were young and bold and strong. As we were.

I knew Dougie from the climbing club I belonged to in Oldham, when I was barely in my teens and we were both roughneck kids from Raggedass Road, out every weekend on the Chew Valley gritstone outcrops. He was a legend. My best buddy of the time, Little Jack Landy, with whom you didn't argue, told me about holding Dougie's rope when he led Erosion Direct on Carreg Wastad after eight pints in the Gwryd one lunchtime. Erosion Direct was the most difficult thing around in those days – horribly awkward and committing, bad and distant protection, smooth rock, right up at the top of that loose and nasty crag. It was *the* required tick for us aspiring young rock-thugs (The Thing on Dinas Cromlech, Gothic preamble to the guidebook description notwithstanding, was always overrated). I asked Dougie about his pissed-up ascent. He couldn't remember a thing except that he'd pissed up it.

I've been trying to remember why we would have been in the Gwryd. It was never our watering-hole of choice. The social stratum from which it drew its clientele was a bit rarefied for most of us northern street-kids, and it was too far from the crags. The main attraction in the summer, I suppose, was the posh tottie who worked there and seemed to prefer hanging out with us in their time off rather than succumbing to the advances of the members of daddy's club who were forever making passes at them in the back bar. Old Jo Briggs made sure there was no hanky-panky of course, so nothing much went on in those unreconstructed times. Briggs himself was fine in his bluff way, despite being from Yorkshire. There was a geniality about him, an undercurrent of good humour.

One wet day, heading down to Tremadoc in Brian Greenall's ancient Austin Devon estate that had no brakes, bald tyres and rust holes in the floor, we overtook the Briggs's Mercedes, 'PYG 1', on the bends just before Llyn Dinas, half a dozen of us hanging out of windows, gurning and shouting. Chris stole a sly look to see if Jo was watching then flashed us a V-sign and an amused smile. I liked him for that. Much later, when I'd become almost respectable and was a regular dinner guest at PyG with the likes of David Cox, Kevin FitzGerald and Jack Longland – great men of the mountains who taught me not to take climbing too seriously and how to elegantly dissect and masticate the shoe-leather that passed for lamb chops at the table – I saw what an attentive, interested and informed host he was, held in universal high regard.

Does his memory still remain bright with the present-day clientele of the PyG and the mountains themselves? Are the old class divisions and their post-Thatcher revisions still prevalent? I wouldn't know. My last memory of the place is of filming a television series on the Welsh mountains there. I had to do a long piece-to-camera in that bath with the great copper shower-impedimenta overhead. It took so long, so many takes, that the water was all but freezing. The director said that she wanted me to take my knickers off. I refused. A man has his pride, after all …

Jim Perrin was born in Manchester and lived in Wales for over 40 years. After leaving school, he instructed mountaineering at several outdoor education centres and at the National Mountaineering Centre in Snowdonia. In his youth he was one of the most notable rock-climbers in Britain with many first ascents and solo ascents at the highest standards of the time to his credit. He has climbed extensively in the European Alps, the Pyrenees, the Moroccan Atlas, Garhwal, Tien Shan, the Bolivian Andes and the American and Canadian Rockies and has travelled extensively from the High Arctic to the Caribbean.

Perrin has written 17 books. His biographies *Menlove* (1985) and *The Villain* (2005) both won the Boardman Tasker Award for Mountaineering Literature, the latter also winning the Mountaineering History Award at Banff Mountain Festival 2005. His collection *The Climbing Essays* received the Mountain Literature Prize at Banff in 2006 and was shortlisted for Wales Book of the Year 2007. His collected travel essays, *Travels with The Flea and other Eccentric Journeys* appeared in 2001. He has published five further collections of essays, a best-selling book on Snowdonia (1997), a 'biography' of Snowdon itself (2012), *River Map* (2001) an essay on love and landscape, and *West: A Journey into the Meaning of Loss* (2010), a psycho-geographical travel book on the nature of grief. Most recently he has published *Shipton and Tilman: The Great Decade of Himalayan Exploration* (2013), which won the 2014 Kekoo Naoroji Award for Himalayan Literature, and *A Snow Goose and other utopian fictions* (2014 – a collection of short stories).

Described by Professor M. Wynn Thomas as, 'The most singular, and the most outstanding, prose-writer of present-day Wales', by Robert Macfarlane as,

'Britain's outstanding outdoor essayist', and by Peter Beaumont in the *Observer* as, 'The pre-eminent writer on the British landscape', he is *The Guardian*'s Country Diarist for Wales, contributes regular travel essays to the *Daily Telegraph* and writes a monthly column for *The Great Outdoors* magazine. A Fellow of the Welsh Academy and Honorary Fellow of Bangor University, he is creative director of the MA course in travel and nature writing at Bath Spa University and is currently working on a critical biography of the eccentric Victorian writer George Borrow and a novel-cycle set in Wales that he describes as, 'a chronicle of witness recording the perverse and vicious Thatcherite legacy of Britain's descent into diseducation'.

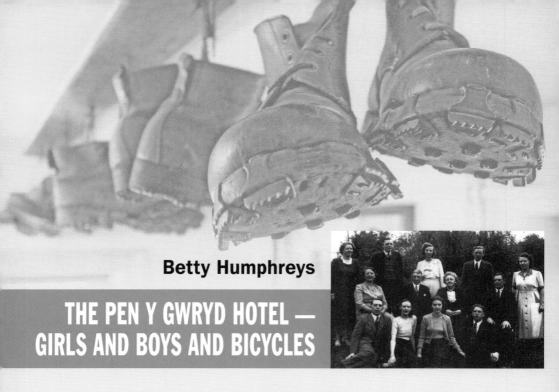

Betty Humphreys

THE PEN Y GWRYD HOTEL —
GIRLS AND BOYS AND BICYCLES

I STARTED WORK at the Pen y Gwryd Hotel for Mr Lockwood in 1939, just before war broke out. Before my time, my mother – whose maiden name was Prichard – also worked at the Pen y Gwryd with her two sisters. My younger sister was named after Mrs Lockwood – Ethel Florence. For many years Mrs Lockwood would send my mother a big hamper at Christmas time, filled with everything you could think of.

In those days, all the young girls went into service – and were taught to be waitresses and chambermaids – and the local boys went to work in the slate mines. During the Second World War, when the PyG was designated as a school for evacuated children, I worked at the Royal Hotel in Capel Curig before joining 'the War Effort' in the aircraft industry in Llanberis. Then, in 1947, I went back when the Pen y Gwryd reopened and Mr Briggs took over the management. Blodwen Griffiths, who devoted her entire life from the age of 14 to her death at the age of 84, also came back to the Pen y Gwryd and nearby Hafod y Gwynt.

It was a very busy and popular hotel – as it still is today. But at that time, there were very few private cars and no coaches. Guests from all

---

Photograph of Betty Humphreys on the far right with her father and mother and brothers and sisters.

over the world, as I recall, came by train to Betws y Coed. They were then brought to the Pen y Gwryd by taxi. In my mother's time they came up by horse and carriage.

My mother Elizabeth came from Capel Curig and, at the turn of the 19th century, she worked at the Pen y Gwryd with her two sisters. My father, Thomas, who was an Owen, lived in Nant Peris and, of course, worked in the Dinorwig quarry at Llanberis. He and my brothers, who also worked in the mines, were bell ringers at the church here in Llanberis. For 120 years the Owen family have been bell ringers – and they still are today.

Well, my father would come to visit my mother – over the pass – on a bicycle. And my mother and her sisters would come from Capel Curig – Mary Jane, Maggie and my mother, Elizabeth: the Prichard girls. That's where my mother and father first met – at the Pen y Gwryd. I suppose they just 'clicked'. It was common in those times for young people to meet there. Girls from Capel Curig and boys from Llanberis meeting at the Pen y Gwryd; and I believe it still happens today.

Actually, speaking of bicycles, during the Second World War I was in the Home Guard and, because I had a bicycle, I was given the job of 'runner'. I guess if the Wehrmacht had invaded Gwynedd, I was going to be the first line of defence. During the war I worked at the North East Coast Aircraft Company (NECACO) in Llanberis. Because of bomb damage to factories further south, aircraft building was spread north and west – including to North Wales. The main slate splitting building in the Llanberis quarry was empty (there was little demand for slates during the war) so we started with building wings for the Boulton Paul Defiant night fighter. When it was fully operational, the factory produced parts for the Handley Page Halifax, Avro Lancaster, Short Stirling and Vickers Wellington bombers. Parts were then transported to Anglesey or to Broughton in Flintshire for assembly.

My mother and father had 12 children. I was number eight. There was Bob, Nellie, Mary, Nesta, Hugh, Dorothy, Tom and me, then Evan, Kate, Ernest and Ethel. Last year we made a list of the children of the children of the children and it amounted to hundreds.

And when my husband Owen Humphreys asked my father for permission to marry me – my father said, 'Of course Owen, yes, you have my permission, but just make sure that Betty leaves the bicycle'.

Our daughter and her boyfriend came up from London to ask permission of my husband to marry too, just as he had with my father – only it was getting on late and they hadn't arrived, so my husband went up to the bathroom and took his teeth out … and who should arrive but my daughter and her then boyfriend Tony. My husband came downstairs and Tony said, 'I would like to marry your daughter', and my husband just nodded and said, 'Yes'. Later he told me he couldn't say the word 'no' without his teeth in.

Betty Humphreys (née Prichard) was born in Llanberis. She is the eighth of 12 children born to Thomas and Elizabeth Owen. Her father worked at the Dinorwig Slate Quarry in Llanberis, as did all of her brothers. She attended Dolbadarn School in Llanberis until the age of 14 when she followed in her mother's footsteps and commenced work at the Royal Hotel, Capel Curig. When war broke out, Humphreys worked at the NECACO aircraft factory in Llanberis where she met her husband Owen Humphreys – a native of Nant Peris. She restarted work at the Pen y Gwryd Hotel when Mr and Mrs Briggs took over the tenancy in 1947. After marrying Owen, she moved to a house in Gwastadnant, Nant Peris, at the foot of the Llanberis Pass. Her husband continued to work at the quarry and she supplemented the household income by keeping visitors during the summer months. When the quarry closed in 1969, Betty and Owen Humphreys managed the Nant Peris Post Office until their retirement in 1977.

Alice Burton

THE SNOWDON CLUB

I VISITED THE Pen y Gwryd as a child of 11 and was fortunate to experience a unique and very special part of the hotel's heritage.

My younger brother and I were brought along for a weekend away with our parents and their friends who had taken over the entire hotel for a wedding anniversary. As part of their celebrations, the party was to convene at the summit of Snowdon, whether by the somewhat tempting mountain railway or by one of the numerous walking trails up the mountain.

It seemed the decision was already made for us. We were to ascend via the Snowdon Horseshoe itself, the most challenging of all walking routes in Snowdonia. Born and raised in the open-field landscapes of the Cambridgeshire Fens, with not a hill in sight, the 3,560 foot (1,085 metre) ascent and seven miles of the Horseshoe seemed agonisingly challenging for our little legs.

The Snowdon Horseshoe is one of the best known high level mountain outings in Britain and definitely not a good idea for anyone with a fear of heights. Its rugged beauty and interesting terrain was obviously one of the reasons why it was chosen as a training route for the 1953 British Everest team, and why it remains so popular today.

A particular highlight is the spectacular Crib Goch; a knife-edge ridge scramble with exposed drops on both sides and one that you definitely want to cling onto at all times. Mum was a nervous wreck by the time we got to the top, having watched her two youngest children gleefully scrambling along the ridge. So she definitely needed the champagne that Dad had carefully transported in his rucksack for a celebratory drink at the top (with orange juice for my brother and me as we still had to negotiate the second leg and, of course, we were not 'of age').

Unbeknown to us as we completed this heroic feat, the effort was all in pursuit of an exclusive opportunity to participate in a very special tradition belonging only to the Pen y Gwryd. We survived the climb unharmed and, in recognition of our success, my brother and I were initiated into the Snowdon Club, reserved for children who made their first ascent of Snowdon under 12 years of age. Our reward was a very distinctive ice axe-shaped members' pin badge and an opportunity to drink from one of the tankards belonging to Everest team members who had stayed frequently at the Pen y Gwryd during their training and later reunions. (It was still to be orange juice though – as I was only 11.) I vividly remember feeling especially privileged when Edmund Hillary's pewter tankard was taken down from display behind the bar in honour of the occasion.

Alice Burton was born in Cambridge and is currently studying for a postgraduate degree in biomedical sciences. She still enjoys spending time outdoors and has climbed Snowdon three times since her induction into the Snowdon Club.

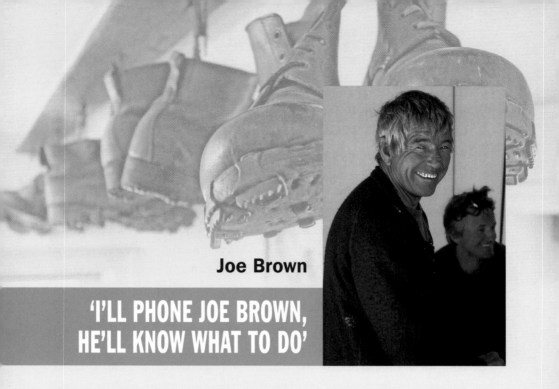

Joe Brown

'I'LL PHONE JOE BROWN, HE'LL KNOW WHAT TO DO'

I F I GO BACK to my earliest memory of Chris Briggs, it was, not surprisingly, in the Pen y Gwryd Hotel. It was during the day and Chris was walking from the front door towards the dining room with either a forked hazel or a birch twig in his hands, 'water divining' with his daughter Jane, who was then about three foot high or five years old. He was just having a good time and Jane believed him, even though it was he who was making the birch twitch and vibrate.

But the way I really got involved with the Pen y Gwryd was through mountain rescue. The rescue work that Chris did was, in my opinion, second to none and, when Chris was given a British Empire Medal for his services, I thought, that's ridiculous, he ought to have had much higher recognition and he should have gone to the Palace to receive his honour. Chris didn't have a mountain rescue team, he *was* the mountain rescue team, and the rescues he co-ordinated were amazing.

Chris Briggs wasn't really a climber but, when you got him out on the crags I often thought, 'He's going to kill himself one of these days'.

The photograph of Joe Brown was taken in 1986 by Ed Webster at Everest Advanced Base Camp (20 000 feet), situated on the East Rongbuk Glacier in Tibet. Webster explains, 'Joe's good mate and long-time climbing partner, Mo Anthoine, is sitting beside him in the picture. They were on a British expedition to Everest's lengthy and difficult North East Ridge. Joe cheerfully volunteered to cook us all supper and I'd like to report that his high-altitude cuisine was excellent! It was quite a memorable evening'.

But the thing about him was that he was such a genuine person and his attitude towards mountain rescue was: the phone rings; climber in trouble; who have we got; we need to go and rescue someone. He might grab a couple of lads from the bar or even drag down the pass to see if there was anyone camping; he would get anyone at all to help. On one occasion, he even came to 'rescue' me.

A group of us were up on 'Cloggy' (Clogwyn Du'r Arddu) on a really terrible day and I had gone across on the West Buttress. I had traversed from near Longlands across White Slab and the wind was very strong. It was a day when you didn't get many runners on and the rope was being blown right up in the air with it.

I was shouting at the top of my voice to the people I was heading back with and so, when we got down, there was no one left on the crag. We went back to Mrs Williams at the Halfway House. (I was very friendly with the Williams family, like one of their own kids: they were terrific.) Anyway, we were sitting in there with Mr Williams who had phenomenal eyesight. He was a very quiet man but he could see right down to the farthest point on the Snowdon Track, and he said, 'There's a group of people coming through the gate and they are carrying a stretcher'. We looked and couldn't see anyone but, about 30 minutes later, in trooped Chris Briggs with about half a dozen drinkers from the bar of the Pen y Gwryd, and Chris said, 'Someone's in trouble on Cloggy'. And I replied, 'I don't think so'. Chris explained, 'Someone on the railway track heard people yelling and weren't able to understand what was being shouted but assumed it was climbers in trouble'. 'Well', I said, 'to save you having wasted your energy and to put it into proper practice, you can carry *me* down if you like'.

Long before we had the climbing gear business, I had been working at the Pen y Gwryd. One of the many jobs I did there for Chris was to change the boiler, taking the old coke one out and putting in the new oil-fired one. Chris said, 'Well, the problem is Joe, we are not closing the hotel, so we want to keep hot water'. And I said, 'That shouldn't be too much of a problem, as long as we have the right ways of cutting the water off when we break into the pipes'. But we hadn't. There were no valves on the circulators. It was a plumbers' nightmare.

The thing was, we had to do it all after the guests had their baths in the evening and be finished by morning, which was a hell of a job. If someone asked me to do that now, I'd say it was ridiculous. Anyway, we really cracked on and we got the thing connected up by dawn. Going to check that everything was all right, Chris and I went upstairs. The main vertical cylinder had collapsed. The suction pressure had folded it in. Chris just said, 'Ahh, don't worry about that Joe, it's of no consequence, the insurance will sort it out'. And that was the sort of typical job at the Gwryd – never easy.

When Val and I did get the first shop in 1965, all sorts of people helped us, like one of the partners from Black's. He was incredibly helpful and offered long credit but what we wanted was a bank loan. We went to the local establishment and they said, 'What security do you have?' We said, 'A building on the Llanberis High Street' (the same one as the shop today) and they were just not interested. I talked to Chris about that and he said, 'I'll get you a bank loan and, if I can't, I'll lend you the money myself'. So he ended up getting us a loan from the bank manager at Birkenhead where we still have our main account today. But, in the end, we also got a loan from Chris Briggs as well.

Although Chris employed me frequently over the years, we were friends – that was the most important part of our association. I would call in to the Gwryd all the time. A really good time for me would be to meet Chris and fish the Lledr on a sunny day after a storm had passed, just after the river had been high and it had dropped and you could go down with polaroids on and actually see the salmon you were going to fish for. I would take some sandwiches, a can of beer and a big cigar. We fished the Lledr hundreds of times together like that.

I was sitting next to Jo Briggs in the Smoke Room one day and she said, 'There was a time when I thought you and Chris had a *thing* going on you know'. 'Well', I just said, '*What?*' She said, 'Because no matter what happens around here', Chris always tells me, 'I'll phone Joe Brown, he'll know what to do'.

What I like to recall about the Gwryd is, it has atmosphere. I always found it interesting to get a pint and look through that little hatch and see who was behind the bar in the Smoke Room, because it could be anyone. You'd get the famous old climbers like Geoffrey Winthrop Young. On a couple of occasions, I remember meeting him there. And all the old Everesters too, not only from 1953 but Noel Odell and the like from the 1924 Expedition as well.

Joe Brown established hundreds of rock-climbing routes in Snowdonia and the Peak District that were at the leading edge of the hardest grades of their day. Many of these climbs were in partnership with Don Whillans. In 1955, as part of a British expedition, together with George Band, Brown was the first to climb the world's third highest mountain, Kangchenjunga in the Nepali Himalayas. Brown and Band stopped just short of the summit, as promised to the King of Sikkim, so that the top of the mountain would remain inviolate. Every climber who has reached the summit since has followed this tradition. In 1956, Brown made the first ascent of the West Summit of the Muztagh Tower in the Karakoram with Ian McNaught-Davis. Apart from numerous classic rock climbs in Britain and mountaineering achievements around the world, he featured in many televised rock climbs in the 1960s, a number in Snowdonia and, in 1967, on a spectacular new route on the Old Man of Hoy, a Scottish sea stack, with Ian McNaught-Davis and Chris Bonington. Fifteen years later, Brown repeated the climb in a television documentary with his second daughter Zoë. www.joe-brown.com

Anna Lawford

THE ALPINE CLUB AND THE PEN Y GWRYD HOTEL

HOW SHOULD THE Alpine Club (AC) celebrate the 60th anniversary of the first ascent of Everest? The decision was easier than many AC Committee decisions over the Club's 156-year history. Clearly there was no better way to celebrate the achievements of fellow Alpine Club members in true mountaineering spirit than with a party in the mountains and there are few more fitting places for a mountaineers' party than the Pen y Gwryd Hotel.

Thus, on 1 June, 2013, the first ascent of Everest and, somewhat prematurely but equally significantly, the first ascent of Kangchenjunga, were celebrated in appropriate style with a PyG party hosted by the Alpine Club and with the assistance of Rupert and Nicolas Pullee. Numerous former presidents of the AC were there: Emlyn Jones, Denise Evans, Tony Streather, Chris Bonington, Doug Scott, Stephen Venables, Tut Braithwaite and President Mick Fowler, together with expedition members Joe Brown, Norman Hardie, Tony Streather (the same) and Jan Morris, the wider families of the Everest and Kangchenjunga teams and many AC members. Memories were relived, news shared, photos enjoyed. The PyG was once again filled with climbers and their families enjoying the warm, comfortable hospitality of the old hotel with an atmosphere and location that are unique.

Over the years, there have been various other occasions that gave an excuse for AC members to meet at the PyG and celebrate as a club: the centenary and 150th anniversaries of the formation of the Club in 1957 and 2007, to name but two. Both events had resulted in the great and the good of climbing (and probably the not so great or good) descending on the hotel for a party.

However, the relationship between British mountaineers and the hotel began more than one-and-a-half centuries ago in 1854 when, three years prior to the formation of the Alpine Club, Charles Mathews, aged 20, visited the hotel and made his first of more than a hundred ascents of Snowdon. Two years later, Mathews discovered the pleasures of climbing in the Alps but, living in Birmingham, Snowdonia continued throughout his life to provide him with wonderful opportunities to enjoy mountain days close to home.

As a founder member of the AC, and its president from 1878 to 1880, Mathews became the first of numerous members over the next 158 years to have used the PyG as their personal base for Welsh mountain excursions; and he stayed more than 25 times. His enthusiasm for Snowdonia and the hotel was such that he introduced many others to both and, since his early trips were to enjoy winter climbing when the hills were usually covered in snow at Christmas and Easter, ice axe and crampons were in use and alpine skills were practised. His patronage seems to have contributed significantly to the success of the PyG and its survival during those early years, when few people other than alpinists chose to holiday in British mountains in winter.

In 1865 Mathews was joined at the hotel by ten fellow AC members, which might be considered one of the first UK climbing meets. In January 1870, during another visit, Mathews, Frederick Morshead and Anthony Adams-Reilly founded the 'Society of Welsh Rabbits', its object being 'to explore Snowdonia in winter'. Adams-Reilly, better known for producing the first detailed map of Mont Blanc in 1865, even designed a coat of arms for the group and its popularity grew so great that it, in turn, led to the formation of the Climbers' Club with Mathews as its first president.

In April 1888 Mathews invited his regular Swiss guide, Melchior Anderegg, to join him at the hotel, and took pleasure in reversing the usual roles by taking his favourite guide up Snowdon in deep, soft snow. Reminiscing about this occasion, Mathews clearly found it entertaining to recall that, on reaching the top of Crib Goch, Anderegg, who was obviously unfamiliar with judging distance in the smaller Welsh mountains, advised his client that they should turn back since Snowdon's summit appeared to him to be far too great a distance to cover that day. It must have delighted Mathews to be able to advise Anderegg that it would take only an hour and then, to prove it, summiting in 65 minutes. I find myself wondering what the great Melchior, renowned guide to so many of the early alpinists, Leslie Stephen, Lucy Walker, Horace Walker, et al, with ten alpine first ascents in ten years from 1858-68, thought of his PyG experience.

It was very much Mathews, visiting the PyG year after year, who helped make the hotel a centre of British climbing in the latter part of the 19th century and, through him, many other AC members experienced the joys of Welsh hills, Welsh hospitality by courtesy of Harry and Ann Owen and, no doubt, Welsh weather.

After Harry and Ann Owen died, from the early 20th century until the 1930s, the Gorphwysfa Hotel at Pen y Pass took over as the main Welsh base for climbers, due to the patronage of Geoffrey Winthrop Young and his famous climbing parties. The PyG had to wait until after the Second World War to resume its place as a centre for mountaineering.

The AC/PyG connection was re-established in 1945, two years before Chris and Jo Briggs took over the hotel. Several AC members returned and another future AC President, John Hunt, and his wife, Joy, arrived on heavily laden bicycles.

Despite strict food rationing and post-breakfast hunger, the delights of the hotel were clearly obvious to the Hunts, though they could have little realised on that first visit the historic association between the PyG and Everest which would be formed within ten years through John Hunt's involvement with the 1953 British Everest Expedition. In the spring of that year, with John Hunt having been appointed the expedition leader, team members met in Wales to train and test equipment, staying at the Climbers' Club hut, Helyg, and spending the more relaxed hours eating and drinking at the PyG. The 1953 Everest and 1955 Kangchenjunga teams were AC members and, subsequent to the successful expeditions, the hotel became their base for reunions and celebrations.

Through the years from Mathews to today, in between the special celebratory occasions, a large number of AC members have found the PyG a fantastic base for days on hills and crags and evenings in the bar and Smoke Room. The desire to have time and space after long mountain days to share stories of climbs and climbers, of routes and lines, remains strong. Informative conversation is punctuated with reminiscences and anecdotes. It seems fitting that the PyG, where the gentle tones of the daily gong at breakfast and dinner give a relaxed structure at the beginning and end of a day in the hills, should be so linked with the AC whose first draft rules in 1857 required members to meet twice yearly to dine together.

The objects of the AC, from its inception, were to share information and encourage climbing, and the AC/PyG association has surely been mutually beneficial to climbers and hotel both; the climbers enjoying the magnificent location, character and welcome of the PyG and the hotel benefiting from the keen climbers who will still come, in sun and rain, snow and ice.

Anna Lawford is the current Honorary Secretary of the Alpine Club and the third of four generations of her family who have been members of the club. Her maternal great-grandfather and father were elected to the club in 1899 and 1967 respectively and her son joined the club in 2013. She is the second of three generations of her family who have enjoyed many occasions at the Pen y Gwryd Hotel over the past 50 years.

The objects of the Alpine Club are to promote mountain climbing and exploration in good style throughout the world, to develop a better knowledge of the mountains through literature, science and art and through its meetings and publications, to encourage protection of the mountain environment and to conserve the club's heritage.

Dane Tobias

PYG ... RICK STEIN ... JAMIE OLIVER ...

M Y FIRST POSITION as a qualified chef was at the PyG. As a 21-year-old, I had the enormous privilege of learning how to prepare traditional Welsh, English and Danish food under the direction of the PyG's long-term cook, Lene Henriette Hampson.

What I took away from the hotel was a deep knowledge of how to keep things traditional, by absorbing the genius of recipes and techniques that have stood the test of generations. I also learnt that cooking in a remote area is not a liability, far from it, but rather an opportunity to use local products to create extraordinary meals for extraordinarily hungry patrons (within a restricted range of produce). This was something of a PyG tradition passed from cook to cook, going back to the hotel's legendary chef, Jack Griffith Williams.

As an 18-year-old non-English-speaking Welsh boy from Blaenau Ffestiniog, Jack learnt his craft in the British Army during his National Service. He later perfected his skills as the catering chef at the Bronaber Residential Village for construction workers at the Trawsfynydd Nuclear Power Station project before starting as head cook at the PyG, a position he held for many years. There is a photo of Jack with Jane Pullee in the *Locked Book*. He is dressed in his chef's whites. And so, true

77

to the expression *nanos gigantum humeris insidentes* ('standing on the shoulders of giants'), in the kitchen of the PyG I discovered the secret of great cooking – to build on previous discoveries.

In turn, this experience opened many doors for me, beginning with the opportunity to cook with Lene for the 50th Anniversary of the 1953 British Everest Expedition, which was held at the PyG from 6 until 8 June, 2003. Guests included over 80 members of the 'Everest family', as Lord Hunt once described the group. This included widows of those now deceased and surviving expedition members including Michael Westmacott, George Band, Michael Ward and Charles Wylie, and many members of their families. It also included the celebrated writer and *Times* reporter Jan Morris. All recalled memories and shared anecdotes of the historic exploit which saw Edmund Hillary and Tenzing Norgay reach the roof of the world for the very first time.

A very special guest at the dinner was Lady Denise Evans from Capel Curig, the widow of expedition member Charles Evans who very nearly became the first man to the summit. He and Tom Bourdillon formed the first assault party but, having climbed higher than anyone before, they wearily turned back after suffering problems with their oxygen equipment. Two days later, Hillary and Tenzing began their successful attempt.

The PyG's 50th anniversary dinner menu included:

Entrée – Seafood Salad

Entrée – Garlic Cream Cheese Soup with Croutons

Main – Roast Leg of Welsh Lamb with Redcurrant Gravy and Mint
Sauce Served with Seasonal Vegetables

Dessert – Sticky Date and Walnut Pudding
with Butterscotch Sauce and Cream

Dessert – English Rhubarb Crumble and Custard.

Dessert – Summer Pudding and Cream or Various Ice Creams

Welsh cheeseboard

Coffee.

And how can I recall such detail of that wonderful night after all these years? The surviving Everesters kindly signed a copy of the menu for me – a priceless memento of my time in the kitchen of 'The Home of British Mountaineering'.

Dane Tobias is head chef at a restaurant in the Illawarra district south of Sydney. He completed his apprenticeship at Piato Restaurant, in Wollongong, New South Wales. After working at the PyG, Tobias had the opportunity to work at Rick Stein's critically acclaimed flagship The Seafood Restaurant in Padstow, Cornwall, where he cooked in the 'mains section' after mastering all food and beverage divisions within 12 months. Tobias then landed a job with Jamie Oliver in London at Oliver's acclaimed restaurant *Fifteen*. He has cooked for, amongst many others, former US President Bill Clinton, actor Brad Pitt, musician Sting, Yogyakarta Crown Prince His Highness Sri Gusti Hadiwinoto, Javanese Prince and Indonesian variety show host Indro 'Kimpling' Suseno as well as Jamie Oliver's mentor Gennaro Contaldo.

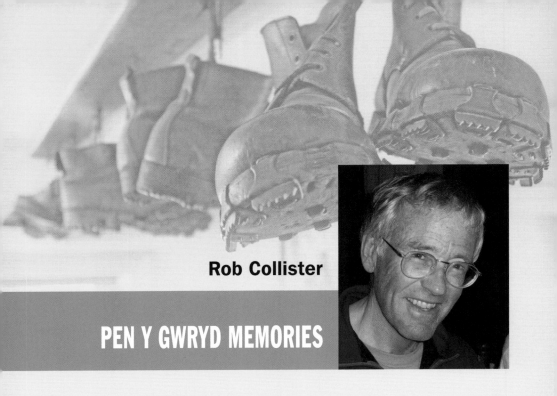

Rob Collister

PEN Y GWRYD MEMORIES

MY EARLIEST RECOLLECTION of the Pen y Gwryd Hotel dates from the mid-1960s when I was a teenager. My brother and I had hitchhiked up to North Wales and were camped at 'Willie's farm', Gwern Gof Uchaf, in the Ogwen valley. We had climbed one day on the Milestone Buttress and, on another, battled our way up one of the long routes on the East Face of Tryfan. On the day in question, we set out for the cliffs of Glyder Fach.

The cloud was right down and visibility so limited that we might never have found the crag, let alone climbed anything. As it was, we had reached Llyn Bochlwyd and had struck out away from the path that leads to Bwlch Tryfan, when we heard a whistle blowing somewhere high above. We recognised it as a call for help and, forgetting about our compass bearing, we headed upwards. The terrain became steeper and steeper, the visibility worse and worse, until we could scarcely see each other and the insistent whistling never seemed to get any closer.

We continued onwards and upwards interminably, conscious that we had absolutely no idea where we were until, eventually, the angle began to ease and we guessed that we were approaching the plateau of Glyder Fach. Only now did the whistle sound fairly close and then, quite suddenly a few yards ahead, we found a little cluster of people. Their faces lit up at the sight of us but, when they realised we were not the rescue team, their expressions crumpled with disappointment. It was a school party, one of whose members had collapsed with hypothermia, in those days known as 'exposure', brought on by cold and wet conditions. It was the sort of incident that was becoming all too common and led, a few years later, to the establishment of the Mountain Leader Training Scheme.

Fortunately for the boys and their teacher, and for Kiff and me as well, the real rescue team arrived from the opposite direction moments later. Its members were all large men exuding confidence and competence and, in no time, the casualty had been manoeuvred into a sleeping bag and lashed on to a stretcher. Kiff and I were handed a carrying strap each and shown how to pass it over one shoulder to take the weight and off we went. We very soon discovered that carrying a stretcher down a rocky, wet hillside, even with plenty of carriers, is an exhausting business. It felt as though we had been slipping and sliding downhill for hours when, abruptly, we dropped out of the cloud to see a road and a cluster of buildings not far below. It was the Pen y Gwryd.

The casualty was loaded into an ambulance, the school group had already been escorted off the hill and we, as members of the rescue team, were ushered into the bar and found ourselves clutching pints of bitter – on the house. I do not remember any faces specifically but I suspect that it was the first and only time that I met Chris Briggs, mine host of the Pen y Gwryd Hotel and mountain rescue supremo of North Wales at the time. At that age, beer was not much to our taste and, when a friendly policeman offered to drive us the ten miles back round to Ogwen, we put down our glasses without regret and headed for the squad car. Fifty years on, I am now a trainee member of the Ogwen Valley Mountain Rescue team, struggling sometimes with the technical complexities of modern rescue methods and communications.

Not long after that, I met Esme Kirby for the first time. Esme lived in Dyffryn Mymbyr farm midway between Plas y Brenin and Pen y Gwryd and was a close friend of the Briggs family. I was coming down off the Glyderau one day and found myself confronted by a stone wall barring access to the main road. I had just climbed over it when an ancient Morris 1000 pulled up alongside. A diminutive figure emerged, bristling with indignation. 'Young man, have you any idea how much I have to spend repairing my walls every year?', she demanded. 'One hundred and fifty pounds' (at least £2,000 today), she continued and, before I could open my mouth, she proceeded to berate me for several minutes before driving off, leaving me thoroughly chastened. Not only had she made it clear that she was extremely angry but, more to the point, she made me understand why. There was no room for excuses but she never became abusive either. I could only humbly apologise and promise to be much more careful in the future about where and how I crossed walls. I have never forgotten the effectiveness of that reprimand and I have kept my promise.

It was only a matter of time before I read *I Bought a Mountain* by Thomas Firbank and realised that I had fallen foul of its heroine; but our paths did not cross again until the 1970s. By then, I was married with a baby son and was living in North Wales. By chance, I picked up a flyer about the Snowdonia National Park Society, which Esme had founded in 1967, and felt that I should support its work. I was never a very active member but Esme used to ring up from time to time enquiring about National Park issues in the Penmachno area and up on the Migneint, or to ask me to write a letter of objection regarding some undesirable development. On a couple of occasions, I was invited to Society HQ in her kitchen at Dyffryn, a low-ceilinged room with tiny windows set in thick stone walls which made it seem dark whatever the time of day. Every conceivable work surface was piled high with books, reports and papers. Cooking was clearly a low priority.

In 1989, the Snowdonia Society (as it became, to avoid confusion with the National Park Authority) bought Tŷ Hyll, the Ugly House, where the A5 crosses the river Llugwy midway between Betws y Coed and Capel Curig, and converted it into an office. Sadly, this was the start of an increasingly acrimonious struggle between Esme, who could not bear to relinquish the reins of the society she had founded, and a committee who found her style too confrontational and wanted the society to be run by a paid director. Four directors came and went in quick succession, quite unable to work with Esme, until finally a bad-tempered extraordinary general meeting in 1992 saw her replaced by David Firth as Chairman. Many of Esme's friends including Jo Briggs and her daughter Jane Pullee, immediately resigned from the society.

For myself, I still liked and admired Esme on a personal level but I could see that, if the Snowdonia Society was to be an effective pressure group on behalf of the National Park, a willingness to negotiate and sometimes compromise was essential. Today, the society's office is at the Caban in Brynrefail, from where it continues to monitor inappropriate planning applications, respond to government policy documents and organise a range of conservation work within the Park with a team of hardy volunteers. Tŷ Hyll is still owned by the Society and is open to the public as a tea-room and honeybee interpretation centre, along with its delightful wildlife garden and surrounding woodland.

You cannot live in North Wales for any length of time without some contact with Pen y Gwryd. Usually, for me, it was calling in for a drink after a day's climbing in the Llanberis Pass but more than once I found myself giving a lift to pretty Danish chambermaids hitchhiking to or from the metropolis of Betws y Coed on their afternoon off. Once, Netti and I stayed the night after a party and marvelled at the shared Victorian bathroom and bedrooms apparently unchanged since the days of the Everesters. Another time, during the making of a Channel 4 production, we came down from a wet, murky Crib Goch to be filmed reviewing the day in the snug behind the bar.

Another link was Chris Brasher, whom I knew initially through running mountain marathons, and later as a trustee of the John Muir Trust. Chris was always keen for the Trust to buy a property in Wales (an ambition that was not achieved despite several attempts) and I remember a convivial dinner which he hosted at PyG for trustees to meet friends like John Disley, John Jackson and Peter Kirby. Chris was well known as an athlete, journalist and entrepreneur and was something of a habitué at the Pen y Gwryd, as he owned a holiday cottage in Nant Gwynant for many years. He was also a good friend of Esme Kirby and it was he who stumped up the cash to buy and then demolish the derelict filling station at Pen y Gwryd, an eyesore that had been the bête noire of both Esme and the Briggs family for years.

Brasher had always been an advocate of the Shipton/Tilman lightweight approach to mountaineering; in particular, he was fond of Tilman's dictum that any expedition worth going on could be organised 'on the back of an envelope'. From this grew the 'OBOE' club, a disparate but sociable group of Chris Brasher's friends who would gather from time to time for a weekend's walking in the hills. I enjoyed a number of these events but could not help wondering sometimes if Tilman would have approved the amount of telephoning required to organise them.

On one occasion Chris employed me professionally to guide the party through the underground caverns of Wrysgan mine above Tanygrisiau and then across the Moelwynion to Nant Gwynant. All went well until the rain set in and Brasher chose to lead us on a fearsome bush-bash through a rhododendron thicket in search of his old house. At some point, he must have communicated with Pen y Gwryd, unbeknownst to me, for just as we were resigning ourselves to a weary trudge up the valley, Brian and Jane Pullee appeared in their cars. Their arrival, like fairy godparents, was as welcome as it was unexpected. Uncomplaining, they conveyed us, dripping and muddy, to the welcome warmth of their remarkable hotel.

Rob Collister is an international (IFMGA) mountain guide who has lived in North Wales since 1976. He is the author of *Over the Hills and Far Away* (Ernest Press, 1996), a collection of mountaineering essays, *Lightwood Expeditions* (Crowood Press, 1989) and *Park Under Pressure* (Pesda Press, 2007), an account of the Snowdonia Society and the Snowdonia National Park.

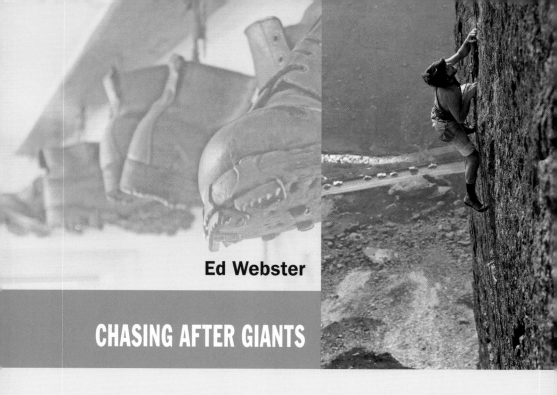

Ed Webster

CHASING AFTER GIANTS

Aↇᴏɴᴇ, I sᴇᴛ ᴏғғ on my very first overseas climbing trip in the
autumn of 1978. I was a fresh-faced, rock-climbing-obsessed
22-year-old from the suburbs of Boston, Massachusetts. My destinations?
London, to visit my father's relatives, but also North Wales. I was well
versed in the cragging history of Snowdonia, having followed on a
tight rope *The Hard Years* exploits of Brown, Whillans and Bonington,
at least in book form. After successes on the finger-destroying vertical
walls of Llanberis Pass, with leads of Cenotaph Corner, the Left Wall of
Cenotaph and Quasar under my waist loop, late one afternoon my rope
mate slowed the car and suggested, 'Let's pop in to the Pen y Gwryd,
the PyG. This is a place you must see.'

He then said reverentially, 'It's where Everest climbers go for a pint!'

I remember walking gingerly through the rooms, gazing in awe at
the 1953 British Everest Expedition memorabilia and drinking pints
with my climbing partner, who might have been Malcolm Creasey
or Nigel Shepherd. During the next decade, I participated in three
separate expeditions to Everest myself, climbing on a different side of
the mountain on each trip, once in Nepal and twice in Tibet. The 1980s
were the innocent, uncrowded, pre-guiding years on Everest. In 1985

I played cards, gambling for rupees at Khumbu Base Camp with Chris Bonington, American mountaineer Dick Bass and several Norwegian climbers, just days before Chris summited. A week later Bass also topped out, completing his quest to become the first to climb the 'Seven Summits'.

While researching Everest's early climbing history, I read up on Geoffrey Winthrop Young's 'gatherings' at the PyG and Pen y Pass that propelled the likes of George Mallory to the forefront of Welsh rock climbing, guideless alpinism and eventually, Himalayan mountaineering. I began to appreciate even more the unique role the PyG has played in fostering a welcoming atmosphere among climbers for well over a century and that virtually all the 'giants', my British climbing heroes, have enjoyed many a convivial evening in the PyG's much loved Smoke Room.

When I embarked on my third Everest expedition in the pre-monsoon spring season of 1988, one of my three partners attempting the great mountain's East or Kangshung Face was the British mountaineer Stephen Venables. And it was Lord Hunt (John Hunt, leader of the 1953 British Everest Expedition) who initially recommended Stephen. Our team's leader, American climber Robert Anderson, left a message on Stephen's mother's answering machine inviting Stephen to accompany us on a brand new route up Everest's so-called 'Forgotten Face' in Tibet. Paul Teare from Canada was already on board. After receiving our invitation, Stephen, to his credit, was not sure that this was an adventure he should embark on with total strangers, joining forces with, as he phrased it, 'three Yanks I don't know'.

'Well, who are they?' asked Stephen's rock-climbing partner Dick Renshaw. Venables replied, 'Let's see, some bloke named Ed Webster is on it, and …' 'Wait!' replied Renshaw. 'I've climbed with Ed, he's a good chap. You should go, Stephen', proclaimed Renshaw. 'You'll have a good time.'

Renshaw and I had climbed together during my 1978 trip to Wales. Based on that single connection, that I'd tied into a rope with one of his trusted partners, Stephen Venables decided to make the journey to Everest with Paul, Robert, myself and two additional Americans, Miriam

Zieman, our doctor and Joseph Blackburn our team photographer. And I know Stephen is glad he did. As are we, for ours was one of a small minority: a happy Everest expedition.

Our 1988 American-Canadian-British team accomplished the seemingly impossible. We achieved the first ascent of a new route directly up the Tibetan side of the South Col, vanquishing, although sustaining serious frostbite injuries in the process, Everest's least visited, most remote and notorious aspect, the avalanche-scoured Kangshung East Face. We achieved success, not just with only four climbers but also without the traditional high-altitude aids of Sherpa assistance, bottled oxygen, and radios. And Stephen, our sole member to summit, became the first Briton to climb Everest without breathing from an oxygen bottle. With appropriate humour, we christened our route the 'Neverest Buttress'. It has been repeated twice. (I unfortunately lost eight fingertips and three toes to frostbite; Venables and Anderson were also frostbitten. After contracting cerebral oedema at the South Col, Paul Teare voluntarily descended 9,000 vertical feet alone, and survived. He was the only one of the four to emerge relatively unscathed.)

The greatest fun I've experienced in my life has been to meet and shake the hand of many of the rock climbers and mountaineers who inspired me as a youth: Joe Brown, Don Whillans, Chris Bonington, Ed Hillary, John Hunt, George Band, Mike Westmacott, Tony Streather, Doug Scott, Peter Boardman, Paul Ross, Hamish MacInnes and more. What exciting and memorable encounters they were! I hold those moments of meeting like precious gems that capture the sunlight and then sparkle within the soft folds of memory.

In March 2013, our 1988 Everest Kangshung Face Expedition, including spouses and children, held its own 25th anniversary celebration. There was only one mountain hotel at which we could possibly meet – the Pen y Gwryd. Another member of our expedition was Norbu Tenzing, eldest son of Tenzing Norgay and, of course, Norbu recalled happy days of his childhood when his father had brought him to North Wales and the PyG for the 1953 British Everest Expedition reunions. Then, who should unexpectedly make our three-day visit even more delightful but Jan Morris, the 1953 team's official correspondent for *The Times*. Such warmth and memories; such exemplary and adventurous people. Socialising together in the welcoming rooms of the Pen y Gwryd, then standing beneath the ivy-covered archway for a group photograph, or two.

That energetic and fearless 22-year-old from Boston striving to repeat the hard rock routes and mountain faces pioneered by my British climbing heroes has aged into a 59-year-old wearing reading glasses and typing on a computer. But my feelings unite. Turning backward to gaze through time and space, I smile when appraising my 'storm years of youth', an expression minted by Geoffrey Winthrop Young. And I know, with complete certainty, that North Wales and the PyG will always be the homes of giants.

Ed Webster was born in Boston and obtained a bachelor's degree in anthropology from The Colorado College in Colorado Springs. Married to Lisa, they reside in Maine, USA with their daughter Joyelle. A veteran of seven Himalayan expeditions and pioneer of many new rock climbs of extreme difficulty in New England, Colorado and Utah, Webster is one of America's best known climbers and Himalayan mountaineers. Hardest of all Ed's routes was his new line up Everest's Kangshung East Face in Tibet in 1988, as part of an international four-man team, a climb hailed as 'The last of the great Everest expeditions'.

A highly accomplished lecturer, author, and photojournalist, Webster has been published worldwide. He has authored over 50 magazine articles, plus five books: three editions of his classic guidebook, *Rock Climbs in the White Mountains of New Hampshire,* as well as *Climbing in the Magic Islands: A Climbing and Hiking Guidebook to the Lofoten Islands of Norway* and his best-selling autobiography, *Snow in the Kingdom, My Storm Years on Everest.* Having achieved a solid five-star rating on Amazon, *Snow in the Kingdom* is available as an eBook, on every platform, worldwide.

Webster is the recipient of the American Alpine Club's 1990 H. Adams Carter Literary Award, and 1994 David A. Sowles Award for saving the life of a fellow climber, British mountaineer Lindsay Griffin, with help from their partner Julian Freeman-Attwood (also UK), in Mongolia. Additionally, Webster is one of just three mountaineers cited in the board game *Trivial Pursuit,* the other two climbers being Edmund Hillary and Tenzing Norgay. Webster's photographs have been published by Sierra Club Books and National Geographic Books, in *Alpinist Magazine, Climbing Magazine, Popular Mechanics,* even in *Rolling Stone.*

Webster's website is: www.mtnimagery.com and he may be contacted for lectures and autographed books at info@mtnimagery.com and via Facebook.

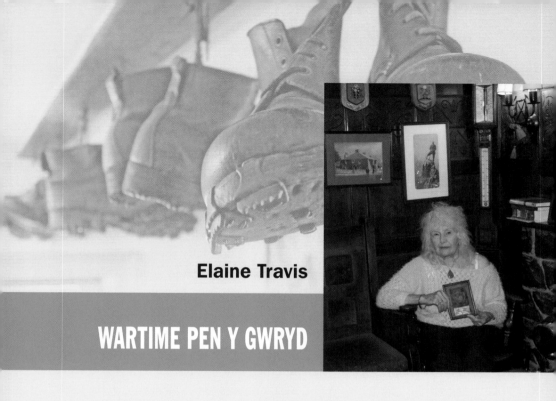

Elaine Travis

WARTIME PEN Y GWRYD

A FEW YEARS AGO, I rediscovered the Pen y Gwryd. It was when my son Howard took me back for a surprise visit, over 60 years since I had left there at the end of the Second World War.

At reception I was given my room and I went up to find that it was the very same one that had been my bedroom for the duration of the war. The Pen y Gwryd seemed not to have changed at all. And so, I promised myself I would come back once a year for the rest of my life. I am 87 years old now and have returned annually ever since.

At the beginning of the conflict I was 12 years old. My father, Eric Dougal, was the deputy headmaster of Lake House Preparatory School for Boys in Bexhill-on-Sea, Sussex. As the war turned against us, Bexhill was not the ideal place to be, as fears of an invasion were so real. The decision was taken to evacuate the school somewhere safer and North Wales was chosen. The headmaster was Alan Williams but, shortly after we moved, he decided to join the Navy. It was at this point that my father became headmaster. (Unfortunately, Mr Williams's ship was sunk and he was lost.)

There were, I think, about 30 boys at the school but, in addition, there was my mother Marie and my brothers and sisters Erica, Marion,

Richard and Malcolm. Miranda came later. We were absorbed into the school to continue our education. My mother became matron. On arrival in Snowdonia, we went for a brief period to the Royal Victoria Hotel in Llanberis but we soon found ourselves at the Pen y Gwryd until the war ended.

Life in the mountains was lovely. The air had purity, a sweet fresh-fulness and, for us children, it was very exciting. Twice a week after breakfast we would be given a packed lunch and were told which mountain to climb that day. They were normally the ones close to the hotel and the masters who were teaching us came along to supervise and we always returned to a generous high tea. There was always plenty of good simple food even though it was wartime. The hotel was always warm and cosy with many fires.

When I was about 15 years old, once a week I had to prepare, cook and serve supper for the staff and then join them to eat it. It was fun and I loved the responsibility. All meals were taken in what is now the hotel dining room. If you look carefully on some of the panes of glass in the hotel dining room and in the Residents' Lounge, you will still see the names of some of the boys who were brave enough (or naughty enough) to scratch their names to mark their stay for the benefit of posterity – a moment in time captured forever.

What is now the Residents' Bar (the Smoke Room) was, for the length of our stay, the staff room. The headmaster's chair remains there to this day; my father's chair. My father was a lovely gentleman and a very good teacher. I think the staff room also served as the staff's evening retreat, for a nightly tipple no doubt! There is also a Lake House School badge in there to this day that has the signatures of various boys who had returned from the war.

My mother, the matron, was very strict. This wasn't just for the boys. My sister Marion was very naughty and constantly in trouble. It seemed almost daily that Marion did something horrendous that culminated in her being biffed on the behind by my mother and sent upstairs to her room, with the words, 'You … are … a … very … very … naughty … little … girl' ringing in her (and my) ears. But Marion was also a lovely, spirited girl. She was very much loved despite this, or maybe because of it. My brother and sisters had an unusual but very happy childhood but the years at Pen y Gwryd were the best by far. There was so much fun to be had.

My two sisters and I slept in a ground floor room which had French windows leading out to a pool. Every morning when the boys were woken up, they had to traipse through our bedroom in the nude and jump into the pool and then rush back downstairs for a shower. My sisters and I were honour bound to keep our eyes shut or our heads under the sheets. The boys were clearly very embarrassed because they all had their hands clamped over their private parts. Obviously I couldn't look … of course Marion told me to. She was very naughty!

On one occasion there was a great palaver when Marion found a boat on the lake across the road and put her infant brother Richard in it with her and cast off. She was now adrift and heading for the weir. Crowds gathered around the lake wondering how to save them. Oh what a fuss! A real drama. They were saved though and once more Marion was off up the stairs to bed early. 'You … are … a … very … very …'.

In this wonderful place of relative safety, the war passed us by. In the holidays, as the threat of invasion diminished, some boys would go home to their parents. Others would remain if their parents couldn't take them, for example, if their fathers were fighting, and my mother was paid to look after them. At this time my father would have to go to Bexhill to join the Royal Observer Corps.

I recall two incidents when the Germans were a little too close. The first came one night when my father returned from Bexhill and decided to take my mother out for a drink in Llanberis. I was left in charge. Whilst they were away, German bombers raided Liverpool. Flying back, they came overhead and there was an air-raid warning. This caused my mother great concern. Back at PyG, I got all the children under the oak kitchen table; we had planned for such an eventuality. We were there for half an hour. But all was well. On the second occasion, a German aeroplane crashed in the mountains. Staff went off to capture the crew. The boys were very disappointed they couldn't go too.

Eventually, with sadness, we left the PyG as the war was won. Lake House merged with a school from Norwich called Town Close House

School and, in effect, ceased to be. We eventually returned to Bexhill to live and were sent off to various boarding schools.

Now, many years have passed. Pen y Gwryd is a hotel again and I am old, but my frequent return visits remind me of that special time at that special place and bring me much happiness.

Elaine Travis (née Dougal) was born in 1928 in Sussex. She is the daughter of Eric and Marie Dougal and the eldest of their six children. Eric Dougal was headmaster of Lake House School that was evacuated to PyG during the Second World War. Travis later became a teacher herself before marrying Edward Travis and having four sons. She regularly stays at PyG and it is her favourite holiday destination.

Bill Roache

WHERE GREAT MEMORIES
ARE ALWAYS PRESENT

FOR MOST OF MY LIFE I have had strong Welsh connections. At the age of seven I was enrolled in boarding school, Rydal in Colwyn Bay, North Wales. (My son Linus also attended the same school.) After 11 years, I completed my education and joined the Royal Welch Fusiliers. (Welch is spelt with a 'c' so as not to embarrass King George III who had written a letter to the Regiment misspelling the name.) I was commissioned and signed on for a further three years, serving five years in all, reaching the rank of Captain.

There then followed a period of theatre work, television and films in and around London when the only Welsh connections were the few friends that I had made at school and in the Army. In 1972 I met Sara and found that we had much in common, especially our mutual links to North Wales. Sara told me about her wonderful childhood memories of PyG. So quite soon I was taken to meet the proprietors, Chris and Jo Briggs, and to experience for myself this legendary mountain inn.

I don't believe that any hotel in the world could boast a more extraordinary location, at the very foot of Snowdon, framed as it is by the majestic backdrop of Glyder Fach and the remarkable shattered pinnacles of Castell y Gwynt. (Each of the main guest bedrooms at PyG is named after one of the 15 local peaks over 3,000 feet.)

The first sight of PyG at the crossroads to Snowdon is an exciting experience, especially if you think of the site's rich history from Roman times to the preparations for the 1953 British Everest Expedition. Inside, I was taken to Jo Briggs's private sitting room and there was Chris Brasher, Olympic gold medal-winning British athlete, sports journalist and co-founder of the London Marathon, and a High Court Judge, John Ramsey Willis. Jo Briggs was holding her own 'court' like the chairperson of a debating society, of which I was the newest inductee. It was just as Sara had described.

Behind the public bar, inside the front door with its distinctive 'Mountain Rescue Post' sign, is a small private area. In those days the Smoke Room was only entered on the invitation of Chris Briggs himself (who was the High Sheriff of Caernarfonshire in 1966, the oldest secular office under the Crown dating back to Richard de Pulesdon in 1284). Apart from running the hotel, Chris Briggs was the local civilian rescue coordinator and it was not uncommon for a notice of 'strictly no entry' to be posted on the billiard room door as the result of the practicalities of managing an unsuccessful rescue.

Over the years, I have often visited the PyG and continue to be warmly hosted by Chris and Jo Briggs's daughter Jane and her husband Brian. For me, the PyG is a lively and vibrant place that lives in a timeless state where great memories are always present. I have never climbed Snowdon, but I am going to very soon. It is the sort of spiritual place to which I am personally attracted. (The name Snowdon is from the Old English for 'snow hill', while the Welsh name Yr Wyddfa means 'the tumulus', which refers to the stone cairn thrown over the legendary giant Rhitta Gawr, after his defeat by King Arthur.)

William Patrick 'Bill' Roache is an English actor. He has played Ken Barlow in *Coronation Street* since its first episode on 9 December, 1960. He is listed in *The Guinness World Records* as the longest serving living television actor in a continuous role.

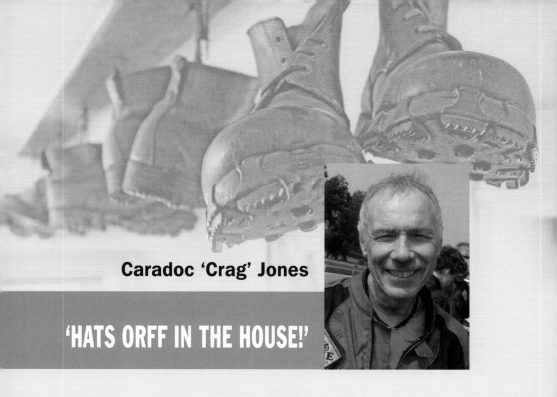

Caradoc 'Crag' Jones

'HATS ORFF IN THE HOUSE!'

THE FREEZING SLEET blew horizontally around the Pen y Gwryd, sweeping away the last of the daylight. Five pm on a winter's evening and, as a climbing-obsessed 14-year-old, I'd stayed on for that one extra route. This left me with the usual empty country road for the 100-mile hitch-hike back to Cardiganshire. It passed through God-fearing country where pubs were closed and I'd often end up sleeping under a hedge. Warm glows flickered out of the windows as the next gust scythed though my bones. The buggers would not let me in, even if it weren't a Sunday.

It was tricky getting a pint as a fresh-faced youth up here in the north. Back home we had special pubs for underage drinkers that adults could avoid to prevent mutual embarrassment. They were looked upon benignly, even by the police, as a sort of kindergarten where you learnt to hold your drink without causing trouble.

Families undertook special expeditions across the Cambrian Mountains to Radnorshire where the pubs were open on Sunday. My great aunt Hilda seemed to own most of them and everyone considered it essential that you learnt to consume beer. But I was losing count of the number of pubs I'd been chucked out of in Snowdonia. The Douglas

95

Arms in Bethesda was the best bet, particularly if you spoke Welsh and deferred to paying in the spirit of 'true pounds sterling'. Yes, they were still holding out against decimalisation in these parts and I was probably one of the last that could still calculate in £ /s /d (at least for the first few anyway). But tonight, it made no odds whether by imperial or decimal reckoning. I was, as usual, broke and starving. And now, in the howling winter darkness, I could not even use my young visage to persuade nervous motorists for a charitable lift. It was going to be a long haul home.

This is what true climbers did; we suffered for our art in an apprenticeship, long before pubs became Victorian-Contemporary and you paid a company to drag you up a mountain. The Pen y Gwryd lets me in these days and, as far as I know, has not succumbed to the make-over. I once made the mistake of loafing in under the latest beanie. 'Hats *orff* in the house' had not even registered as words before I had saluted and plunged it shamefully into my deepest pocket. The instantaneous obeisance to Jane Pullee's barked order gave way to my own bemusement at that startled reflex action. Architecture, age, class, language, dress, authority and deference: cultures of a kind had suddenly leapt into sharp focus out of nowhere. My surprise gave way to a broad grin as her son Nicolas rolled his eyes and served me up a pint.

Two nights at 8,300 metres Camp III on the North Ridge of Everest in gale force winds and my Danish climbing partner and I started to use oxygen. 'Could we speak to Michael please?' I handed over the radio. A quick bout of Danish sarcasm disarmed their worry that I might be detaining Michael Jørgensen against his will, forcing him to go on against his better judgement. Michael and I had become firm friends during the expedition. I could not ask for a better companion. We were both relaxed, but equally determined to hang on for a clearing in the weather which was now, at long last, forecast for the next morning. During the storm, it had become a bit of a public relations exercise to placate the concerned voices from down below.

Henry Todd had kindly given me this chance to attempt Everest in the style we wanted, guideless, staying true to his word all those years before when our expedition to Tierra del Fuego had imploded. Michael and I had put in the hard miles, carrying loads, cutting platforms, erecting tents and stocking them with Sherpa help, gradually working our way up the mountain. Because of the storm, it was clear that above the North Col, the two of us would have the route to ourselves. Henry and I had been in a few tight corners before so we both knew the score but kept up the moral support despite his worries. We also had Eric Jones and Leo Dickinson at base camp to keep the natural concerns of other expeditions from denting our determination. Our high camp days were spent crawling around on all fours sifting through the rubbish for extra food and cooking gas. Gone were the visions of cloud-puffing cherubs adorning the sky as I scavenged for extra oxygen. When the heart yearns for home, it's time for the head to hold steady. Now was our opportunity. We could finally make our summit attempt.

Back at the Pen y Gwryd, Nicolas Pullee pointed to the ceiling of the Everest Room, handed me a large marker pen and invited me to 'Choose your spot!' I proudly added my name amongst those of my illustrious heroes. Many of them I had come to know in the intervening years for their unstinting work to help young mountaineers from all walks of life as well as the peoples of the Himalayas. They seemed a certain type, a product perhaps of their more enlightened post-war times. Don Whillans, no less, said of their ilk at the time, 'Those university wallahs could have regarded me as just another monkey from the city. But they didn't'. Despite their privilege, they seemed to truly believe in equality, whatever your class, and opportunity for all. These were redeeming establishment qualities that are now becoming increasingly rare in regressively selfish and divisive times and thus need to be encouraged and emphasised more than ever before.

Caradoc 'Crag' Jones is a Welsh climber and fisheries consultant. While he has achieved a number of first ascents on peaks around the world, he is best known for being the first Welshman to reach the summit of Mount Everest, on 23 May, 1995, at the age of 33. The ascent via the North Ridge from Tibet was made with the late Michael Knakkergaard-Jørgensen, the first Dane to the summit. Jones, a former Vice President of the British Mountaineering Council, was born and raised in Pontrhydfendigaid, a village near Tregaron, Ceredigion, in mid Wales and climbed from there at an early age. He continues with exploratory climbing expeditions and climbs as hard as his training, household duties and opportunities for escape allow.

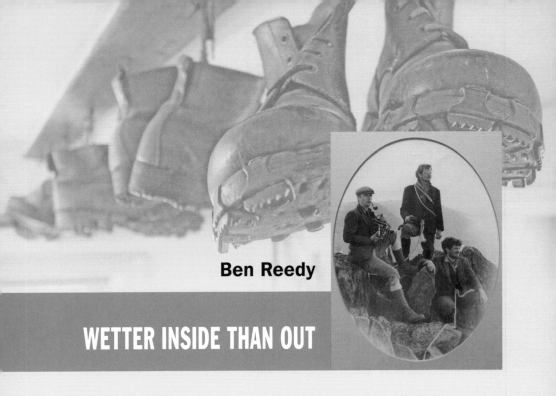

Ben Reedy

WETTER INSIDE THAN OUT

THE VERY FIRST thing I did as a fresher at my Midlands polytechnic was to join the mountaineering club and hence embrace the tradition that every third Friday, regardless of study commitments, we would cram into the student union minibus and race up to the Lakes or Wales, in the latter case stopping on the way for a late pint at the Star in Llangollen.

As impoverished students, we either camped or borrowed huts from other clubs. The tradition continues today as members of our club still hold an annual reunion somewhere hilly, 38 years after we graduated. Kids have come, grown up and moved on and many of the original members are beginning to look distinctly middle-aged. You may miss the odd year but the loyalty engendered by holding someone's life on a rope endures for a lifetime and members always make the effort to travel.

From the age of eight I was hauled up mountains, starting with Moel Hebog in Snowdonia. Every family holiday was camping and climbing in Wales or Scotland, for as long as we could tolerate the midges. My father was a country general practitioner and he was invited to join the Climbers' Club so, later on, we had the use of their huts too. In the

1960s, mountaineering was still something of a middle-class pursuit and I have a vivid memory of a group of gents, clad in breeches and jackets, encouraging a novice to climb a short chimney on the Glyderau, heavy boots scrabbling on damp rock and a hawser-laid rope knotted around his waist while his mentors enthused, 'Well done old chap!'

Initiated in this late-Edwardian tradition of mountaineering, I was always thrilled to visit the Pen y Gwryd as a student. The Mountain Rescue Post plaque on the wall outside gave the building a look of serious purpose and I sensed that the Everest Room was a hallowed place. I would spend a few minutes peering reverently up at the yellowed ceiling, which is densely scribbled with the signatures of famous climbers (and a few not so famous) who managed to immortalise themselves before the ceiling received its protective covering of perspex. Admiration for the pioneers of mountaineering even led me and two pals to bumble up Tryfan's East Face where we shot a black-and-white 8mm movie, dressed in tweeds and cords and using a frayed old caving rope, which upset some modern climbers so much that they were rather rude to us and called us 'irresponsible'.

The legendary mountaineer and raconteur Tom Patey penned 'The Manchester Delinquent's Song', which goes to the tune of 'The Manchester Rambler' and includes the lines:

> When I'm in the Gwryd my language is lurid,
> the landlord is pregnant with gloom.
> I've soiled his amenities and scribbled obscenities
> all over the Everest Room.

This was one of the songs we used to belt out gleefully in the public bar of the PyG, an establishment with a long history of tolerating climbers, tired and wet but happy after a day on the hills. I haven't heard anybody sing in a pub for 30 years but, in the mid-1970s, it seemed to be acceptable to be drunkenly rowdy. Usually, we would be in the PyG early enough to be able to occupy the Everest Room entirely; any non-members hoping for quiet conversation would be driven out by the sheer noise. We were proud of our collection of folk and climbing songs and, once we had ensconced ourselves in the room, packed in like mice in a nest, it would only be a matter of a couple of pints before somebody struck up with the club signature song and then on we'd go into the club's repertoire with gusto. Twenty or so damp bodies in a small unventilated room would produce a stink of wet wool and a level of humidity to rival the tropics, and the single-glazed windows would run with condensation.

The magazine *New Scientist* has confirmed what every beer lover knows: that in moderation, fresh, unpasteurised session bitter with about 3.8 per cent alcohol is a healthy natural drink. The diuretic effect of the ethanol is balanced by the water content, and beer contains minerals, vitamins, carbohydrates and pectin for regularity. The bonus is the relaxing effect of the ethanol and the sociable environment in which it is consumed, making beer the perfect post-exercise relaxation and recovery drink.

In the mid-1970s, one British pound was still enough for three or four pints of this elixir. Somebody would elbow their way through the crowded hallway to the small bar to buy a round, and jug after jug would be passed precariously back and loaded on to a table. This operation was especially slick when closing time approached, as there was a need to build up a good stock for after the final bell. On my 21st birthday I remember swallowing a very large number of pints far too quickly and, in one of those occasional moments of lucidity, I can still see the baleful stare of an older drinker as he watched me struggle to hold down the huge volume of liquid.

I drank a substantial part of my student grant at the PyG, so I hope to have the pleasure, once retirement allows me the time, actually to stay there. I'm told that the food is robust and I remember climbing friends of my parents enthusing about an Edwardian shower that gave you an invigorating blast of hot water from several directions at once. I travel widely for business and sometimes use TripAdvisor to find hotels; I see that for the PyG, TripAdvisor has more than ten 'excellent' reviews for every 'terrible', so it looks as though the few who disliked the hotel went with the wrong expectations. It is not necessarily right to modernise such an historic hotel, especially when most of your clientele enters so willingly into the unique spirit of the place.

Ben Reedy was born in London, in a hospital that is now a hostel for the homeless. In 30 years of export business travel, he has drunk lager in 20 different African countries, most frequently Nigeria, and concedes that there are some quite good ones out there if he's forced to drink 'Euro-fizz'. To stay fit and healthy and counteract the effect of all the carbs, Reedy goes road cycling and, on retirement, Reedy says he plans to get back into ski touring, mountaineering, rock climbing and skinny-dipping in mountain streams, if he still 'has his marbles'.

Before specialising in Africa, Reedy sold perfume to the French and, before that, he graduated in modern languages; the degree course included five months in France and five as an English assistant at an Opus Dei college in Spain. Before college, he had a variety of jobs including rambling leader in the Alps, ski chalet odd-job, hotel night porter and a variety of labouring and driving jobs.

Photograph of Andy Forsyth, Ben Reedy and Dick Moore on Tryfan, 1979. Moore says, 'The image was taken with a Russian Lubitel 2 that cost me £11 at the time. It used the '120' film format giving 12 exposures per roll of film with a negative size of 35×35mm. The lens gave a pin-sharp centre and soft outer edges. Running back over the rocks from the tripod to get into position before the timer went off, was 'interesting'. I still have the leather gaiters'.

Doug Scott

THE PYG, UNDENIABLY THE CENTRE
OF BRITISH CLIMBING LIFE

W ITH FRIENDS from Nottingham, I was a frequent visitor to North
Wales in the late 1950s and throughout the 1960s. Our form of
transport was hitch-hiking and accommodation was camping, usually
down the Llanberis Pass and quite often under the Cromlech Boulders.

Generally we gravitated to the pubs down-valley at Nant Peris or
Llanberis. There were exceptions as, on our honeymoon in 1962, Jan and
I slept our first night in what was then the hotel at Pen y Pass (another
famous climbers' hotel, soon to become a prime youth hostel). The beds
were hard and the old ladies running the place were buttoned up to
their neck ruffs, never smiling. We only had five pounds and so spent
subsequent nights under the Boulders. This was a good thing because
camped alongside us were Harry and Shirley Smith of the Rock and Ice
Club. Harry led me up Cemetery Gates in big chrome-leather Alpine
boots and I led him up Cenotaph Corner in my new Pierre Alain rock-
climbing shoes, the revolutionary 'PAs' that Dez Hadlum and Dennis
Gray had bought me for 'our' wedding present.

We did stray occasionally into the august atmosphere of the Pen y
Gwryd, once by appointment to meet, cap in hand, Wilfred Noyce of
Everest South Col fame, to discuss climbing in the Atlas Mountains.

There were other times, however, when we did drop in en masse for refreshment and a singsong (that usually got out of hand). I was so impressed at the way the landlord, one Chris Briggs, handled ribald behaviour, bouncing the young ones out of the public bar with his strong arms and holding the delinquent tight against his barrelled chest. I can vouch for the fact that there was no escape until outside, where he politely asked the offender to calm down before re-entry.

The last time I spent any time with Chris and Jo Briggs was in Darjeeling, way back in 1985. It was a real gathering of the clans at this meeting of mountaineers and trekkers. An untold story of that particular conference of the Himalayan Mountaineering Institute was that, if it hadn't been for Chris Briggs, the cream of the international climbing fraternity could all have been incinerated in a blaze of Sikkim whisky.

The conference gala dinner was sponsored by Air India and Old Gold Himalayan Premium Single Malt. At some time during the evening, the planets aligned and those responsible for guarding the entrances abandoned their posts in favour of free liquor. Gatecrashers poured in in their hundreds and invaded the buffet, which collapsed under the sheer weight of their enthusiasm. And so, at that very same instant, there was an electricity blackout. In the pitch darkness the organisers lit the hall with flaming torches of rolled-up copies of the *Times of India* (remember that the venue was a wooden, 100-year-old colonial-era ice-skating rink). Chris must have seen a vision of what was probably about to happen ... and calmly organised guests to leave the curry-splattered maelstrom by the rear entrance.

I was billeted with Mike Westmacott and, during numerous conference sessions, met Ed and Peter Hillary, Tenzing Norgay and other well-known climbers from just about every country that had ever climbed in the Himalayas. I recall a constant throng of well-wishers surrounding Chris and Jo, most of whom, at some time or another, had stayed at the Pen y Gwryd and enjoyed the splendid atmosphere in what was undeniably the centre of British climbing life.

Doug Scott is a British mountaineer noted for the first ascent of the South West Face of Everest on 24 September, 1975. (He and Dougal Haston were the first native Britons to reach the summit of Everest and return successfully.) Scott is a past president of the Alpine Club. In 1999 he was awarded the Patron's Medal of the Royal Geographical Society. He received the Lifetime Contribution Award at the 2011 Piolet d'Or awards in Chamonix. Scott founded the charity Community Action Nepal (CAN) and spends much of his time in fundraising. CAN is supported by mountaineers and mountain-lovers from across the globe. Funds are raised from donations, fundraising events, and the sale of Nepali-produced goods, grants and Scott's lecture tours.

Special note: The April 2015 Nepal earthquake killed more than 8,800 people and injured more than 23,000 others. CAN's role involves long-term support, including the rebuilding and rehabilitation of remote mountain communities. CAN ensures that all donations go directly to project areas without any deduction for administration costs, which are covered separately from sales and auctions at lectures and events held in the UK. www.canepal.org.uk

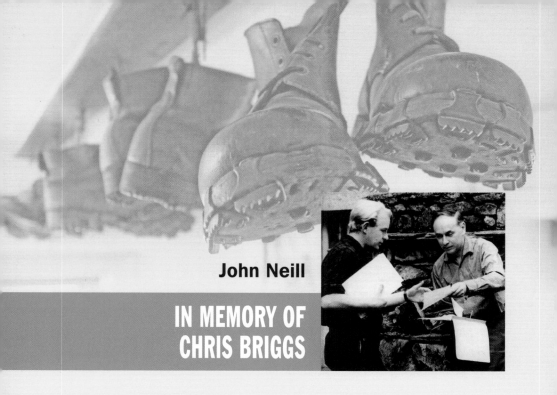

John Neill

IN MEMORY OF CHRIS BRIGGS

CHRISTOPHER PERCIVAL BASKIN BRIGGS (1913–1992) was a member of the Climbers' Club for 41 years. He is remembered primarily as landlord of the Pen y Gwryd Hotel, which has always occupied an important place in the life of the club and from which the club sprang in 1898.

After the Second World War (during which time the PyG had housed a school), fellow Climbers' Club member Arthur Lockwood, who had owned and run the Pen y Gwryd since 1921, retired to Hafod y Gwynt nearby, which he had rebuilt and enlarged, and sold the hotel to Mr Redditt, also a member of the club. During a visit to PyG in 1947, we found that Mr Redditt had, in turn, sold the hotel to Leslie Mather (who was a member of the Rucksack Club) who installed one Chris Briggs as manager. This was a turning point in the history of the hotel, which had become somewhat run down. Chris Briggs and his wife Jo put all their energy into restoring the hotel's past glory, in which they acquired a part-ownership, ultimately becoming sole owners.

In the above photograph John Neill (right), is handing over Climbers' Club Journal papers to his successor as Editor, Nigel Rogers, 1966. This contribution is reproduced with Ruth Neill's permission and with the permission of the Climbers' Club.

In the 1940s and early 1950s, the PyG increasingly became *the* place where the British (and international) climbing community congregated, to meet friends and to drink. My particular recollection of those years is of late nights in the Smoke Room with other Climbers' Club and Rucksack Club members, with Liar Dice sessions going on far into the night. The Climbers' Club Committee held most of its meetings there as, in due course, did the British Mountaineering Council (BMC) North Wales Committee (which was also formed there) and later the BMC Committee for Wales.

The successful 1953 British Everest Expedition also met at PyG both beforehand and on its return, and frequently thereafter. Members of the expedition signed their names on the ceiling of the new public room which had been created by the front door; this henceforth became 'the Everest Room'. Each expedition member was given his own tankard, kept hanging over the bar in the Smoke Room, for use when drinking in the hotel. Climbers making first ascents of new Welsh climbs were given the privilege of drinking from these same tankards when the owners were absent, after putting details of the route in the *Locked Book,* the use of which was revived by Chris.

There had been a mountain rescue kit at the hotel since 1936; Chris took it upon himself to lead a mountain rescue team based on the use of this equipment. In the early days mountain rescue was not the professional activity it has now become and Chris assembled his team for any particular rescue from competent guests, plus any climbers in the vicinity.

During the Easter of 1951, we were staying at PyG when conditions became extremely wintery, with heavy snow cover and the main slopes turning to continuous sheets of ice. My party were aiming for the Trinity Gates on Snowdon when we came across a dead body at the foot of the gullies. (This turned out to be that of Peter Koch who had fallen from the Central Gully.) We were setting off to raise the alarm when we were hailed by another member of Koch's party who had told us that the PyG rescue team had already been sent for.

When the team arrived, we joined in the carry down and, for the rest of that Easter ('Death Easter 1951', when many serious accidents occurred), we spent all our time with the team taking part in rescues or carrying bodies down from the mountain. Chris later wrote an article for the Climbers' Club Journal on the activities of his team at this period; it was at this time that he was elected to the club. He continued to run the PyG Mountain Rescue Post for over 20 years and, in 1956, he was awarded the BEM for his services to mountain rescue.

Chris was never what you would call 'a great climber', in latter years doing more skiing than climbing. He always, however, took a tremendous interest in the affairs of the Climbers' Club and served as Vice President from 1976 to 1979. He put much effort into both support and actions to conserve the beauty and amenities of the district, gave Esme Kirby backing in the work of the Snowdonia National Park Society and was a member of the North Wales Protection Committee.

Other than climbing and mountains, Chris's leisure interests lay with rugby, football and fishing. He was appointed High Sheriff of Caernarfonshire in 1966 and later became Deputy Lieutenant of the County. Chris was always a great friend to climbers. His daughter Jane and her husband Brian Pullee took over the running of the hotel from Chis and Jo and continued to maintain the same atmosphere.

John Neill (1917-2002) was a British climber (often in partnership with Mike Harris, who tragically disappeared with George Fraser on Ama Dablam in 1959). Neill's climbing high point was Mount Gestola in 1958, in the old Soviet Union with Eugene Gippenreiter and Dave Thomas, as part of the British Caucasus party (of which Neill was a driving force, responding to the Russian visit to Britain). He is, however, best remembered for his unrivalled scholarship and service to the climbing world as a writer, editor and archivist. He was the Climbers' Club Guidebook editor from 1961 to 1970 and presided over the publication of eight important guides including seminal works on Tremadog, Clogwyn Du'r Arddu, Llanberis Pass (north and south) and Bosigran.

He was also the editor of the Climbers' Club Journal from 1960 to 1966. In 1985, John became President of the British Mountaineering Council and was supported by a group of notable vice presidents including Chris Bonington, Alan Rouse, George Band and Paul Nunn. Neill met his wife Ruth in 1959 when she was working at the Pen y Gwryd Hotel.

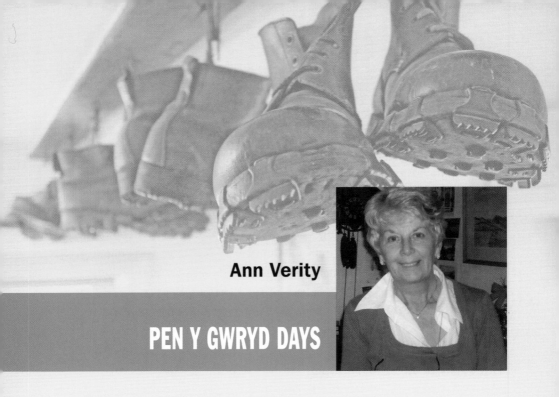

Ann Verity

PEN Y GWRYD DAYS

IN SEPTEMBER 1959 I arrived at the Pen y Gwryd Hotel as a 17-year-old, not as a guest or visitor but to work. I had spent the previous three years studying catering at college in Liverpool. Every year or so, Mr and Mrs Briggs would visit the college to see if any of the young ladies wished to follow a career in hotel catering and would like some hands-on experience at the PyG. I thought it was a good idea, applied and luckily I was accepted. It changed the course of my life.

My first journey to PyG was by motorbike. I shall never forget the amazing final miles of ups and downs and winding bends on the narrow road from Capel Curig to the hotel. From the beginning, I worked with five other girls. We all got on very well; the work was hard but great fun too. I remember the first morning both my roommate and I overslept and Jane, Mr Briggs's daughter, had to wake us up. Not a good start!

Memories start to flood in. During the first winter, a reporter from the local *Daily Post* visited to take 'winter photographs' for the paper. My friend and I volunteered and Mr Briggs found some very old wooden skis which we donned to pose in the snow (the pictures made the Liverpool Edition). By December the nearby Lockwood's

Lake had frozen and we were treated to a wonderful display of figure skating by Sylvia Disley. The hotel had some distinctly unusual traditions. At Christmas, when all the residents had been served their festive dinner, they, in turn, served the staff theirs. On our one day off a week we were also allowed to choose our breakfast, which was brought up to our rooms. Happy memories.

An important member of staff was Blodwen who appeared very old to us and may have been over 80 years old at that time. Born in Llanberis, she had worked all her life at the PyG. She had her own little room at the top of the stairs in the staff quarters and looked after us all. Mischievously, if she heard we had a honeymoon couple staying, she would enthusiastically burst in, after knocking of course, but not quite waiting for the reply. The highlight of her week was visiting the town of Caernarfon where she could shop at Woolworths. One year, Chris and Jo Briggs took Blodwen to London. They stayed at the Cumberland Hotel near Marble Arch. Blodwen maintained her professional role taking the Cumberland staff in hand to make sure Mr Briggs had his morning tea served on time.

At weekends and holidays the bar at PyG was always absolutely jam-packed with customers and collecting glasses was quite an ordeal. Well before days of piped barrels, the beer had to be transported from the storeroom to the bar in jugs. This frantic job fell to a Yorkshireman and climber, Doug Verity. We fell in love and married in 1963 in the church at Capel Curig. Jane Briggs, Liz Roberts and Helen Brown, Joe and Val's daughter, were my bridesmaids.

After leaving school, Jane Briggs moved to London and joined BOAC, the forerunner of British Airways, as a stewardess. On her visits home, she was always ready to give a helping hand in the hotel or do some cooking in the kitchen as her mother had done for so many years. She later became a personal assistant to the comedian Peter Cook. In time, she met Brian Pullee, an interior designer, and together they moved back to the hotel. Over the years Brian has made a major contribution to restoring, maintaining and developing the PyG, cleverly avoiding any unintentional or unnecessary changes to its unique character.

Life at PyG was a fantastic experience and I look back with great joy at the years I spent there.

Anne Verity was born in Liverpool. She lost her mother when she was very young and was brought up by her father and grandparents. It was her grandmother who introduced Ann to cooking. This encouraged her to apply to the Mabel Fletcher College and finally to pass her City and Guilds course in Catering. She worked at the Pen y Gwryd from September 1959 until the late 1960s.

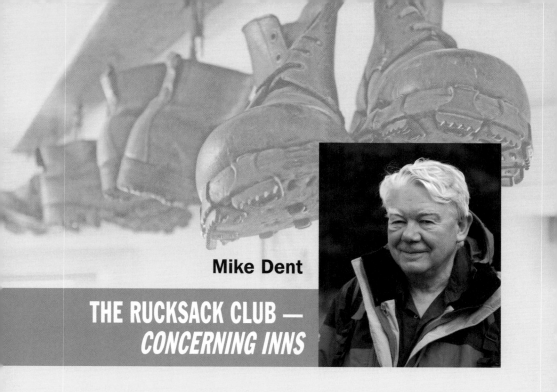

Mike Dent

THE RUCKSACK CLUB —
CONCERNING INNS

IN MAY 1902 John Entwistle, a young Manchester man, took a solitary
walking tour in North Wales and stopped for lunch at the Pen y
Gwryd Hotel. Whist relaxing there, he came across a recently published
Journal of the Yorkshire Ramblers' Club. This contained a report of the
previous annual dinner at which Joe Collier, a Manchester surgeon and
Alpine Club member, proposed the toast. In his well-received speech,
Collier regretted that no similar club had arisen in Lancashire. Later
that year, a leader appeared in the *Manchester City News*, 'In Praise of
Walking Tours', which gave rise to a lively correspondence in which such
a club was mooted.

A meeting called on 13 October, 1902, attracted men from a wide
range of backgrounds. Arthur Burns noted an uncanny number of
lawyers with broad interests, ranging from ramblers to those with
ambitions to explore the Alps and beyond. (Burns was Entwistle's regular
walking companion. The pair worked closely together and were elected
joint-secretaries at the club's foundation, remaining in office for many
years.)

Two of the lawyers were bidden to draw up a provisional set of
rules of The Rucksack Club. This included Rule 9: 'The Club shall

whave an Annual Dinner'. This was duly enforced some 53 days after the club's foundation (surely claiming some sort of record). A query by a founding member as to the admission of 'ladies' was quietly shelved and it was not until 1990 that the club elected to admit women to membership.

Members of the club have always been involved in rock climbing, long-distance walking and mountaineering. The 2,500ft Corbetts are named after one of the original members, and members of The Rucksack Club featured as the male half of both the first and second married couples recorded as Munro Compleaters. The club was the first in the UK to have its own hut as a mountain base, firstly in Cwm Eigiau and now in Nant Peris, resulting in the Pen y Gwryd no longer being the base for meets, while remaining a regular and much-loved watering hole.

In 1987 a small group of members persuaded the committee that a club archive should be established. Two archivists set about discovering what was kept and by whom. An amazing amount of material was uncovered, dating back to the founding of the club in October 1902. (Fortunately, one of the original archivists had an empty wardrobe and an understanding wife.) Subsequent projects have included the digitising of all club journals with a full index, newsletters, photographs, handbooks and minutes. Recently, a study of the activities of members during the First World War was commissioned; a most rewarding and moving experience.

Archival research is always interesting and sometimes uncovers areas of club history rarely explored. To this end I have chosen a delightful journal entry from 1923 and 'a climbing song' from 1953, both of which exemplify the long and affectionate association between The Rucksack Club and the Pen y Gwryd.

> **RCJ 1923 Vol. V., No.1. Issue 17**
> Extract from '*Concerning Inns*' by Charles H. Pickstone.
>
> In thinking of these things, other memories of the land of yesterday 'rush upon me thronging'. Now it is Pen-y-Gwryd. What associations this inn has! What lasting friendships it

has given birth to! Doubtless there are other equally deserving inns, but this was my first and (with the exception, perhaps, of the little inn in Upper Eskdale) has remained my best love. An early episode stands out. I was on a walking tour in North Wales, into the hazards of which I had inveigled a complete novice – a youth who had been strictly brought up in the singular doctrine never to 'darken the doors of a public house'. He was only allowed to come on the strict understanding that we put up at *temperance* inns. This happens to be a type of house which (originally) instinct and (later) experience taught me to avoid.

After miles of road walking, Ogwen was reached en route for Beddgelert, which place it was intended to make via Capel Curig. But the thought of those nine long miles of hard road which lay between Ogwen and Pen-y-Gwryd was too appalling, especially as I knew it could be avoided and halved in distance by a bee-line. An impish fancy seized me. He should have one experience of what real mountaineering was like. Accordingly, we left the road for the well-known route by the pass over Col Tryfan. Ere the summit was reached my friend had clearly had enough and, as night was coming on, the thought of my own responsibilities somewhat damped enthusiasm. There will be few members of the club unacquainted with the kind of ground which has to be negotiated on the descent to Pen-y-Gwryd. There is no more awkward two miles in Great Britain on which to be benighted. To add to our troubles mist came down. My friend had, of course, no sense of direction and his faith in me and my compass was lamentably weak. Suddenly, the mist lifted and disclosed a distant light. I knew that light; it was Pen-y-Gwryd. It put new life into my friend. I shall never forget his excited exclamation, 'I see a house!', and my crushing reply, 'But it is a *public* house.' 'Never mind what sort of a house it is; let us go for it' was the eager rejoinder. This we did, and the memory of that bee-line haunts me still. Incidentally, the episode was the means of undermining the faith in which he had been nursed that licensed premises are necessarily the way to the abyss. Pen-y-Gwryd was his first experience of a licensed house, and I believe he has never since stayed at a temperance house – certainly not with me.

P. Y. G.
Words by John Hirst
(Air: 'Wonderful Copenhagen')

RUCKSACK CLUB LADIES' NIGHT, APRIL 10, 1953.

Some folk like formality, and some hospitality,
Some like luxury and some good cheer,
And some just beer! But have no fear,
We cater for everyone here.
Wonderful, wonderful Pen-y-Gwryd,
Here you will get your desire.
You may sip your wine as you sit and dine
Or eat snacks before the fire.

Wonderful, wonderful Pen-y-Gwryd
Caters for girl and for boy,
You may climb or walk, or play bridge or talk,
While at Pen-y-Gwryd, wonderful, wonderful,
Wonderful days you'll enjoy.
There's some who like scrambling and some just go rambling,
Some climb buttresses and scrape their knees,
And some like ease – I'm one of these –
But here you can do what you please.
Wonderful, wonderful Pen-y-Gwryd,
That is the place when you're wet,
You may toast your toes, while we dry your clothes,
And a welcome you will get:
Wonderful, wonderful Pen-y-Gwryd,
That is the place when you're dry.
There are some whose dream is a mountain stream
But at Pen-y-Gwryd, wonderful, wonderful,
Wonderful drinks you can buy.
Some climb with a dexterity, and some with temerity,
Most climb carefully, but sad to say,
Some go astray and lose their way,
And return on a stretcher next day.
Wonderful, wonderful Pen-y-Gwryd,
That's where we Rescue Lads are.

We will scour the ground 'till the corpse is found
And first-aid it at the bar.
Wonderful, wonderful Pen-y-Gwryd,
Gently we'll put it to bed
If we can contrive, 'twill remain alive,
But the Pen-y-Gwryd will still be a wonderful,
Wonderful place if it's dead.
Wonderful, wonderful Pen-y-Gwryd,
Cambria's hotbed of vice.
You will drink a pail of our export ale,
And be fleeced at Liar Dice.
Wonderful, wonderful Pen-y-Gwryd,
Once you come here you will stay,
It's a princely pub, you'll get "gradely" grub,
Because Christopher Briggs is a wonderful, wonderful,
Wonderful hotelier.

(This version is taken from Hirst's book *Climbing Songs* published by the Rucksack Club about 1960. John Hirst was a prolific entertainer, with contributions such as these being responsible for the 'Pinnacle Ladies' poem, and much in demand at various clubs' dinners.)

Mike Dent was elected to the Rucksack Club in 1961. He has walked and climbed in the UK, the Alps, Norway and Canada but with a good deal of his time on the hills spent introducing young people to the outdoors. Club secretary from 1999 to 2008 and vice president in 2009, he took over as one of the archivists in 2008. In this current post, he can indulge in the delightful pastimes of exploring the club's history and helping researchers.

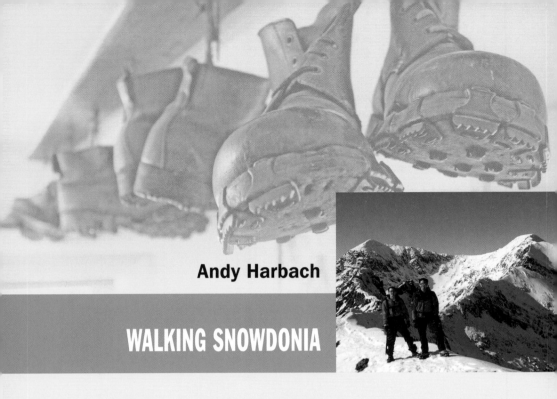

Andy Harbach

WALKING SNOWDONIA

THE SNOWDON HORSESHOE is the classic ridge walk of North Wales. Snowdon itself is the highest mountain in England and Wales, with a height of 1,085 metres. The highest car park surrounding the mountain is at Pen y Pass, which is about five minutes' drive from the Pen y Gwryd Hotel.

The walk itself is approximately 11 kilometres in length, with an overall height gain of 910 metres. It normally takes five to six hours to complete.

If you want to complete the Snowdon Horseshoe, then you begin by following the Pyg Track. Because of the expensive parking at Pen y Pass, I usually choose to leave my car near the Pen y Gwryd Hotel, in one of the less expensive park-and-pay lay-bys; then I walk up a track just below the road. This adds about half an hour in each direction to the adventure.

The mountain you see ahead of you when leaving Pen y Pass is not Snowdon but Crib Goch. This catches a lot of people out. The

In the above photograph, taken from Crib Goch, in full winter conditions, Snowdon is on the left and Crib y Ddysgl on the right. Harbach is on the right facing the camera.

www.walk-snowdonia.co.uk

Llanberis Mountain Rescue team often get calls from people who have underestimated the challenges of the mountain's characteristic knife-edged ridges. For this reason, the Pyg Track and Crib Goch are both well marked at the diversion of paths at Bwlch y Moch. Before heading up Crib Goch, you can look across to the imposing cliffs of Y Lliwedd where the 1953 British Everest team did some of their training.

The Welsh name Crib Goch can be translated as 'Red Ridge' and in the right light you can see why. As you ascend, the path loses its definition and you end up scrambling up rocky ground. This is no place for those who are afraid of heights.

Eventually you come out on a sharp summit and can see the knife-edged ridge ahead. It is a particularly enjoyable to traverse in winter but only if the conditions are right (especially with no strong winds and if you are equipped with ice axes and crampons and have the skill to use them). Some weekends during summer you may have to queue to get across the ridge and then over the Pinnacles at its far end. An early start is recommended at this time of year if you want to beat the crowds.

After crossing Crib Goch, the path becomes clear until you reach the Crib y Ddysgl ridge of Carnedd Ugain, at which point you start to scramble again. At 1,065 metres, Carnedd Ugain is the second highest mountain in Snowdonia. It has a trig point on its summit and this is where I often have lunch before heading on to the summit of Snowdon itself.

When you join the Llanberis Path for the last part of the walk up to the summit of Snowdon, you sometimes again find a crowd. There is a large standing stone marking the point where the Pyg Track meets the Llanberis Path and, to cut my walk short, I sometimes descend this way.

After a photo stop at the summit and possibly a snack in the café, which is open during the summer months in good weather, I leave the crowds behind and descend south-westwards until I reach another large standing stone. This marks the top of the Watkin Path. This path initially starts as steep scree and is tricky to walk down. Eventually, you reach a flat section which you proceed across and then ascend the three peaks of Y Lliwedd, West, East and Bach (meaning small). Shortly after the last peak, there is a path off to your left which takes you down to Llyn Llydaw.

From there you follow an obvious path called the Miners' Track and then continue back to Pen y Pass.

If you chose not to park at Pen y Pass, as I usually do, you will now need to walk back down to your car. At the end of a long day in the mountains, I usually stop at the Gwryd for a beer (assuming someone else is driving).

The bar is a friendly place and you can sit by the fire and look across at a photo of Hillary and Tenzing on Everest, taken in 1953. It shows them sitting on boxes and drinking tea. You can see the type of clothing they were wearing. It makes you realise how much things have moved on. There is also a photo from 1897 when the Abraham Brothers attempted Slanting Gully on Y Lliwedd. Again, this shows the advances in mountaineering equipment from the 19th century when 'the leader must not fall' was the inescapable maxim, to current times where a leader can usually continue climbing after falling on to a good gear placement.

As I make my way out of the Pen y Gwryd's public bar and into the brisk mountain air, I immediately start to consider my next adventure in Snowdonia, where the mountain playground on which I was scrambling today was the training ground for the first successful expedition to reach the summit of the highest mountain on earth.

Andy Harbach was born in Sutton Coldfield, West Midlands, England, in 1978 and went on numerous walking trips to North Wales with his parents and where he went to Bishop Vesey's Grammar School. This kindled his love for the mountains and influenced his choice to attend the University of Wales, Bangor, where he studied computer systems engineering. Harbach continued to go out walking each weekend whilst a student and created his Walking in Snowdonia website during this time. He has been a member of the Ogwen Valley Mountain Rescue Organisation for the past six years, a voluntary team which helps people in difficulty in inhospitable terrain.

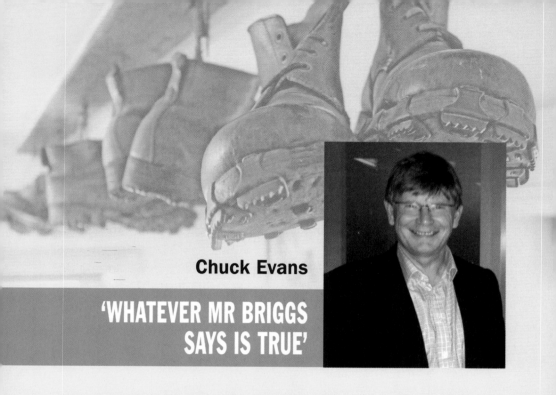

Chuck Evans

'WHATEVER MR BRIGGS SAYS IS TRUE'

Living in Bangor and then Capel Curig, my brothers Robin and Peter and I were often taken to the Pen y Gwryd when we were boys and, later on, with my father (Robert Charles Evans, deputy leader on the 1953 British Everest Expedition and leader of the expedition which first climbed Kangchenjunga in 1955) and my mother, Lady Denise Evans (the first female president of the Alpine Club) for the regular Everest and Kangchenjunga reunions. Later still, many times, it was after completing the Snowdon Horseshoe for a well merited pint.

The PyG was, and still is, a magical place. As children, we were often installed in the snug behind the bar and Blodwen, the 'maid of maids' (dressed in traditional Welsh black), would look after us by serving hot buttered toast, forever after known in our family as 'Pen y Gwryd toast'. And I recall that there were funny napkins with a few choice phrases written in both Welsh and English. (This is still probably the limit of my Welsh.)

As a boy, I was fascinated by the oxygen cylinder and other holy relics of the 1953 British Everest Expedition in the glass case in the Smoke Room. And every member of the expedition had a silver pint beer tankard; and, when my father was not there, I got to drink from it too.

119

One story I like to recall is about the police visiting the hotel, questioning Blodwen about after-hours or Sunday opening. Blodwen gave the policeman a stern look and despite persistent interrogation all she would say was, 'Whatever Mr Briggs says is true'.

I also remember Jane Pullee organising Halloween parties where the staff were dressed up as ghosts. Such happy times!

In the year that my father died (1995), we celebrated the 40th anniversary of the ascent of Kangchenjunga and my two-year-old daughter Natasha made the first cut in the cake, whilst my then six-month-old boy, Charlie, lay asleep on a blanket on the floor in the PyG dining room as we drank champagne opposite the 'captain's table', where for many years Chris Briggs would host, amongst others, the likes of David Cox and Kevin FitzGerald, two real gentlemen!

Wonderful memories!

Chuck Evans (1959-2016) was the eldest son of Charles and Denise Evans. He also did some Himalayan exploration in the late 1980s and early 1990s, including Jaonli in India, Churen Himal and Saipal Nepal, as well as a visit to Khumbu. When not enjoying the mountains or sailing, Chuck advised French companies in difficulties with their respective banks. He passed away in March 2016.

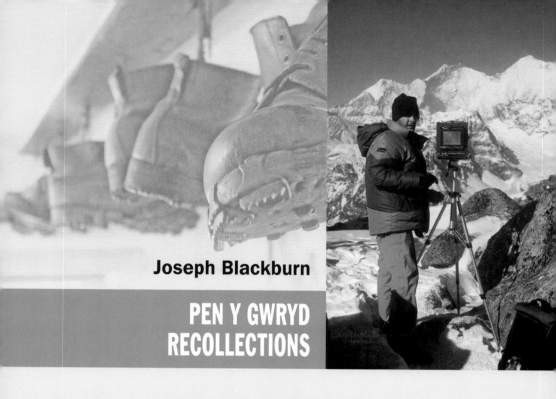

Joseph Blackburn

PEN Y GWRYD
RECOLLECTIONS

W E WERE SPEEDING through the English countryside on the wrong side of the highway, at least wrong in my mind. This was an adjustment, since I was sitting on the side of the car that I would be normally driving on, at least back home in Canada or the USA.

London had been a whirlwind trip; our 25th anniversary reunion of the Everest 88-Kangshung Face Expedition had been held at the Royal Geographical Society the evening before, with the presentation introduced by Ranulph Fiennes. Expedition leader Robert Anderson and the rest of the team gathered once again for 'the party of the century' as team member Stephen Venables had coined the gathering of Paul Teare, Ed Webster, Mimi Zieman, Miklos Pinther, Sandy Wylie, Norbu Tenzing Norgay and me, along with spouses and close family members. Yes, the team which established a new route, without the use of supplementary bottled oxygen, on the notoriously dangerous East Face of Everest in 1988, was together again.

The evening at the Royal Geographical Society had been a huge success. Significantly, the night was organised as a fundraiser for the charity www.brainstrust.org. All participants who filled the great theatre enjoyed the full expedition story as each of the climbers spoke

121

in turn. My photographs of 25 years earlier came to life, once again revealing the hardships encountered, the logistical challenges of scaling the Kangshung Face from Tibet and the joys and friendships shared that have kept this close-knit group of friends alive. But that was kilometres away now as we sped closer to Mount Snowdon in North Wales.

Pen y Gwryd, a quaint mountain inn in North Wales, has a long history. It has drawn almost all of the world's most famous climbers (and countless less-known ones) to gather and share the adventures of the day, or of their lifetimes. Moments after depositing my luggage and camera gear at the head of the stairs, I descended to find Norbu Tenzing Norgay. I was directed to a small room just off the central hallway, a part of the bar, the Smoke Room. As I entered, Norbu turned to me asking how the drive from London was and did I want a beer. I said, 'Sure'. Then Norbu handed me the silver flask he was holding and said, 'Here, have a drink from my father's mug.' The flask I was now holding had been the very one his father would drink from when staying at the Pen y Gwryd in the years following his first successful ascent of Everest in 1953 with climbing partner Edmund Hillary. I felt honoured to have had this opportunity to drink from Norbu's father's flask, usually reserved for immediate family only. It was a token of the close friendship we had forged since 1987 when we both resided in Connecticut. Then, Norbu's employer was Lindblad Travel, our expedition's transport organiser, and I was self-employed as a professional photographer in New York City.

The famed Smoke Room walls were filled with photographs of the past and featured history of those who had come to hike the trails of North Wales, climb the rocky crags and reach the summits of Snowdon and other surrounding peaks. As a photographer, I spent a good deal of time studying the images, admiring some of the photographic techniques and simply enjoying taking it all in as I sipped on a wonderful local brew.

I gazed into the shadow box on one wall adjacent to the bar; its contents held the rope that tied Hillary and Tenzing together on that successful first ascent of Everest's South East Ridge, over the now renowned Hillary Step on 29 May, 1953. The metal cup portrayed in the iconic photo of Ed Hillary taken after summiting – which John Hunt had given to Hillary to rehydrate, was there too, as he and Tenzing shared their story with the others in the climbing party. We made our own toast, relived our climb of 25 years earlier, discovered what had transpired in our lives, learned about children born since, and got to know new faces. I walked the halls, visited rooms with other photographs and enjoyed the ceiling of signatures of successful Everest climbers and icons of the climbing past, all part of the history of this remarkable hotel.

Breakfast was early, a full course of eggs, sausages, toast and lots of coffee, as well as almost anything else you might want. We stored some calories and then were off for the crags of nearby Snowdon. Despite the foggy, overcast and threatening sky, we slipped through the gate near the roadside parking and hiked across the meadow, past lakeside foliage and up to one of the rocky buttresses. It was time to test out skills on a bit of North Wales wet rock.

Stephen Venables took no time gathering rope in hand and making his way up the crack, running upwards on a damp face, as Norbu, Teare, Webster, Anderson and myself watched his balletic moves in mountaineering boots. No sooner up, he was down, having secured a 'top rope' for each of us to have a turn at climbing and belaying, all the while sharing the stories of our respective lives during the 25-year interim.

Most of us had kept in touch. Robert Anderson and I had done so, especially during the two years of the Seven Summits Solo, his odyssey to be the first person to climb the highest mountain on each of the seven continents, solo. As he needed a photographer to document the quest, Robert and I had travelled together during 1992 and 1993 when he successfully climbed a new or difficult route on Aconcagua, Kilimanjaro, McKinley (Denali), Elbrus, Vinson Massif and Kosciusko. The summit of Everest came several years later. On occasion, when time permitted, I checked a few off the list myself. This included my favourite, McKinley's knife-edged ridge to the summit. This was on 5 July, 1992, the day after my 46th birthday.

The Pen y Gwryd was our base while in North Wales, as we had another climbing presentation to do just down the road at the Climbing

Training Centre, a gathering point for climbers to sharpen their skills and meet up with others or to gain rescue and training skills. The audio-visual room was filled with guests wanting to hear a first-hand account of our climb, on a side of the mountain of which George Mallory's 1921 journal entry noted, '...others less wise may choose this way if they should, but emphatically it was not for us.' Stephen Venables' lanky figure silhouetted the show screen; Ed Webster's image of Stephen hanging on the Tyrolean traverse over the Jaws of Doom was revealed floor to ceiling. Another eventful night of memories shared with others and then a quick return to the Pen y Gwryd for our last nightcap.

Shortly after breakfast a long-time friend of Norbu (and of his father Tenzing Norgay) arrived. This was Jan Morris, celebrated author and *Times* correspondent. Coffee, snacks and tea were served as we listened to stories of how the news was announced to the world the day Elizabeth II was crowned Queen of England. Everest has been conquered; England and the whole world celebrated joyously. I clearly recall the *LIFE* magazine cover and the story within. *LIFE* was one of the magazines that had so influenced my subconscious and later, in part, led to choosing a career as a professional photographer.

Time was running short; we had to depart and go our separate ways. But first, the entire group gathered for me to make an official photo at the Pen y Gwryd entry doorway with Jan Morris; it was a momentous occasion to share and remember.

Joseph Blackburn graduated from The Art Center College of Design in Pasadena, California, with a BA (Hons) in 1977. After graduation, he worked as a staff photographer for Hallmark Cards. He then relocated to New York City in 1980 where he opened his own professional photography studio, servicing advertising agencies, design firms, media publications and private clients, creating images both in-studio and on location. In 1988, Robert Anderson, leader of the Everest '88 Kangshung Face Expedition invited him to be the official photographer. Then again in 1992, Anderson asked him to join his odyssey Seven Summits Solo, documenting the climbs and producing images for the corporate sponsors. Images from both expeditions were used in numerous books, publications, televised broadcasts and multimedia presentations worldwide. Joseph now resides in Vancouver, British Columbia. www.everest88.com

John Disley

IN MEMORY OF JO BRIGGS

THE FORMING OF A 'Climbing Club' was first proposed at the Pen y Gwryd Hotel at a dinner in December 1897. The first president, C. E. Mathews, was elected at that meeting and the Climbers' Club was inaugurated in London a few months later on 28 April, 1898.

During the next 50 years, landlords came and went, including Arthur Lockwood of Lockwood's Chimney fame, but, no doubt, the Climbers' Club members still stayed on and drank at this most convenient hostelry, a continuity only broken by the Second World War when the PyG was used to house an evacuated school.

By 1947, the hotel was run down and unloved and, when Lockwood put it up for auction, Chris and Jo Briggs acquired the PyG and began the daunting task of resurrection. They had never owned a hotel, or any other business for that matter. Jo Briggs later admitted that she believed that all the mine host's wife had to do was '… to arrange the flowers and discuss with the cook the day's menu'.

This elegant young lady, raised in Newfoundland of English parents and sent back to England to be 'educated' in the mid-1930s, suddenly found herself, together with a six-year-old daughter and a chemist husband (who was equally devoid of hotelier skills) owning a broken-down establishment in an era of rationing and quotas, as well as staff and supply shortages, all in 'a foreign country'. And there was no cook to instruct, just one middle-aged Welsh maid named Blodwen. The only factor that Jo Briggs found that was positive about this fraught situation was that this ivy-clad building had a history; and what a history. It made a good claim to be 'The Home of British Mountaineering'.

The Climbers' Club, at her suggestion, held its committee meetings in Jo Briggs's sitting room and abandoned the Pen y Pass and Cobden's hotels for their Christmas dinners, returning to their spiritual home.

Jo capitalised on this historical asset. She was a networker par excellence, long before the term was in common parlance. She spent the next 35 years of her life cultivating friendships, not only with the élite of the world climbing fraternity but also with the great and good of Caernarfonshire society. She sent her daughter to Penrhos School for Girls in Colwyn Bay, and young Jane brought home her school friends. Their influential parents were soon visiting the PyG and were enrolled on Jo's own social register. Witness to her charm and networking ability is that her husband Chris, leader of the local mountain rescue team based at the hotel and with not much else on his curriculum vitae, became the High Sheriff of Caernarfonshire. No mean feat for a non-Welsh speaking, taciturn Yorkshireman.

The Smoke Room at the PyG was Jo Briggs's 'salon' inhabited by masters of the well-turned phrase and bon mots. These doyens of conversation, such as David Cox, Kevin FitzGerald, Jack Longland, Emlyn Jones, Dick Viney, Wynford Vaughan-Thomas, Cliff Morgan and Huw Wheldon graced her after-dinner soirées. During the period of the Llangollen International Eisteddfod, it would seem that half the BBC was there.

Jo Briggs had style. Where she got it from is hard to say. She certainly didn't bring it from Newfoundland, or get it from the Pitman's Secretarial College she attended, or from her Manchester-based husband, Chris, or his Prestwich Rugby Club. But it was there in spades; chilled dry sherry at precisely 12.30pm and 6.30pm in slim glasses and an annual round of the Henley Regatta, the England v Wales rugby match, skiing in Kitzbühel and the Glyndebourne Opera, when, on return, she could reel off the names of all the celebrities who were picnicking there but had more difficulty remembering what she had heard on the stage.

'Everest' was the pinnacle of her life and the life of the PyG. The symbiotic relationship between the Everest team and the hotel was sustained over many years of reunions by Jo's unremitting attention to the cultivation of friendships. Yes, she was a snob but she had a wonderful talent for making even a humble young climber who had come to her attention feel part of some grand design in the annals of her historic home. After all, 'he could be the next Joe Brown'.

I remember as a young man standing with Chris Brasher in the lobby of the PyG and being fulsomely introduced by Jo to that Grand Old Man of British Mountaineering, Geoffrey Winthrop Young. I read later in one of his writings that he recalled being introduced to Brasher and me. He wrote, 'They seemed nice enough young lads'. I can't recall if Jo was mentioned in connection with his visit. Bound to have been!

'The Queen's telegram' eluded Jo Briggs and she died – in the late Spring of 2007, in her fine apartment overlooking the Menai Strait and Snowdonia, at the age of 91.

John Ivor Disley (1928–2016) was born in Corris, a village in Merioneth (now in present day Gwynedd). He competed for Great Britain in the 1952 Summer Olympics held in Helsinki in the 3000 metre steeplechase where he won the bronze medal. (He also competed in the 1956 Melbourne Olympics.) Disley was responsible for setting five British records in the steeplechase and four at two miles as well as setting Welsh records at six other distances. Disley also broke the record for the traverse of the Welsh 3000 Foot peaks.

Disley was appointed as the first Chief Instructor and Acting Warden of Plas y Brenin, the Central Council for Physical Recreation's new Centre for Mountain Activities. He then served as Inspector of Education for Surrey Education Authority for 13 years (1958-71). During this time, he was also named Vice Chairman of the National Sports Council (1965-71) and, later, Vice Chairman of the UK Sports Council (1974-82).

He is, however, best known as the co-founder of the London Marathon, launched in 1981, which now attracts over 35,000 runners who raise significant sums of money for charity. He has also been a leading pioneer of orienteering in the UK, organising the World Championships in Scotland in 1976.

He was Vice Chairman of the UK Sports Council in 1974, a post he held until 1982. He was a former President of the Snowdonia Society and a member of the Welsh Sports Hall of Fame. (Reproduced with permission of the Climbers' Club.)

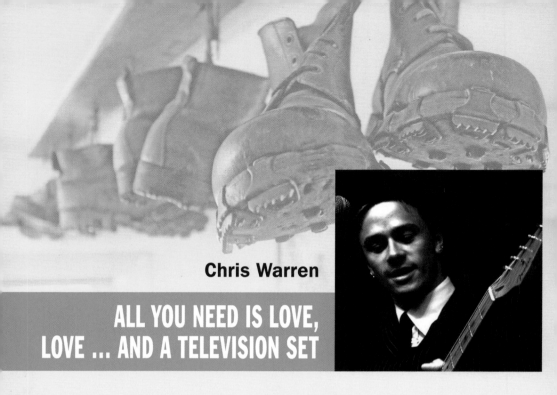

Chris Warren

ALL YOU NEED IS LOVE, LOVE ... AND A TELEVISION SET

T HERE IS A WONDERFULLY quirky connection between the Beatles and 'The Home of British Mountaineering', a story from the time of Chris Briggs, then the proprietor of the Pen y Gwryd.

The Beatles undertook several brief residencies in 1963, mainly in coastal towns in England and Wales. One of these was a six-night season in Llandudno on the North Wales coast. Also on the bill for the week were Billy J. Kramer and the Dakotas, The Lana Sisters, Sons of Piltdown Men, Tommy Wallis and Beryl, and none other than Tommy Quickly. The compère was the redoubtable Billy Baxter. The shows began promptly at 6.30pm and 8.50pm; both were sold out. Tickets were priced at 4/6d, 6/6d and 8/6d. (One of the audience members was Mary Hopkin, then just 13 years old, who would later be mentored by Paul McCartney.)

On 14 August, 1963, the band returned to the Granada Studios in Manchester to record 'Twist and Shout' and 'She Loves You', which were broadcast a week later on 19 August. On their way back from the Odeon Cinema, Llandudno, after completing the Monday 12 to Saturday 17 August performances, the 'Fab Four' were looking for a television set to watch themselves perform. What the 'mop tops' were doing in that part of North Wales is not known because it was definitely the long way back to Liverpool; perhaps they were lost? Or confused? Or sightseeing? But one thing is certain, televisions weren't as plentiful in those days and so the story was often told by Chris Briggs that the band stopped at the first hotel they could find, which just happened to be the Pen y Gwryd. Chris (soon to be High Sheriff of Caernarfonshire) was in his office, which in those days was to the right just inside the main door (where the 'boot room' section of the public bar is now.) He is recounted to have said, 'Help yourself lads, there's a set in the staff lounge'.

And so ... John Lennon, Paul McCartney, George Harrison and Ringo Starr trooped through the Swiss-chalet-styled Everest Room, past a wall-mounted 'Testo Reaction Meter', a public phone and a coin-up cigarette dispensing machine to a humble, airless staff sitting room and watched themselves perform on a black-and-white television set mounted on the wall. It was reported that each had a lemon squash at the bar and Ringo also had a pack of bacon and onion crisps; they all used the public facilities and drove away – and life went on at the Pen y Gwryd as it had before; but the rest of the world was never the same again.

Chris Warren is a guitarist and backing vocalist from the south of England. He holds a BA Honours Degree in Professional Musicianship from the Brighton Institute of Modern Music. Warren is a member of the band *The Slytones*. Chris describes the Pen y Gwryd as his 'favourite hotel in Snowdonia'.

www.theslytones.com

www.chrisjwarrenmusic.com

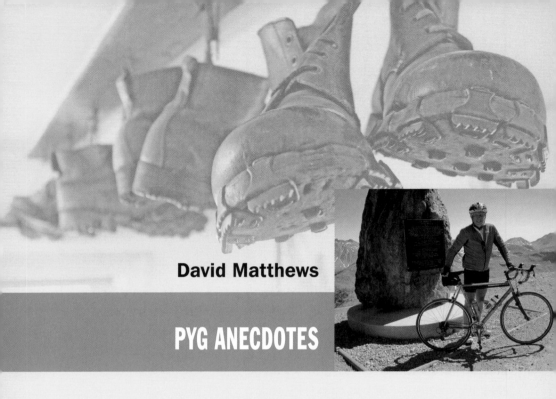

David Matthews

PYG ANECDOTES

I HAVE THREE particular memories of the PyG, which relate more to its surroundings than its interior. This is because, as an extremely impecunious student in the early to mid-1960s, I could not afford to linger in the hotel longer than the time required to purchase half a pint of bitter. (All of my limited funds in those days went on climbing gear and on a motorbike, which was essential for getting to the crags).

These significant memories are not in chronological order and the specifics are hazy given the intervening 50 years; but I am sure that many will be interested in these tales and can relate to some of the experiences (well, maybe not the last one!).

For many years, I travelled to the Pass on a 350cc Matchless bought for £15 from a fellow climber in the Mynydd Club. Friday night in those days was race night from Altrincham to the PyG, often more exhilarating (and dangerous) than the weekend's climbing exploits.

There is a series of 'S' bends when you approach the PyG that are taken at maximum speed (as is every other bend on the way). One night as I was well cranked over, an out of control SS Jag with massive headlights came around a blind bend towards me on the wrong side of the road but just flicked back on line sufficiently to let my bike on to the verge. I can still see those headlights today and how close I came to bringing my climbing career to an early end.

As I approached those same bends one dark night, the fields on the left were ablaze with light. A large crowd was watching some spectacle or other. The entertainment turned out to be filming 'The Lady Loves Milk Tray' advert which involved a guy driving an E-type Jag up a ramp and flying over a stream to deliver the chocolates; all very impressive, especially given that the driver successfully recovered from being knocked out on landing.

My third story takes in the long holiday between school and university, I was staying with Audrey and her son David (known at the time to one and all as 'Dogsbod'). Dogsbod, aged around 15 years, had been diagnosed with a serious eye illness which would eventually lead to blindness, so Audrey had given up her job in Manchester and moved to a small cottage in the Pass to allow her son to enjoy the hills whilst he could still see them, accommodating a few other broke young climbers in her cottage as well.

One night, we wandered up to the PyG to be astonished to see jets of flame zooming into the sky outside the hotel. These turned out to be the result of a group of ten macho Bavarian mountain troops demonstrating their prowess at fire eating (and generally showing off to the assembled crowd.) A couple of us got talking to them and eventually offered to take these tough troops on a moonlight expedition to climb Lockwood's Chimney, a few miles away down the valley. (The 1960 guidebook written by the incomparable Trevor Jones along with John Neill says of the climb: 'Lockwood's Chimney: Difficult. About 400 feet. A very traditional climb. It is customary to do this climb by moonlight in the worst possible conditions. The party should preferably be large, of large men, and incompetent.')

We got the troops to follow us up the first couple of hundred feet of straightforward, grassy climbing to approach the chimney proper. We were soloing but they were all roped up and following orders barked out by their commandant. As we rapidly gained height, and they rapidly became stuck all over the crag connected by a network of ropes, it seemed like a good plan to clear off up the crag at high speed and leave the troops to sort themselves out.

So we sprinted up the chimney, walked back over Snowdon's southern slopes to Audrey's cottage and got our heads down under the kitchen table for a short sleep as dawn broke over the Pass. We never did hear what happened to the troops, probably it was too embarrassing for them ever to mention it, and so we laid very low and didn't dare go near the PyG for a couple of weeks … in case Germanic retribution lay in wait for us.

David Matthews first climbed a significant hill in 1948 aged three, by ascending Rhinog Fawr with his father. Since then, he has climbed all the English and Welsh 2000 feet hills, the Munros and tops and 80 Corbetts, along with devoting 20 years to rock climbing during the 1960s and 1970s. These days, he enjoys long distance cycling in the UK and Europe to maintain his long love affair with hills and the outdoors.

David adds: 'The photo was taken in 2012 at summit of the Cime de la Bonette (2,802 metres) during a ride from Geneva to Nice along the line of the Grand Alpine route … proof that I am still out on the hills'.

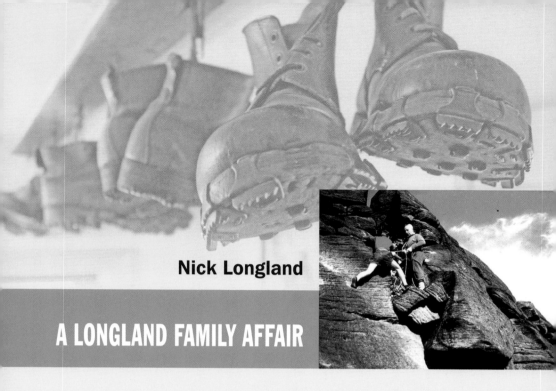

Nick Longland

A LONGLAND FAMILY AFFAIR

In 1956, Jack Longland's family spent Christmas at the PyG. It was cold and there was lots of snow about and I believe we skated on Llyn Lockwood opposite the hotel. My sisters and I remember one morning the diminutive but quite fierce hotel chambermaid Blodwen (who dressed in traditional Welsh costume, without the distinctive tall black hat) coming into the dining room and announcing in Welsh, 'Mae 'na oen yn un o'r ystafelloedd gwely'. (It sounded to us like 'there is an owen in the gwely'.) At the time, the table napkins in use illustrated Welsh-English translations of basic words and we established that what Blodwen had said was, 'There is a lamb in one of the bedrooms'. How it got there is not known but we suspected it was not entirely there by its own design.

In the Everest Room, there was a wall-mounted 'Testo reaction meter' that amused me endlessly as a pre-teen in the early 1960s (while the grown-ups got stuck into the drinks in the Smoke Room, which is why the Testo was there in the first place). It theoretically tested your reaction speed to brake in time for hazards while driving. You placed a

Photo of Jack Longland with his son Nick Longland taken at Birchen Edge, a gritstone edge in Derbyshire, around 1957. 'Shoulder belays were de rigeur and none of this modern nonsense of climbing harnesses or sticky rubber boots!'

threepenny bit in a slot at the top of the machine and pressed the green button to position the coin in the transparent, vertical chute that had a sliding scale from 'Excellent' (when you got the coin back) to 'Very Slow'. An alarm gave warning and you hammered the red button to stop the coin as it dropped. If your reaction time measured 'Very Slow', presumably someone more sober would take over your vehicle. Regardless of any serious intent, it was a great game and the till must have been well stocked with threepenny pieces.

The relationship my father had long established with the PyG was to grow. In 1957 my brother John was joint leader of the Cambridge Andean Expedition. This group were all young men in their early 20s. They went especially to climb Mount Pumasillo in the Peruvian Andes, then probably the highest unclimbed mountain outside Asia. As Simon Clark says of the entirely successful expedition in his book *The Puma's Claw*, PyG was the group's 'spiritual home'. They even called base camp, PyG and Camp 1, PyP (after Pen y Pass).

On the expedition's return, Chris Briggs allowed them to sign one of the ceiling panels in the Everest Room, a rare honour indeed, alongside the much more illustrious 1953 Everesters, 1955 Kangchenjunga team and even veteran Everesters, which included my father. My sister and her son checked the ceiling recently and the signatures are still intact, if faded, in the near left-hand corner as you enter the room.

In May 1978 the 50th anniversary celebrations of the first ascent of Longlands Climb on 'Cloggy' (Clogwyn Du'r Arddu) were based, not surprisingly, at the PyG. Three of Jack Longland's children and a nephew climbed the route and there was a party and meal afterwards at the hotel. The menu included Bow-shaped Melon Slab, Fresh D'ur Arddu Salmon with Parsley Fern Sauce, Cox's A.B. Pie (in honour of David Cox, ex-Alpine Club President, who was affectionately known as A.B.) and Bilberry Terrace Crumble.

As a reflection of the significance of the occasion that night, four Alpine Club and four Climbers' Club past presidents were also at the dinner as well as Eleanor 'Len' Winthrop Young, the first President of the Pinnacle Club and Kevin FitzGerald, the writer and mountaineer.

Nick Longland is a graduate of Sir John Cass College, then a technical college, but, being located in London (Aldgate), he was permitted to study for an internal London University degree. After graduating, he did geological research into gabbroic rocks on the Isle of Mull before working for the Opencast Executive of the National Coal Board (British Coal). Later, Longland ran a café above the 'Outside' climbing shop in Hathersage, Derbyshire. Early family holidays were usually in the British hills and he was first taken climbing by his father, Jack, on the Idwal Slabs where he was ignominiously lowered off after a few feet. However, the spark was lit and he has been a very keen climber for over 60 years.

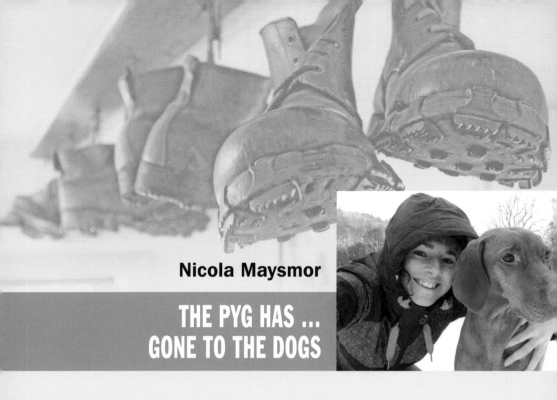

Nicola Maysmor

THE PYG HAS ...
GONE TO THE DOGS

Economic activity based around tourism is very important to communities and businesses in North Wales. The forest provides a major attraction to tourists bringing them into the area and also offering activities once there – like going on holiday and walking with dogs. Welsh forests provide a great opportunity for people to exercise dogs. In fact, over 50 million visits are made each year to woodland managed by Natural Resources Wales with around 40 per cent of those made by people with dogs.

I have a favourite walk that I do almost every day with my hyper-active hound Luna – an eight-year-old Hungarian Vizsla. It is in Bryn Engan forest, Capel Curig, which is owned by Natural Resources Wales. It is at the foot of Moel Siabod, which is very close to the Pen y Gwryd. (One of the rooms at the hotel is named after the mountain.) And, not surprisingly, the PyG is dog friendly. Luna and I often run through Bryn Engan forest, up Moel Siabod and then take the West Ridge down to the PyG where I have a brew and we both warm up in front of the fire before getting a lift back to Capel Curig.

For a small charge, dogs are welcome in bedrooms and in the bar areas of this wonderfully traditional old hotel. And a walk up

Snowdon from the front door of the Gwryd must be like some sort of dog nirvana. Luna and I have done it many times together and, as a bonus, Luna helps with my training for the Snowdon Race (Râs yr Wyddfa), an annual ten-mile endurance running competition from Llanberis to the peak of Snowdon and back – which is challenging for me – but not a problem for Luna.

Nicola Maysmor works as a forester for Natural Resources Wales. Her duties include land management – fencing, the network of forest roads, public right of way paths through the forest, tree safety, and conservation – mainly irradiation of invasive species such as rhododendron. Maysmor works closely with local community groups, local councils and Snowdonia National Park as well as other Natural Resources Wales teams involved in harvesting and planting, as well as recreation teams that all ensure the successful and sustainable management of the forest in her area of responsibility – Coed y Brenin.

www.naturalresources.wales

www.theruffguide.co.uk

www.snowdonrace.co.uk

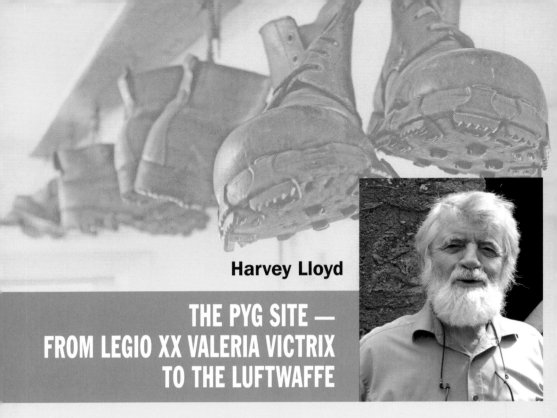

Harvey Lloyd

THE PYG SITE —
FROM LEGIO XX VALERIA VICTRIX
TO THE LUFTWAFFE

D URING THE FIRST or second Roman campaigns in Wales, AD60
or AD78, a Roman legion (Legio XX Valeria Victrix) under the
command of Governor Gnaeus Julius Agricola arrived at the Pen y
Gwryd site. Here they built a marching camp covering nearly ten acres,
surrounded by a defensive turf and stone embankment, in a strategic
location at the junction of three valleys, to guard against the local native
tribe, the Ordovices. The size of the camp suggests it would have held
around 1,000 men.

The territory of the Ordovices covered most of what is today mid
Wales and parts of north and west Wales. They farmed and kept sheep,
and built fortified strongholds and hill forts. The name of this tribe
appears to be preserved in the place name Dinorwig or 'Fort of the
Ordovices' in North Wales. (The Celtic name *ordo* is related to the word
for 'hammer', in Welsh *gordd*.)

The site was partially excavated in 1960 by surveying courses from
Plas y Brenin under the direction of Dr Josephine Flood. The camp
had no permanent buildings, as it was used mainly as an overnight
stop, probably on the march to or from Segontium (on the outskirts of

present day Caernarfon). Marching camps were often built for only one night's use – it is not known how long the Romans occupied the site.

In 1198 the whole vale of Nant Gwynant was granted by Llewelyn the Great to the Cistercian Abbey of Aberconwy, including the lands of Kemen Trinemt (Trawsnant) and Gwryd, whose boundaries ran from Pen y Pass to the summit of Moel Berfedd (400 metres from Pen y Pass) and down to the waterfalls on the Mymbyr river. By 1506, much of Nant Gwynant, including the lands of Gwastadannas and Gwryd, was leased to the Abbey's Steward, Maredudd ab Ieuan ap Robert, the founder of the Gwydir estate. Maredudd built a farmhouse at Gwastadannas shortly afterwards, with the Gwryd as part of its lands.

After the Dissolution of the Monasteries in 1537, Abbey lands passed to the Crown, through Maredudd's son, John Wynn of Gwydir. When the male line of the Wynns of Gwydir died out in 1681, Gwastadannas and other Wynn properties in Nant Gwynant were bought by John Rowland of the nearby estate of Nant, Betws Garmon. The Rowland family continued to own Gwastadannas and the Gwryd lands until Emma Rowland married Viscount Bulkeley of Baron Hill in 1749, when her lands became part of the Baron Hill estate.

The site enters history again in 1810 when it is reported that there was a small squatter cottage at Pen y Gwryd built by John Roberts on the lands of Gwastadannas, owned by William Bulkeley. The idea of an Irish Sea crossing from Porthdinllaen was promoted by W. A. Maddocks and others in 1802. This required an upgrading of the Capel Curig road via Pen y Gwryd to Traeth Mawr. It was reported in August 1808 in *The North Wales Gazette* that celebrations associated with the road opening in Porthdinllaen took place. In the same year, the General Post Office finally adopted the Capel Curig to Holyhead route, and so, the Porthdinllaen scheme perished. However, it had created the new turnpike route from Capel Curig to Beddgelert. The toll house was situated where the Dyffryn Mymbyr cottages are now. The first road created over the Gorphwysfa/Llanberis Pass to Nant Peris was built in 1828, linking into the turnpike, opening up access to Caernarfon and making travel much more convenient for visitors.

The first published mention made of the Pen y Gwryd was by J.G.

Benet in 1830 when he wrote in *Pedestrian Tour of North Wales,* of staying overnight; he was not impressed. He described John Roberts as 'a silent but importunate monster'. (Does this remind you of a bad TripAdvisor review?) However, Roberts clearly saw the value of tourism over farming and improved the building and coach stop facilities.

The Reverend D. E. Jenkins in *Beddgelert: Its Facts Fairies and Folklore* describes how John Roberts discovered a hoard of Queen Anne coins near the Pen y Gwryd site. John Roberts subsequently emigrated to America in 1842, with his wife and children, and settled in Welsh Prairie, Cambria, Wisconsin. They were among the first group of European settlers in the area; he named his property – 'Penygwryd Farm'. John Roberts also changed his name to 'Rowlands', perhaps because he did not have a legal claim on the hoard.

Following John Roberts the Pen y Gwryd was tenanted by a Mr Benjamin from Bethesda. It then passed to Mrs Hughes who was connected with the Royal Hotel (then the Capel Curig Inn) Capel Curig; and she, in turn, appointed Benjamin Williams as manager for two years. As a new centre for tourism the Pen y Gwryd's fame continued to grow when, in 1847, Harry Owen became a tenant of the Pen y Gwryd with his new wife Ann Prichard; it had eight acres of land attached. He also acted for six years as foreman of the stone polishing mill sited next door to the Pen y Gwryd. The mill was powered by a water wheel fed by a leat from the Mymbyr River. To ensure a sufficient water supply, a sluice gate was constructed at the outflow from Llyn Cwmffynnon, which was closed every night and opened every morning by one of the workmen. When the mill closed, Owen diverted water from the leat to feed a mill pond behind the hotel to drive the small watermill used to churn butter and cut chaff for animal feed.

By 1849, Owen, then aged 25, bought the lease from the Bulkeley Estate. In 1851, Charles F. Cliffe wrote of 'The solitary roadside inn' as a 'useful station for anglers and artists who do not mind roughing it'. He described the host and his wife as being 'remarkably civil'.

Tourism continued to grow and, in 1847, the traverse of the Snowdon Horseshoe was first recorded by a Pen y Gwryd resident, Mr C.A.O. Baumgartner. To meet the increasing demand in the 1850s, the bedrooms at the hotel were increased in number from two to four. (The 1851 Census lists Henry Owen, a Copper Mine agent, with Anne and two children. They have one visitor, and a servant Jane Owen.)

In the late 1860s, Owen persuaded the Baron Hill estate agent to transfer the lands of Pen Lan and Geufron, Gwastad Annes and Penlan, four farms in Cwm Dyli, to his hotel. Jenkins writes of four thriving farms in Nant Gwynant being taken over by Owen. 'Mr Owen worked up the sleeve of Richard Bulkeley's agent and got all the land, it was painful to observe.' Jenkins strongly states,

> All these were thriving farms … having well stocked pens and cattle folds. The tenants were evicted, and the productivity of the farms declined. At the turn of the century, two were in ruins and the other two 'simple dwellings'.

Although Jenkins did not have anything good to say about Harry Owen and his farming methods, his guests certainly appreciated the service he and his wife provided; Jenkins closed his writing on Owen by praising him as a hotel keeper and admiring his knowledge of 'the geography of Snowdonia'.

At about this time (1855), Mr Burtells of Stockport gave Harry Owen £5 towards buying a boat to put on the Llyn Cwmffynnon. Owen is described as having a wide knowledge of the best fishing in the area.

Owen was impressed by having important visitors and saw the value of expanding the hotel's accommodation facilities. In 1858 and 1859 he commenced major improvements, including a new roof, a dining room and four more bedrooms, as well as new stables, at a cost of £600, the mortgage raised with the Bangor and North Wales Building Society. It could be said that these improvements led to a golden future for the hotel.

Charles Edward Mathews, with a party of 13 people, first visited Pen y Gwryd in 1854, and booked the entire hotel. Nearly 50 years later he writes, summing up the Owens' management,

> All the visitors who stayed at the Pen y Gwryd in the days of Mr Owen received a courtesy and attention which irresistibly compelled him to return; all of them forming a friendship,

141

indeed an affection, for of the worthiest souls ever born and bred in the principality.

Fishing remained popular with visitors in the early days. Arthur Lockwood moved into the hotel in 1908 and saw the advantage of a lake on the hotel's doorstep for the use of enthusiastic fishermen visitors. In the early 1920s, Lockwood viewed the boggy low-lying site as being ideal; unfortunately, Richard Bulkeley owned the land and was not eager to sell. However, Lockwood had a persuasive manner and an agreement was reached, although Bulkeley chose to continue to own the mineral rights of the land that the lake was to be built on, insisting on a drainage valve being installed in the dam with the idea that copper might be discovered in the strata below the lake.

Instead of using contractors to construct the earthworks, Lockwood persuaded volunteers, casual labour, tramps, friends and acquaintances to build the dam. Improvisation also played a great part in the construction work. A variety of materials were used. It is said that Lockwood learnt about two First World War submarines that were being scrapped in Porthmadog harbour and used parts of them in the construction of the dam. What the parts were or how he obtained them is not known, but the nature of the finished project suggests that this would have been a very small challenge for Arthur Lockwood. The project was finished in 1927.

The first winter guests staying at the hotel used the lake as a skating rink when it froze over; even students came from Bangor University and joined in the fun. Another tale which reflects Lockwood's sense of humour was that he offered a shilling to anyone who could ride a bicycle across the frozen surface without falling off.

Lockwood also built a boathouse to service the lake, again largely using recycled materials. In 1946, he received a grant of £50 from the River Board to set up a trout hatchery at the back of Hafod y Gwynt. This ensured that the lake was well stocked with the native brown trout which travel up the Gwryd and down from Llyn Cwmffynnon.

The next part of the tale of the Pen y Gwryd site jumps forward about 15 years from the lake building era. Great Britain was again at war with Germany and the year was 1940. The British government was expecting the Germans to invade Britain, with a likelihood that they would use Ireland as a jumping-off point for an invasion, via the deep-water harbour at Holyhead.

Anticipating invasion, local defences were erected between Bangor and Porthmadog (Stop Line Number 23). At the Pen y Gwryd (the junction between the A498 and A4086), which, as in Roman times, was considered to be a strategically important road junction, four defensive pillboxes were erected. History tells us that the Germans decided against this action but there is no doubt that at the time there would have been a great deal of military training in the area. These fortifications are now preserved and are considered to be of national importance, listed as scheduled monuments.

The Second World War has left a further impression on the site. It is said that that the disrupted earth across the road and down the valley from the Pen y Gwryd is actually a bomb crater from a 500lb Luftwaffe bomb (*Sprengbombe Cylindrisch 250*) jettisoned after a raid on Liverpool. Likewise, further bombs were dropped near to Nant Peris and Betws y Coed.

Harvey Lloyd was introduced to the hills some 60 years ago through his active involvement in the Scout Association and was greatly influenced by *Mountain Craft* written by an early visitor to the PyG, Geoffrey Winthrop Young.

In February 1972, he took up the position of joint manager of Pen y Pass Youth Hostel, one mile from the Pen y Gwryd. Through this role, Lloyd became a leading member of the Llanberis Mountain Rescue team and, over 25 years, was directly involved in many search and rescue operations. Additionally, he set up, organised and instructed on courses in mountaineering and outdoor pursuits based at the Hostel.

Harvey Lloyd has walked and climbed extensively within and outside Europe and has been involved in organising seven mountaineering/trekking expeditions to Nepal. He is a founding member of the Eryri Harriers and was treasurer for the early years. He is the secretary of the Gorphwysfa Club.

www.gorphwysfa.org

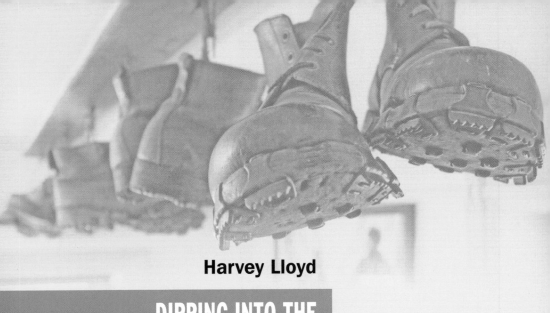

Harvey Lloyd

DIPPING INTO THE
LOCKED BOOK, 1884–1953

Holidaymakers staying at the Pen y Gwryd Hotel during the Victorian era were generally aristocratic, academic and wealthy. It was fashionable at that time to leave notes recording visits, accounts of activities, and generally writing comments in a visitors' book provided by the proprietors. The first visitors' book at the Pen y Gwryd Hotel is mentioned by Herbert Carr in his book *The Mountains of Snowdonia* (1925), where he notes that such a book at the PyG dates from 1854.

> This and other subsequent books became mangled and torn, entries of interest were cut out and stolen and whole pages were intentionally or accidentally destroyed.

The more learned visitors to the hotel were becoming upset by the standard of entries. In Easter 1884, Mr Hugo J. Young, KC, set out to reverse this 'vandalism' when he presented Mr and Mrs Harry Owen with a thick black leather-bound quarto book with a metal lock. Young had the cover embossed with the words 'Not the Visitors Book'; he specified that it was never to be used as an ordinary visitors' book, but rather for 'more serious matters' such as Mountain Rambles, Botany, Geology and other subjects of interest connected with the Pen y Gwryd.

In this way, information would be available to future visitors and reminisces and otherwise would not be lost or defaced.

Through his action over 130 years ago, it is now possible to explore today the fascinating accounts of those many visitors who have shared their adventures within its covers. Today, the *Locked Book* forms a unique record of the social history of the hotel over four generations.

Hugo Young wrote the first entry on 10 April, 1884:

> On my visits to the Pen y Gwryd I have noticed that your visitors' book has become a receptacle for all sorts of nonsense scribbled by the casual passer-by. On the other hand, many notes are recorded of lasting use and interest to many who delight to stay weeks with you.

Today, the reader is rewarded for his foresight. On 5 August, 1885, the Reverend Hibbert Newton (1817–1892) from Saint Michael's, Southwark, who was a writer and an early proponent of British Israelism, is recorded trying his hand at poetry with 'Snowdonia Personified'. This is followed by a visitor who lists 26 species of fern found around the Pen y Gwryd. (Fern collecting was very popular in the Victorian age.) In October 1890, after a traverse of the Glyderau, a writer mentions 'the Canon on Glyder Fawr' – perhaps the observer was a soldier. The 'canon' is still there today but it is the massive rock called the cantilever and it is to be found on Glyder Fach.

The *Locked Book* is full of the great and the famous. On 11 April, 1887, on page 15, there is to be found the first entry by Oscar Eckenstein (1859–1921), the railway engineer, who was the first person to study technique, balance and holds on rock. His entry describes the First Ascent of Central Gully on Lliwedd with Thomas V. Sculley, branching out on to the West Peak. In 1896 he is recorded climbing East Gully on the same face with J.M.A. Thomson and others. This became a very popular route on Lliwedd and, effectively, the sport of rock climbing was born.

With the deaths of Mr and Mrs Owen in the 1890s, an era ended. The hotel passed through a transitional period until, in 1906, William Hampson of Walsall purchased the lease and appointed Florence

Bloomfield as manageress. After a short courtship, Florence married Arthur Lockwood in Beddgelert church on 10 May 1909. Sadly, this is not recorded in the *Locked Book.*

Reading through the *Locked Book,* it is soon apparent how many other important events are not recorded. The Pen y Gwryd Hotel is noted for the foundation of The Climbers' Club; although conceived at the Pen y Gwryd in December 1897, it was inaugurated in London in 1898. It grew out of a group called the Society of Welsh Rabbits at the hotel; the support of the early membership was very much dominated by rock climbing in North Wales. Sadly, this momentous event is not recorded either.

In 1909, Arthur Lockwood climbed Lockwood's Chimney on Clogwyn y Bustach, above Cwm Dyli Power Station where he worked, again not recorded, but history tells that he was the only hotel proprietor to be credited with the lead climb on any rock face in Snowdonia. Following this, on 16 June, 1911, the second ascent is listed with a full account of the route by Mr J. Brian Burrell of Liverpool. Lockwood writes, 'The approach to the route has now been clearly marked, the cave has a large cross painted over the opening, and the large trees on the way to the foot of the crag are blazed with an axe'.

Arthur Lockwood actually made his first entry in the *Locked Book* in 1908, when he noted that there had been 'extreme rainfall'. On 15 September 1910, Lockwood enters a table of rainfall and temperature weather records. He notes that, 'A self-regulating maximum thermometer was placed on Glyder Fach on 29 May, 1910, for W.P.B.'s records, note above'. (Lockwood identifies W.P.B. as 'William' but no further details are provided.) Below this, W.P.B. notes on 19 September, 1910 that, 'Mr Arthur Lockwood will continue to record…'. This, of course, indicates that Lockwood, having come from Yorkshire, was taking a strong personal interest in the mountains.

Details of mountain accidents are dotted throughout the writings. The obituary for Leonard Salt, a businessman and experienced mountaineer, appears on page 160. He died on Easter Monday, 1910. The entry is noted by 'GSD' and 'CMM'. There is a good reason to presume that Lockwood would have been involved in the attempted rescue. Salt had been staying at the Royal Hotel, Capel Curig. The accident was on Lliwedd and he is buried in Capel Curig churchyard. On two further pages, it is noted that Charles Donald Robinson, staying at the Pen y Gwryd, had an accident on Glyder Fach, East Gully. He was evacuated by stretcher to Ogwen Cottage where he died. He is buried in Bethesda hillside cemetery.

In February 1911, Lockwood notes that someone was blown off the causeway and drowned. This time he signs his name, 'A. Lockwood, Fellow RMS' (Royal Meterological Society). Other sources tell us that it was the local postman delivering post to mine workers who actually came to grief.

The period of the First World War is blank, except for weather readings. On 21 October, 1917, page 189 records that 'Weather data is available from Arthur Lockwood, Cwm Dyli'. On 29 October, 1919, Grace Zangwill signs her name under the couplet,

At Gelert's Grave
Pass on, O tender-hearted, dry your eyes,
Not here a greyhound but a landlord lies.

In April 1938, on page 202, there appears the account of Thomas Firbank and his wife Esme (later Kirby) and their attempt on the Welsh 3000s in two teams, in miserable weather. It is recorded that Esme combined with their farm shepherd Thomas Davies, whilst Thomas joined up with Mr Rex M. Hamer and Mr Eddie Capel Cure. They took the freight train to the top of Snowdon. The first team took nine hours and 29 minutes and the second eight and a quarter hours. The full story is told in Thomas Firbank's book *I Bought a Mountain*.

The next significant entry is a poem addressed to Mr and Mrs Lockwood, again on page 202, but this time dated June 1940.

A Lockwood Lament
If you want a drink at the Pen y Gwryd
Don't be cross and don't get worried,
For Mr Lockwood is at the garage,
Or fixing up the Snowdon barrage,
A pint of beer perhaps you're wishing,
"Oh Mr Lockwood's still out fishing",

> A stranger might with reason think
> That someone else could serve a drink
> Oh, foolish one, for thoughts like these
> For Mrs Lockwood has lost her keys!
>
> Allan Moutsdik

On 28 August, 1940, Ann Larmon, aged four years ten months, whose mother was a friend of Arthur Lockwood, climbed Snowdon; Lockwood would have been their guide. From September 1940 to May 1943, the hotel was taken over by Lake House Preparatory School for Boys. An account of their years in the PyG was slipped into the *Locked Book* in 1950, by a former pupil, A. F. Rogers.

A tragedy is recorded on 22 May, 1948, headed 'Death on Lliwedd'. This gives a lengthy account of the accident. Cyclist Paul Hermansson, leaving his bike at Pen y Pass and setting off into the hills, went missing and, after extensive searches, his body was found at the base of Lliwedd.

The first entry by John Disley appears on 17 December, 1950. Disley ascends Snowdon with the Briggs family, Ralph Jones and Jack Henson, in heavy snow. It is reported that ice axes were needed at the top of the Zigzags. Five pages later, on 26 December, 1951, is recorded the history of the oak furniture in the Smoke Room, which was being presented on that day by Captain Peter Kirby and Esme Kirby to the Briggs's. It was constructed by Peter, Adam Crossier and apprentice Bernard Pettifer, in his workshop at Dyffryn Mymbyr.

From 1951, a number of various group attempts at the traverse of the fourteen Welsh 3,000-foot mountains are recorded. On 13 September, 1952, Chris Brasher and Dr John Mawe record details of their successful attempt on the Welsh 3000s in a new record time of six hours 37 minutes.

The first mention of the Everest team training in the area appears on 17 January, 1953, page 234. In particular, this involved testing oxygen equipment and breathing apparatus on Tryfan. This is described in the *Locked Book* as 'a dismal business'. It is noted that Banks, Noyce, Hunt, Bourdillon, Gregory, Rawlinson, Wylie, Emlyn Jones, Westmacott, Cox, John Jackson and Ralph Jones were all involved.

On 12 April, 1953, page 236, holy communion is recorded as having been celebrated in the hotel's games room, for the second year, starting at 8am. It is noted by Stan P. Meadows that there were fourteen communicants.

On 25 April, 1953, page 238, the Lliwedd Jubilee Dinner celebrating the 50th anniversary of the ascent of the East Peak of Lliwedd is recorded. Twenty-three people attended, including Herbert Carr, Douglas Milner and A.B. Hargraves.

On page 239, the first entry mentioning the first ascent of Everest is recorded. The news reached the Pen y Gwryd at 1.04am on 2 June, 1953, on the day of the Coronation (guests had previously toasted the Queen at midnight). A party left the Pen y Gwryd at 1.30am and arrived on the summit of Snowdon at 4am. They announced the news there and drank a toast to the victorious climbers on Everest. The group included Jack Longland and six others. Pictures of Hillary and Tenzing are attached to the next page, followed by small pictures of all expedition members.

Following 1953, there are still many archival treasures to be found. However, it is noticeable that, with the passage of time, scientific entries diminish as sporting events take over. These include heroic first ascents and challenges by some of history's greatest climbers, adventurers and athletes; there are records of visits and reunions, signed comments, press clippings and photographs, the notification of public honours, the posting of obituaries and the announcement of marriages and births.

H.P.S. Ahluwalia

REACH HIGHER AND SEEK THE STRENGTH WITHIN

THE MEMORY OF reaching the summit of Everest on 29 May, 1965, is still very clear in my mind. It was 30 degrees below zero centigrade but, suddenly and very unexpectedly, the wind dropped. I remember thinking, 'This is indeed a special gift from the Goddess Mother of the Earth'. From that extraordinary place closest to heaven, I could see Lhotse, Nuptse and Makalu with Kangchenjunga looming on the far horizon, along with a host of other seemingly endless peaks far below. The view was unforgettable.

The experience of Everest changes you, completely; it makes you conscious of your smallness in a vast and immeasurable universe. But then, before descending, something else overwhelms you, a sense of pride for having achieved the ultimate in climbing. This euphoria, however, is, in turn, tinged with sadness as, henceforth, all trails would seem to lead down with nothing higher left to climb. Little did I know that Everest was just a training ground for me and that the true test of my spirit lay ahead.

Three months after climbing the highest mountain on earth, I was wounded in the Indo-Pakistani War. Unfortunately, there was no spinal cord injury management in India at that time. No one could even tell the difference between quadriplegia and paraplegia, let alone determine an appropriate course of treatment. After struggling for a number of years in various Indian hospitals, I heard of Stoke Mandeville Hospital in the UK. This hospital was especially designed for the care of injured Second World War veterans. I arrived in England broken in body, but not in spirit. I was determined to rebuild my life against all the odds.

Over the years I revisited Stoke Mandeville many times. Every visit served to reinforce my conviction that India desperately needed such a centre. Ludwig Guttmann, Stoke Mandeville's founding chairman, inspired me to pursue this dream, while Dr Walsh, his successor and my physician, helped me to establish my project with financial assistance from the governments of India and Italy.

Today the Indian Spinal Injuries Centre is a landmark healthcare institute on a par with the best in the world. We provide comprehensive medical care and rehabilitation of the highest international standard. From the beginning, however, our vision went far beyond merely setting up a hospital. Our aim was to return people with a spinal cord injury to the mainstream of society, providing them with a complete regimen of care, treatment and rehabilitation.

The success of our institute is based on many things: my experience of climbing Everest, which taught me to always reach for the highest, by the extraordinary dedication of our exemplary team of specialists and staff, and the strength and courage of our patients.

At the entrance to our spinal injuries centre, a painting of the Himalayas greets every visitor. My hope is that this will motivate everyone who sees it to reach higher, to seek the strength within, and to know that they too can conquer any fear and surmount any challenge!

While I was undergoing my own very challenging rehabilitation in England, I was determined to visit the Plas y Brenin National Mountain Sports Centre and, as a climber, I very much wanted to stay at the Pen y Gwryd Hotel. The hotel has mountaineering records dating as far back as 1837. An Everest autograph book contains the signatures of many notables including the distinguished British adventurers Eric Shipton and Harold William 'Bill' Tilman and, coming to later times, Lord Hunt. Importantly, the hotel was where the teams from the first successful ascents of Everest (1953) and Kangchenjunga (1955) later met for their regular reunions.

The Pen y Gwryd's proprietor, Chris Briggs, who was a mountaineer himself, had received a note from Lord Hunt about my forthcoming visit. Jenny Walker of the Aylesbury Climbing Club made all the arrangements. For me, driving through North Wales, it was like driving up to an Indian hill station. I felt excited seeing snow for the first time since climbing Everest. And, on entering the hotel, I saw a large slate with the following inscription:

> This plaque commemorates HARSH BAHUGUNA, Major in the Indian Army, who died on Everest, 18 April 1971, during the International Himalayan Expedition.

Harsh Bahuguna was one of my companions in the last camp on the 1965 climb.

Chris and Jo Briggs were generous hosts and introduced me to all of their friends, on the very first day of my visit. The next day Chris accompanied me to the mountaineering centre, which I discovered was run, more or less, along the lines of the Himalayan Mountaineering Institute in Darjeeling.

What I also discovered was that there were many connections between Wales and Everest. The mountain itself is named after Crickhowell-born surveyor, George Everest. (Crickhowell [Crug Hywel in Welsh] is a small town in south-eastern Powys, mid Wales). And the Western Cwm of Everest is named after the valleys of Snowdonia, *cwm* being the Welsh word for valley.

After that auspicious first visit to the heart of Snowdonia, my wife Bholi and I continued our connection with North Wales. For many years, we met Chris and Jo Briggs almost every summer. Either they would come to India or we would go to the Pen y Gwryd. Chris and Jo Briggs were not only part of 'the Everest family' but were also our great friends.

H.P.S. Ahluwalia is a retired Indian Army officer and mountaineer. On 29 May, 1965, 12 years to the day from the first ascent of Everest, he was part of the fourth and final summit party of the successful first all-Indian expedition (together on that day with H.C.S. Rawat and Phu Dorji). Ahluwalia set up the Indian Spinal Injury Society in 1993. He is the Chairman of the Indian Spinal Injuries Centre and the Rehabilitation Council of India. Ahluwalia has written several books, including *Higher than Everest, The Everest Within, Eternal Himalaya, Beyond the Himalayas, Everest – Where the Snow Never Melts, Hermit Kingdom Ladakh, Ladakh Nubra The Forbidden Valley* and *Tracing Marco Polo's Journey.* Details of the Indian Spinal Injuries Centre, New Delhi can be found at www.isiconline.org

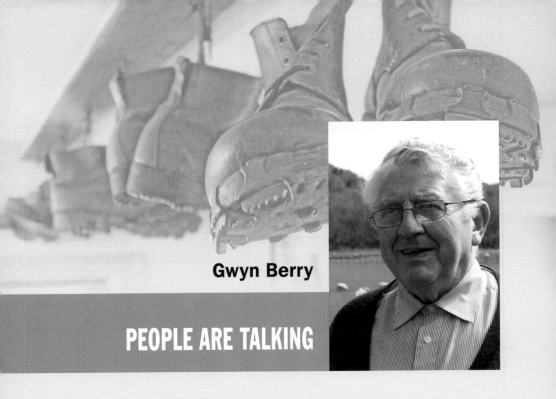

Gwyn Berry

PEOPLE ARE TALKING

THE PYG IS MY LOCAL PUB. I have a favourite place to sit just inside the front door on an old oak wall pew. From here not much misses my attention. When my group of friends come in to the Gwryd for a pint, many of whom are Welsh-speaking local farmers, we usually move to one of the tables opposite the open fireplace.

I have very deep roots in these parts. Seven generations of John Berrys (I am John Gwyn Berry) have lived and worked on the land in and around Llanrwst. My great-great-grandfather, John Berry, for many years a long time ago, held the world record for honey produced in one hive in one year: 168 pounds. (A Mr Smith of Australia reportedly holds the current world record, an astounding result for an apiary at 762 pounds, and that was apparently the average for a very large number of hives!) My grandfather (also John Berry) bred pit ponies for work in the local slate quarries and I continue that tradition, although the mines have long closed.

I have been on the Welsh Pony and Cob Society panel of judges for 54 years and have judged the prestigious Royal Welsh Show twice. Among many notable ponies, I bred the Supreme Royal Welsh Champion Betws Gwenno and the Royal Welsh Male Champion Betws Flach. It

154

is a lifetime's work to breed the perfect horse or pony by selective line breeding (and involves a lot of luck too).

What I have observed over the years is that, at PyG, people talk to each other. They have actual conversations. This is in no small part because the hotel doesn't have televisions in the rooms and there is no juke box in the public bar. Within a very short time, total strangers from almost every imaginable walk of life will be sharing stories about their adventures in Snowdonia, be it in the Everest Room, the Boot Room, the Residents' Lounge or the famed Smoke Room.

And it's not just tales about the mountains and walking and climbing. The PyG is in the geographical centre of all of the great 13th-century castles of North Wales built by warring princes, including Castell y Bere near Abergynolwyn, Castell Dolwyddelan in the valley of the Lledr and Castell Dolbadarn in Llanberis. Others, including the mighty fortresses at Harlech, Conwy and Caernarfon, as well as Beaumaris on Anglesey, were either taken into Norman hands or constructed when Edward I began his conquest of Wales. Indeed I wonder how the local landscape would look today if either the Welsh princes or the English Edward I had adopted the Roman marching camp at PyG as one of their forts?

Gwyn Berry lives near Capel Curig, in Conwy, North Wales, with his wife Sandra. Throughout his career, as a representative with Novartis, customers consistently rated him as one of the top sales people in the Animal Health business, because of his knowledge of the products and, even more importantly, his knowledge of their needs. Berry is also well known in the world of Welsh mountain ponies as a long-standing member of the Welsh Pony and Cob Society. Breeding ponies goes back several generations in his family and he runs the Betws Stud, which has won countless medals, rosettes and sashes at shows over the years.

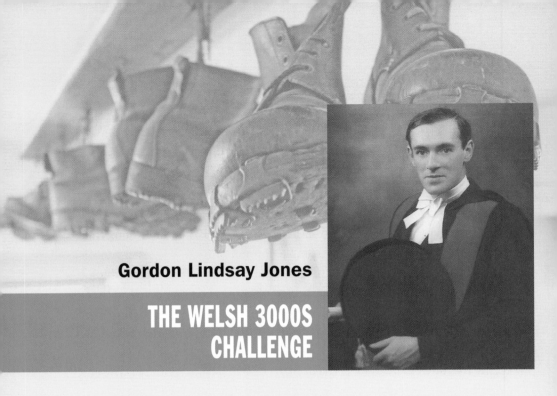

Gordon Lindsay Jones

THE WELSH 3000S CHALLENGE

Thirty-three miles and 14,500 feet of ascent. That was the day's walk ahead of us as we started from the Pen y Gwryd Hotel at five in the morning. The round trip was to include the fourteen 3,000-foot summits of Wales.

Thick cloud prevented the moon from illuminating our path but the road to Pen y Pass glinted like a dull ribbon as the padding of our feet echoed off the boundary walls. At the pass we swung from the highway on to the start of the Pyg Track. On the broad lower slopes leading to Crib Goch, startled sheep made way for two shadowy figures.

Intimate knowledge of the lower part of the scramble made the dark climb both safe and enjoyable. As we reached the summit, the horizon behind glowed a dull red and, almost imperceptibly, the light increased. The gentle wind nudged us along the knife edge arête. The Pinnacles were unashamedly bypassed to save a few precious minutes. It was a rare experience to traverse Crib y Ddysgl on to Snowdon without any other climbers in sight. The reigning peak, hiding in cloud, was reached through the drizzle at ten minutes to seven.

It was too cold to linger with no view to admire so, after the briefest stop, we trotted down the railway track. From Clogwyn station there was a glimpse of the panorama unfolding. We slid off the edge of the ridge into the gloomy depths of Cwm Glas Bach and my knees took their first real punishment as the remaining 3,000 feet of height was quickly shed.

A scheduled rest at a climbing hut in Nant Peris gave us a chance to gather strength for the longest ascent of the day, the heartbreaking pull up the grassy flank of Elidir Fawr. This, the biggest re-ascent of the fourteen peaks, is the key to its successful accomplishment; it is here that the unfit climber will fail and where the battle is fought between mental stamina and the temptation to abandon the endeavour.

After an hour of relentless slogging the boulder strewn slopes below, the summit was reached and the crowning cairn found. We flopped down in relief but were soon pounding along the wall of the Nant Ffrancon valley. This grassy ridge leading to Y Garn is one of the easiest sections of the walk, allowing time to admire the Snowdon and Carneddau massifs on opposite sides. On our right, coal smoke pinpointed the first steam train ascending Snowdon; on our left, the Carneddau seemed to be gathering clouds in preparation for our welcome. Down in the Nant Ffrancon valley, the holiday traffic crawled in slow procession along Telford's highway.

By comparison with the earlier gruelling ascents, Y Garn appeared level, but we were working up a thirst and we hastened down to the refreshing streams above the Devil's Kitchen. The ascent of Elidir Fawr had taken its toll and it was here that my companion reluctantly had to retire and take the direct track down to Llyn Ogwen.

I now made a solitary effort on the scree to reach the summit of Glyder Fawr. Like Snowdon, its plateau was strangely deserted as I crossed over the rocky bastion of Castell y Gwynt to Glyder Fach. These wild, splintered summits conjured up visions of what mountaineering on the moon might be like but, in reality, they formed a central viewing platform for the whole of Snowdonia.

I plunged down the screes and scrambled over huge blocks up to the summit of Tryfan. This was the popular peak of the day and it was the only one where I met other climbers. Clattering ponderously down the steep, stony groove of the West Face route, I reached the halfway stage at Glan Dena where my friends were waiting with a hot drink.

The 20-minutes' refreshment sent me off feeling as if it were the beginning of the day. Speeding past Tal y Llyn Ogwen Farm, I pounded up the grassy slopes near the white ribbon of the Afon Lloer to the hidden Llyn of Ffynnon Lloer and followed the East Ridge of Pen yr Ole Wen to reach its summit in 51 minutes, an encouraging boost to morale. Tryfan was now seen end on, a formidable rock bastion backed by the dark precipitous north wall of the Glyderau. By contrast, the Carneddau looked calm and tranquil with broken cloud producing dappled sunlight effects on the vast grassy expanse. To the north-west, the whole of Anglesey sprawled across the sea like a map.

The urgency of the business at hand soon had me scampering along the broad grassy ridge to the rough stony top of Carnedd Dafydd, one of the few 3000 footers favoured with a concrete triangulation pillar. The mists descended again and the compass was brought out to check the direction of Craig Llugwy. While traversing the narrow undulating ridge, glimpses through the mist revealed the expanse of elevated moorland of the Carneddau. A few hundred feet below the summit of Carnedd Llewelyn, a swing to the north-west was made to meet the ridge between Carnedd Llewelyn and Yr Elen near its lowest point, thus saving a few hundred feet of re-ascent. Yr Elen was clear of mist and, from this vantage point, the scene extended from the Black Ladders to Bethesda, with Anglesey seemingly only a stone's throw across the Menai Strait.

Now a helicopter appeared and, after several practice landings on the lower slopes, it circled overhead like an eagle searching for prey. I did not dare to wave, lest a misunderstanding might cause me to be winched off the mountain. A short re-ascent led to the stony wastes of Carnedd Llewelyn, only a little lower than Snowdon, and the summit cairn was located after a brief search in the mist.

The vast distances across comparatively level grassy moorland were covered at a brisk trot, once the slippery rocks on the north side of Carnedd Llewelyn had been negotiated. Soon the stony top of Foel Grach was reached and its new emergency refuge passed immediately north of it. As mist still covered most of the vast plateau, Garnedd Uchaf was used as an intermediate objective before changing compass bearing for the distant Foel Fras. After following the wall to the cairn, the last of the fourteen 3000s, a rest was taken; this was the furthest point from the start and, now, the shortest possible return route remained. Looking back at Carnedd Llewelyn, which was beginning to shed its misty veil, and the Glyderau beyond, the distance to be retraced could be seen and I began to wonder whether I could complete it on schedule.

I reached Carnedd Llewelyn in a shorter time than on the outward trot; perhaps the thought of hot tea waiting at Glan Dena spurred me on. After checking with the compass on the summit to avoid the mistake of following the Pen Yr Helgi Du ridge instead, the connecting ridge to Carnedd Dafydd suddenly appeared in verdant green splendour. The clouds rolled back and now the Glyderau sparkled in the sun as the sky provided a beautiful blue backcloth.

The traverse to Craig Llugwy provided a few minutes to contemplate before bounding down boggy slopes and finally running to Glan Dena where my supporters were waiting. There was a mere three-and-a-half miles to go over the wall of the Glyderau. At this point my companion joined me for the last stage. Crossing the A5, some extremely wet bog was waded through to reach the old valley road; the ground became drier as it rose into the defile between the smooth rock slab of Tryfan Bach and the boulders at the foot of its more distinguished parent. There was a semblance of a path but rough heather covering it made this the hardest struggle of the day.

Legs which had been trained by ascending Mont Blanc, the Matterhorn and Monte Rosa now wilted on such rough ground. The only reward was an even steeper scree slope on to the Miners' Track on the shoulder of Glyder Fach. Together again, we laboured up on to this col but there the Miners' Track vanished through lack of cairns, so we aimed in the direction of Pen y Gwryd, hidden beneath the brow of this vast mountain.

As we laboured, the Snowdon range ahead basked in the pinkish low sunlight and reminded us of our visit there 12 hours previously. To our left, Moel Siabod sulked, not having received a visit owing to its lack of a few extra feet of height. The distant sea in Cardigan Bay sparkled, and mountains, lakes, sea and sky contributed to the feeling of elation as the walk now seemed certain to be completed ahead of time.

Suddenly the Pen y Gwryd appeared and we corrected our course. The ground now dropped steeply in rock-strewn heather slopes but speed was maintained with the end in sight. The final run beside the Gwryd stream was a veritable gallop, so much so that my companion tripped on the turf, fell forward, and rolled back on to his feet with no change of pace.

At Pen y Gwryd, our watches showed that we had completed the course eight minutes ahead of the 15-hour schedule, beating my previous time for this round by 35 minutes. The fourteen 3000s are among the finest mountains in these islands and few expeditions could be more satisfying than a traverse of all these summits in a single day.

Gordon Lindsay Jones studied Natural Sciences at King's College Cambridge, where he also ran the Cambridge Astronomical Society and played the King's College organ. After completion of his doctorate, Lindsay Jones went on to teach at King's College Cambridge and then Clifton College. It was here that one notable pupil was John Cleese. (Lindsay Jones is mentioned in Cleese's latest book.) After Clifton, he went on to teach at Oundle for the rest of his working life.

Lindsay Jones has climbed extensively throughout the UK and Europe. Notable climbs were the North Wall of the Eiger, The Matterhorn and Mont Blanc. Lindsay Jones's love and passion, however, was Snowdonia and, until recently, he was a very regular visitor to the Pen y Gwryd. His first ascent of Snowdon was when he was 20 years old and, by the time his climbing career had finished, he had amassed 312 logged ascents. After his 200th ascent, he was presented with a piece of the original railway track by representatives of the Snowdon Race Committee.

Lindsay Jones knew and climbed with members of the 1953 British Everest team and his record for climbing the backbone of Wales stood for many years. Lindsay Jones was a keen marathon and fell runner who was introduced to orienteering by the much respected Olympic athlete John Disley. He then went on to compete at a national level.

Lindsay Jones continues to have many interests including astronomy, music, photography and computing. (His photographs of Snowdonia can still be found in many of the residential rooms at the Pen y Gwryd Hotel.) He is a long-serving member of Mensa and has been a member of the Institute of Advanced Motorists for over 50 years. He was a regular visitor to the Jodrell Bank Observatory and was invited by Bernard Lovell to track the Apollo moon landing on the smaller of the radio telescopes.

A special note of appreciation to David Booth and to Ken Jones for their assistance in organising Lindsay Jones's contribution, and to Snowdonia-Active Eryri-Bywiol, a social enterprise and creative consultancy established in 2001 with the aims of supporting and developing the outdoor sector in North and West Wales. www.snowdonia-active.org. For more about the Welsh 3000s Challenge, visit www.14peaks.com and www.welsh3000s.co.uk. A special thank you to Matt Elliott for editorial assistance. The photograph of Lindsay Jones was taken after he received his PhD from Cambridge (in the presence of Queen Elizabeth II).

Norbu Tenzing Norgay

FLYING IN TO THE PYG

IN 1993, in my father's absence, I was invited to celebrate the 40th anniversary of the first ascent of Everest. In the Sherpa language we call Mount Everest 'Chomolungma', which means Mother Goddess of the World.

Following a lecture and a reception attended by Her Majesty Queen Elizabeth II at the Royal Geographical Society in London, the group set off to the Pen y Gwryd Hotel in Snowdonia for a reunion, just as they had done every five years since 1953. It was a special weekend; it was my first time at the PyG but, sadly, the last time I would meet the entire group again.

Colonel and Mrs Charles Wylie hosted my cousin Nawang Gombu and me during our time in London. There were more people than there was room for in the available cars so, somehow, Colonel Wylie arranged for a helicopter. We took off from his backyard for a spectacular flight over the rolling English hills and Welsh hinterland and landed in a field directly opposite the hotel – framed by the panoramic peaks of the Glyderau, Moel Siabod and the Snowdon massif. Much to the disappointment of the waiting press who thought Edmund Hillary was on board, it was only my cousin and I who disembarked to meet our hostess Jane Pullee.

I immediately felt at home at the PyG, which is steeped in Everest history. This first visit was especially important for me, as PyG was where my father so often came to see his friends. Behind the bar is a small room filled with historic Everest memorabilia – including the rope which held Edmund Hillary and my father Tenzing Norgay together on the summit. And there, displayed on shelves, were beer tankards with the names of each member of the 1953 British Everest Expedition etched in silver. Jane looked at me, filled the tankard that had my father's name on it and said, 'It's your turn to take your father's place'.

In the spring of 2013, I was again back in London for another reunion – this time the 25th anniversary of the successful 1988 Everest Kangshung Face Expedition when Stephen Venables became the first Briton to climb Everest without oxygen. I was part of the support group and went partly to honour the memory of my father who died in 1986 but also to see Chomolungma – the sacred mountain that my father had so often dreamt of climbing since childhood. This time I was joined by my daughter Kinzom and our group set off to spend the weekend at the PyG. We went on long hikes, did a little climbing and spent the evenings reminiscing about our expedition – just as my father had done before me.

The highlight was a surprise visit by Jan Morris who joined us for a delightful afternoon tea. It was a wonderful time of friendship and it was especially poignant as Jan is the last surviving member of that historic expedition. And, just as I had taken my father's place at the PyG years before, on this trip I met Rupert Pullee who now runs the PyG with his brother Nicolas. And, together, they too have taken their place and are wonderfully preserving the hotel's rich history – just as their parents had done for theirs.

Norbu Tenzing Norgay is a vice president of the American Himalayan Foundation and the eldest son of Tenzing Norgay.
www.himalayan-foundation.org

Margaret Clennett

REMINISCENCES OF A PYG MAID – A FICTIONAL ACCOUNT OF THE FOUNDING OF THE PINNACLE CLUB IN 1921

I SERVE THE TEA unobtrusively and clear the dining room tables quietly. I've always been a good maid, as is my cousin who works at Pen y Pass. Between us, we know everything that's going on between Llanberis and Capel Curig and a great deal about the visitors to our hotels as well. So I knew all about climbing when the ladies came to the PyG to start the Pinnacle Club.

The first I heard about a rock-climbing club for women was when Mrs Winthrop Young contacted Mr Lockwood about booking a meeting room for Easter Saturday, 26 March, 1921. My guess was that they wouldn't be able use the Pen y Pass because it was fully booked with the Mr Winthrop Young party but Mr Lockwood kindly said that the ladies could use the hotel billiard room.

Mrs Winthrop Young is a lovely lady: vivacious, poised, very capable and self-assured. Her father, Mr Slingsby, was a celebrated climber and explorer. Her brother was killed in the Great War and Mr Winthrop Young lost a leg; she insisted that the Pen y Pass parties start again after the war – she thought, quite rightly, they would cheer her husband up. Although to the world at large she lives in the shadow of her famous husband, everyone who meets Mrs Winthrop Young is enraptured by her.

The prime mover behind the club was Mrs Kelly. She was from a prosperous Manchester family and was married to one of Lakeland's top climbers. When he joined the 'men-only' Rucksack Club, she joined the Fell and Rock Climbing Club where she met and climbed with other ladies but, even so, she found the Fell and Rock too male-orientated and decided there was a need for a club for women where they could learn to climb, share responsibilities and enjoy companionship on equal terms. She was adamant that women should climb independently if they wished. She was committed to helping novices and encouraging other women to learn technique and lead routes.

Rock climbing has developed from the days when men used brute force to conquer the gullies. Today, there are new routes on ridges, slabs and walls requiring technique and balance and, not surprisingly, these climbs are much more attractive to women. Anyway, over a couple of years Mrs Kelly canvassed throughout the Fell and Rock, contacted other women climbers and hill walkers, and inspired them all with her enthusiasm. The men of the Fell and Rock and Rucksack Clubs too were incredibly supportive and some came to Wales to cheer on the new club that Easter.

The climbers called Mrs Kelly 'Pat', although her first name was actually Emily. (Perhaps they thought she was Irish because she had a brother, four sisters and five half-siblings.) With no children of her own and access to office equipment through her job as a secretary, she was ideally placed to do the administration for the new club.

We were expecting about 16 ladies for the billiard room meeting. Mrs Winthrop Young and a friend walked down from Pen y Pass and a group of eight came over from Ogwen. At the top table sat president-elect Mrs Winthrop Young, a beautiful lady in her mid-twenties, and the honorary secretary, Mrs Kelly, a petite, dynamic woman in her late 40s who exuded energy and enthusiasm. With them sat Mrs Eden-Smith who would be voted recording secretary and then promptly nicknamed

'Gabriel'. (Everyone had a nickname or was addressed by their surname – which was very fashionable.)

Mrs Eden-Smith was a friend of Mrs Kelly and is quite a character herself. Mr Winthrop Young would probably describe her appearance as androgynous; she has very close-cropped hair and dares to wear trousers in public. She rides a motorbike and takes her sister, Miss Michaelson, as pillion passenger. That Easter, the two of them came up to Wales on the train to Llandudno and then biked up to Ogwen. Yet, despite her unorthodox dress, she is a modest person and a very graceful climber. Over the past decade she's made some impressive first ascents with Mr Kelly in the Lakes, including the famous route Moss Ghyll Grooves, on Scafell.

The ladies staying here were actually late for the meeting. On Good Friday there had been torrents of rain in Snowdonia so, although Saturday was dry, most of the PyG party decided to do Lockwood's Chimney, just a couple of miles from here. The walk to the crag was extremely muddy; the ladies had problems getting over the awkward, greasy chockstone. Of course, the top pitch was wet and slimy too and the sudden exposure made it very intimidating, so the whole excursion took much longer than they had planned. They looked a sorry sight as they crept in; one had ripped the elbow of her tweed jacket, their socks were caked with mud and their hair was all over the place. At least they had left their nailed boots outside!

Miss Bray – one of the latecomers – is an unforgettable lady. Tall, with an imposing presence, she is forthright and autocratic. She doesn't suffer fools gladly and some of the club members find her rather frightening. In her mid-40s she wore proper tweed breeches, while most of the others had trousers that they tucked into their socks just below the knees. She's a member of the Ladies Alpine Club, a highly select group of skilled mountaineers who can afford to climb abroad.

The other ladies present are a blur now; slim figures in thick, dark trousers, knee-length socks with ankle socks on top, some in sweaters, others wearing long tweed jackets, mostly middle-aged, all keen to establish the new club. They didn't look like upper-class or business ladies, which most of them actually were.

The late arrivals missed Mrs Winthrop Young's inspirational speech in which she encouraged novice climbers to become good seconds and, as their confidence and expertise grew, become leaders and take a full share in decision making. After that, the draft rules were discussed. The first amendment was the name of the club. Originally, it was to be called the Women's Rock Climbing Club but Mrs Winthrop Young proposed changing it to the Pinnacle Club. Miss Bray didn't like this at all; she said the name would leave the club open to ridicule but she was outvoted. She tried again at the next AGM and, although the name change was discussed, it was to remain the Pinnacle Club.

Next were membership qualifications: to become a full member you had to be a proven leader of a rock climb of moderate difficulty; those who lacked this expertise, but had an interest in rock climbing, could become associate members. The annual subscription was set at five shillings. Officials were elected unanimously, including four committee members. The first official climbing meet was the very next day.

After that, the committee looked at all the applications – most had come by post – the new club had 20 Full members and 22 Associates. Two ladies who couldn't come to the PyG had been so keen that they had sent their applications by telegram. There was such an exciting atmosphere at the PyG that day.

Then it was all very quiet; an anti-climax after such an historic afternoon. Mind you, after dinner when the usual sing-song began, the Pinnacle Club ladies were chaffed unmercifully by the other hotel residents – though Miss Bray gave as good as she got and belted out tunes on the piano with skill and good humour. And they did go climbing the next day – in the rain, and all were pleased because the party found the climbing shoes the Ogwen team had lost on the Milestone Buttress the day before and hadn't had time to search for.

I never saw Mrs Kelly again. She had booked in a party of ladies to stay at Christmas but, when Mr Lockwood told her the price had gone up from 14/6 a night to 17/6, she was incensed. She accused him of wanting to attract motorists rather than climbers and moved to Pen y Pass instead. At Easter 1922 the Pinnacle Club met at Ogwen and, tragically, Mrs Kelly had a fatal accident descending Tryfan. Everyone was devastated but members decided they must carry on the club she had worked so hard to found.

We didn't see much of the Pinnacle Club after that; for most of them, the Lakes or Peak District were more accessible. Then last year (1932), the club acquired a hut near the power station in Cwm Dyli, a stone's throw from Lockwood's Chimney, so I expect they will be in Snowdonia more often. The bus from Betws y Coed stops outside the PyG where their club began so, these days, Pinnaclers still call in for tea or to collect a hut key.

Margaret Clennett joined the Pinnacle Club over 30 years ago at the suggestion of her partner, himself a keen rock-climber. Margaret says, 'It was one of the best things I ever did. Thanks to the club, I have made good friends and climbed and walked throughout the world, from Greenland to Australia, the Himalayas and the Americas.' She has held various posts within the Club, including honorary secretary and president, but is currently the club archivist. Since moving to the beautiful countryside of mid Wales in 2004, Margaret Clennett has had an enviable conflict of interest between developing her large garden and going on the hill. So far, she is managing to pursue both occupations reasonably successfully.

www.pinnacleclub.co.uk

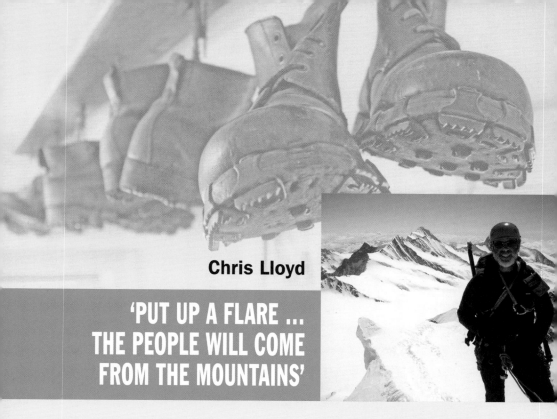

Chris Lloyd

'PUT UP A FLARE ... THE PEOPLE WILL COME FROM THE MOUNTAINS'

T HE PEN Y GWRYD HOTEL became an unofficial mountain rescue post in 1904. As mountain rescue developed, the landlord, Arthur Lockwood, was appointed Mountain Rescue Co-ordinator for northern Snowdonia. When Chris Briggs became landlord in 1947, he assumed this position, one which he held until late in the 1960s.

In the post-war years, the popularity of Snowdonia grew, largely thanks to improved public and private transport infrastructure. In fact, today a staggering ten million people visit North Wales every year and this number is growing. With the increase in mountain users has come a commensurate increase in accidents and incidents. Historically however, small groups of mountaineers, staying at various hotels and guest houses such as the Pen y Gwryd Hotel, the Gorphwysfa Hotel at Pen y Pass (now the Pen y Pass Youth Hostel) and Ogwen Cottage in the adjacent valley, would rescue their own.

Naturally, Chris Briggs took an active interest in mountain rescue. Supported by local friends and regular patrons of the bars of the Pen y Gwryd and Gorphwysfa, for two decades, Chris organised countless rescues and searches on Snowdon. Frequently, he would call upon the

169

trained and equipped members of the Royal Air Force Valley Mountain Rescue team, especially when technical rope rescue was required. This increasing demand for specialised expertise was the catalyst for change in the way mountain rescue was carried out, how it was staffed, and how staff were trained and equipped.

In the late 1950s, two young climbers from Birmingham, supported by a local land agent, bought Ogwen Cottage. They converted this climbers' guest house into a privately-run outdoor pursuits centre. The parting words from the previous owner, Mrs Williams, to the newcomers, Ron James, Trefor Jones and Tony Mason-Hornby were, 'In the event of an incident on the mountain, put up a flare; the people will come from the mountains and congregate here. Appoint the man with the cleanest boots the team leader.'

But the world was changing and mountain rescue was changing too. With a staff of experienced mountaineers and with the support of local outdoor pursuit centres, Ogwen Cottage Mountain Rescue team was formed in 1959. The young and dynamic Ron James looked to the Alps for ideas and equipment for mountain rescue. More and more frequently, the Ogwen Cottage team was called to assist Chris Briggs on the cliffs of the Snowdon massif. In 1965, the Ogwen Cottage Mountain Rescue team evolved into the Ogwen Valley Mountain Rescue Organisation. OVMRO continued to carry out rescues on Snowdon until the 1970s when the Llanberis Mountain Rescue team (although formed in 1968) established a base at Nant Peris. Soon, Llanberis MRT was to become the busiest mountain rescue team in Wales and busier also than any in England.

Chris Briggs was a man of his time. With restricted and, by contemporary standards, primitive equipment, very limited communications and only basic first-aid training, he and his teams of enthusiastic on-the-spot volunteers carried out numerous challenging – and even dangerous – rescues. Today, mountain rescue teams are still staffed by volunteers, as they were in Chris Briggs's day; however, they now have extensive, formal and accredited training in the many skills required for effective and coordinated mountain rescue. These vary from a high standard of casualty care, to technical rope rescue and search management to 'blue light' driving, as well as working with helicopters and investigating fatal accidents for the coroner. In addition, there is the use of specialised information technology to assist the police to manage a mountain rescue incident or to locate a casualty by use of their mobile telephone. Both of these initiatives have been developed by Ogwen members and are now used extensively throughout the UK and beyond.

Today's volunteers provide a professional service, but not at a cost to casualties or clients. Each MRT is a registered charity and has to raise tens of thousands of pounds every year to deliver this free service. Between Llanberis and Ogwen MRTs, they service over 300 incidents per year – and not just for weekend visitors (as the mountains are used throughout the working week as well).

While the days of 'Put up a flare; the people will come from the mountains' has passed into history, Chris Briggs's exploits are not forgotten and are a significant part of the story of mountain rescue in Snowdonia.

Christopher Lloyd became a trainee with Ogwen Valley Mountain Rescue Organisation in 1975, being appointed a full member in 1977. Since then, apart from attending numerous rescues, he has served on committee, has held the posts of equipment officer, communications officer, secretary and has served as chairman twice. He remains an active member as well as being a trustee and the press officer and the archivist.

Ogwen Valley Mountain Rescue Organisation (OVMRO), or Sefydliad Achub Mynydd Dyffryn Ogwen as they are known in Welsh, is a voluntary mountain rescue team responding to incidents in the mountains and valleys surrounding the Ogwen Valley, the Glyderau and Carneddau mountain ranges and surrounding area in northern Snowdonia. OVMRO are on call 24 hours a day throughout the year. The OVMRO team is made up entirely of volunteers who have a wide variety of day jobs. Team members are all mountaineers with vast local knowledge as well as first aid training. Many have expertise in casualty care, advanced first aid, emergency driving and water rescue.

www.ogwen-rescue.org.uk

Hugh Brasher

CHRIS BRASHER

MY FATHER CHRIS BRASHER was a man of enormous energy and determination. He was an Olympic Gold medallist and co-founder, with John Disley, of the London Marathon, as well as an award-winning journalist and broadcaster, successful businessman, racehorse owner, mountaineer and tireless campaigner for conservation in Snowdonia.

(His place in sporting history was sealed when, as a pacemaker, he helped Roger Bannister smash the four-minute mile on 6 May, 1954. He then earned his own place by winning the Steeplechase in the Melbourne Olympics of 1956.)

Chris Brasher was indeed 'a Pen y Gwryd regular' and became a close friend of Chris and Jo Briggs after they bought the hotel in 1947. He was often to be seen in the Smoke Room where his after-dinner stories were the stuff of mountaineering legend. As Chris and Jo's daughter Jane Pullee once said, 'Chris Brasher loved the mountains. He loved the Pen y Gwryd and the Pen y Gwryd loved him'.

In his 'retirement', my father continued to write, broadcast and indulge his love of the British countryside. He personally donated money to protect the Torrin Estate on Skye and Ladhar Bheinn, a mountain in the wild Knoydart peninsula in the north-west of Scotland. The Chris Brasher Trust also donated £250,000 to help buy a part of the summit of Snowdon for the National Trust after it was placed on the market by farmer Richard Williams. (The funding announcement was made by the Oscar-winning actor and president of the National Trust Snowdonia Appeal, Anthony Hopkins.) And my father also bought a parcel of land in the very heart of Snowdonia, 'lock stock and barrel', as legendary conservationist Esme Kirby rejoiced at the time, directly opposite the Pen y Gwryd Hotel, in order to knock down a particularly unsightly derelict petrol station.

The land was cleared and rehabilitated by the Snowdonia National Park Society (now simply the Snowdonia Society) with a grant from the Welsh Development Agency. It was then quietly reincorporated back into the Snowdon National Park, without fuss or fanfare. A private celebration took place the following year, in the summer of 1991, when the native grass finally erased the last physical evidence of the 'eyesore'. Together, Chris Briggs, Esme Kirby and my father symbolically planted a Welsh oak tree. For my father, knowing that another part of his beloved mountains was to be protected in perpetuity, was recognition enough; a measure of the man and a true legacy.

Hugh Brasher is the son of Chris and Shirley Brasher. He is married to Claire, they have two daughters, Skye and Rosie, and he has two sisters, Kate and Amanda. He is Event Director of London Marathon Events Ltd, which organises some of the most iconic mass participation sports events in the world, including Virgin Money London Marathon and Prudential RideLondon. To date the London Marathon has raised over £770 million for charity. As a not-for-profit organisation, its profits are donated to the London Marathon Charitable Trust who have given over £50 million to improve sport and recreation projects in London, Surrey and Northamptonshire.

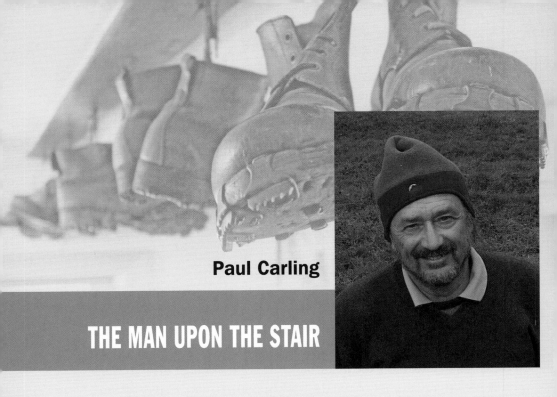

Paul Carling

THE MAN UPON THE STAIR

'Yesterday, upon the stair, I met a man who wasn't there.'

IT IS OVER 40 YEARS since the event I am now going to relay. The detail remains uneasily in my mind, whereas so many other days out in the hills leave positive images or have faded from memory. I was around 19 years old and, together with a couple of companions from Leicester University, we decided to climb Snowdon by the Pyg Track, which for many years started opposite the youth hostel at Pen y Pass but has now been extended to start from the car park opposite the Pen y Gwryd Hotel.

The night before, I had drunk beer with friends in the hotel bar where climbing memorabilia and signatures of famous mountaineers on the ceiling were an inspiration for a young man. The timeless, comforting atmosphere of the hotel does not seem to change as the decades pass but the evening's conviviality did not prepare me for the following day's event. It was a clarty day, otherwise we would have gone rock climbing but, nevertheless, we departed early at around 7.30am from Pen y Pass so we could get a place in the small car park there.

(These days the Pen y Pass car park is often full. The Sherpa bus travels

174

in circuits around Snowdonia's most popular destinations, including the Pen y Gwryd Hotel – the 'spiritual home' of the Climbers' Club and, so, is a local transport solution well worth considering.)

At Pen y Pass, we mounted the initial steep rocky staircase until the point where the gradient eases. Here a small grassy shoulder provides opportunity for some rough camping. It was often the case that a scattering of small tents was to be found there. On this day the low cloud began to lift as we topped the initial ridge. Weak sunshine bathed the wet grass in a baleful light. Rather than a group of tents, a solitary one-man tent was pitched on the shoulder. It looked damp and forlorn after the night's rain. I felt drawn to the seemingly deserted shelter but, as we came nearer, I could see there was an individual crouched in the doorway beneath the low fly. The man was trying to prepare a breakfast on a Primus stove in the cramped alcove. I expected to exchange the usual grunted greetings but the wan face of the man just looked at me impassively; and so I felt it was not appropriate to say 'Hello'. I had a strange barely perceptible feeling of unease and as we continued along the track, I felt the need to look back on the lonesome scene a couple of times, but the occupant did not emerge.

I kept thinking about the tent and the sad face in the doorway as we continued to the summit. Either because of the weather or due to a lack of imagination, my companions and I returned later in the day by the same route. As we descended, I thought again about the tent and fully expected it to be gone along with its occupant by the time we reached the shoulder. To my surprise the tent was still there, albeit now struck, and three fellows from the local mountain rescue team were engrossed in sorting out the contents and packing it into rucksacks. Although an inner sense already told me why they were there, I enquired as to the reason for their presence. Whereas two of them continued packing without looking at me, the third merely stated that they were clearing the tent as the owner had died in a fall whilst walking on Snowdon the previous day. Of course I said I was very sorry to hear that and asked what the man looked like. As I received the summary explanation, I recognised in his descriptions the face of a man I had seen before but never actually met, as we had not exchanged any greeting.

….He wasn't there again today; I wish, I wish he'd go away…

William Hughes Mearns *Antigonish* (1899)

Paul Carling took up climbing at the age of 16 after a few years caving in the British Isles and climbed at many locations around the world. He has been a member of the Climbers' Club for most of his adult life. A keen rock climber and mountaineer in his younger years, he still enjoys mountain walking and bouldering. His career as a professor of Physical Geography has allowed him to travel extensively, including exploration of remote locations across the planet, for example, Argentina, Australia, the Mekong River in northern Cambodia, Laos, Chile, Mongolia, the headwaters of the Amazon in Peru, New Zealand and the mountains of southern Siberia. He lives in a remote farmhouse in the north of England.

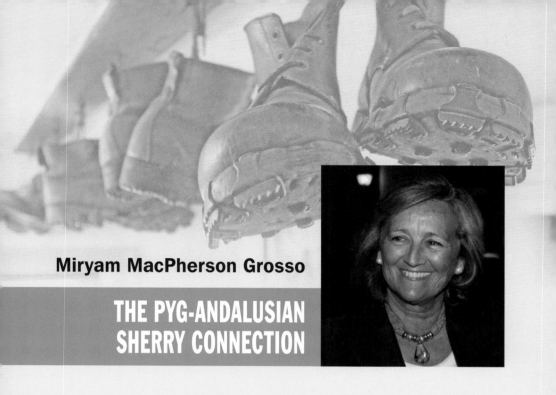

Miryam MacPherson Grosso

THE PYG-ANDALUSIAN SHERRY CONNECTION

M Y NAME IS MIRYAM MACPHERSON; I am the daughter of Guillermo and Lalo and the niece of Luis Gómez and Maridu. The MacPhersons established themselves in Cádiz in 1820, led by the Scottish immigrant Daniel MacPherson, who was born in Inverness, Scotland. He moved to Cádiz for business in what, at the time, was one of the biggest ports in Spain.

My story begins in the Easter of 1979 when I visited Chris Briggs at the Pen y Gwryd Hotel and Jo Briggs at her cottage in Bangor. Chris Briggs was like a father to me; he was so caring, gentle, amusing and sweet. I begged him to let me return to Wales during the summer to practise my English at the hotel – and he agreed. (In those days, Chris's daughter Jane Pullee and her husband Brian were still living in London, where I also stayed.)

One day, Jo Briggs showed up unexpectedly in her white Triumph Stag convertible and, after a very witty chat, took baby Rupert in her arms, threw her car keys in my direction and 'instructed' me to drive us all to Betws y Coed. I was shaking and sweating because I had only just passed my driving test and been given my licence in Spain the previous month. On the way home, I became a little confused and stopped on the wrong side of the street at a crossroads. I dropped the clutch and the engine stalled abruptly. Jo started to laugh and said, 'Oh my dear girl, you look as if you just got your driving licence …'. After a few very long seconds – and a deep breath – I nervously replied, 'Well, just a month ago, in fact!' She was horrified. She grabbed little Rupert and commanded me to VERY carefully drive home. I don't think she ever fully forgave me for not telling her in the first place.

Chris Briggs first met Uncle Luis Gómez (one of the owners of Bodegas Miguel M. Gómez in El Puerto de Santa María) in the early 1960s. They had a common friend who told Chris about the outstanding quality of Gómez Sherry. On this recommendation, Chris travelled to the south of Spain to sample the wines that, at the time, were only available in the UK in Harrods.

After their visit to El Puerto de Santa María, the Briggs left a sherry barrel inscribed with both their signatures (representing their VIP customer status). Not long after that, boxes of Gómez's sherry wines – mostly Fino Alameda and Oloroso Mentidero – began to arrive at the PyG. This commerce was to continue for over 20 years. (These days, the Osborne Bodega is the last operating in our area and Rafael Osborne, who also worked at the PyG, is the company public relations manager; and, not surprisingly, the UK is still the largest consumer of Jerez wine.)

The Gómez children (Patricia, Miguel, David, Helena, Luis, Lorena, Ariadna, Aznamara, Isabel and Irene) clearly remember the Briggs showing up regularly in November driving their lovely Triumph filled with presents for them all, and how they would take them for trips around the area while their parents were busy at work. Gatherings were religiously organised either at La Luisiana (Gómez's home), the Gómez Bodega or at close friends' homes of the Osbornes (Ignacio and Cristina), the MacPhersons (Guillermo and Lalo) and the Terrys (Fernando and Elisa). Often they would come together for wonderful trips to La Barrosa in Chiclana.

In parallel, many of the Briggs's friends in Puerto Santa María began to visit them at the PyG or send their children there to improve their English, as my parents had done. I fondly remember shared days of lovely icy Alameda drinks with Chris Briggs before lunch and afternoon teas with Jo at her cottage in Bangor or at one of those lovely mansions she looked after while her friends were abroad.

Later in the summer of 1979, with my cousin Begoña Grosso, we helped out at the hotel while Chris Briggs was on an extended salmon fishing trip with Joe Brown. At this time, Jane was beginning to take over the running of the PyG from her father. (It was also when I got to meet their Australian cousin, Rob Goodfellow, who also worked with Begoña Grosso, Rafael Osborne and me at the hotel and was followed in turn by Rob's younger brothers, John and Fred.) At this time, Lorena Gómez and Mauricio Osborne spent quite some time with Jane and became good friends with Rupert. Much later, Aunt Maridu and Lorena Gómez travelled to PyG to celebrate Jo's 90th birthday, which was a marvellous experience for everyone.

After more than 25 years, the Briggs stopped coming to Puerto Santa María but Brian and Jane Pullee visited frequently with their children, Rupert and Nicolas. Parties, gatherings and trips continued among the younger generation and that is how Jane started to receive the children and friends of many of these same Cádiz families – all wanting to improve their English and, when required, all happy to help with the running of the hotel. Nowadays, Rupert Pullee keeps this tradition alive and visits Puerto, regularly keeping in touch with Lorena Gómez, Mauricio Osborne and myself.

All of us who have stayed at the PyG cherish such great experiences and especially remember the dinners around the family table, the gorgeous PyG breakfasts and the after-dinner gatherings. We especially remember meeting all kinds of interesting guests and hearing the most astonishing stories about famous climbing expeditions from all over the world; and then our rest breaks in the Smoke Room or playing ping-pong and pool in the hotel's games room, rowing in the lake (despite being fully soaked with rain) and quickly changing to babysit Rupert and Nicolas.

The PyG-Puerto connection continues – originating from the unique friendship initiated by Chris, Luis, Jo and Maridu back in the 1960s – a bond that has spanned three generations and remains as sincere and vibrant as when it began.

Miryam MacPherson Grosso was born in Cádiz, Spain where she studied to become an English philologist at Cádiz University. MacPherson Grosso loves sailing, photography, music, yoga, adores travelling, is keen on family trees and is an expert in taking care of elderly people. Miryam studied English in West Kent College in 1978 and 1979 for eight months and spent Easter and summer of those years at the Pen y Gwryd Hotel with the Briggs. She has worked in vocations as diverse as management, administration and sales. She holds a degree in French from the Official Language School in Chiclana, Spain.

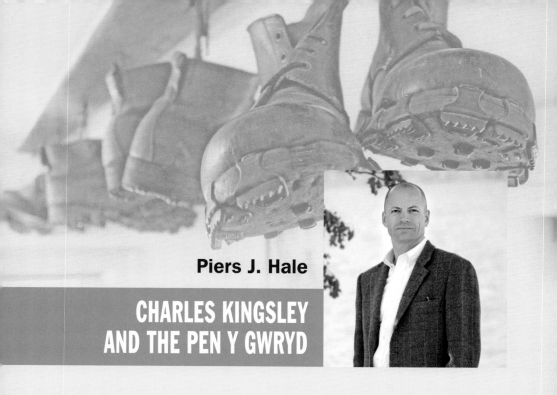

Piers J. Hale

CHARLES KINGSLEY AND THE PEN Y GWRYD

THE REVEREND CHARLES KINGSLEY is no longer the household name that he used to be. Those who are familiar with Kingsley will most likely know him as the author of the charming children's fairy story, *The Water-Babies*, which, while written in 1863 and 400 pages long, has remained in print ever since.

I read it first back in the 1970s, but in an edited version, beautifully illustrated by Mabel Lucy Atwell, and only some 60 pages long. As I later found out, however, Kingsley was famous for much more. He was a successful poet and a nationally recognised and popular author. He was an accomplished naturalist and geologist, and had been elected a Fellow of both the Linnean Society and the Geological Society. He was an active campaigner for social reform: he championed the introduction of sewerage systems and the provision of clean water into the typhoid-ridden inner cities; the reform of the child labour laws (the bill proposing the regulation of child chimney-sweeps became known as The Water-Babies Bill) and educational reform. After his appointment in 1859 as Chaplain in Ordinary to Queen Victoria and in 1861 as tutor to the young Prince of Wales, Kingsley moved in the highest society. At the same time, though, he was not above controversy. Kingsley was among the first to embrace Charles Darwin's theory of evolution by natural selection. Indeed, he took it upon himself, in his sermons, lectures and public speeches, to promote Darwinism as being compatible with a God that did not trouble himself to make every individual creature, when he could make them make themselves. And, if you recall the story of *The Water-Babies*, you will perhaps recognise that spreading this message was his aim in that book too.

It was in the summer of 1856, however, and before he reached the height of his fame, that Kingsley stayed for a 'parson's week' of twelve days at the Pen y Gwryd. Kingsley, his friend Thomas Hughes and Tom Taylor made the trip. They had settled on the place as their base-camp for a holiday of fishing, sketching, climbing and manly adventure. Kingsley knew the area well. His brother-in-law, the cleric and author James Anthony Froude, had a house at Plas Gwynant (now an outdoor adventure centre) at the foot of Snowdon and the two had fished the area before. Familiar too with the unpredictability of the weather, Kingsley described the area to a friend as 'the original Eden (for three months in the year only, though)'.

Kingsley had had a particularly gruelling year and a fishing trip was to be the remedy. Fanny Kingsley, his wife, had given her blessing; he had originally asked her to come along but, evidently aware that he hoped to make the trip a boys' week away, she made it clear that she had no desire to accompany them. She had an aversion to North Wales, she said, on account of her sister Charlotte Froude's 'bad experiences there as a new wife'. Kingsley did not press for further explanation.

Inviting Hughes to come up to his home in Eversley, Hampshire, for a planning session, Kingsley was overjoyed to tell him the trip was on and that 'Mrs Kingsley and the infantry [as he referred to his children] are gone to the sea'.

The trip was to be both a test and an embodiment of the masculine characteristics of the 'muscular Christianity' with which Kingsley had become associated; he had long championed the healthful and spiritual benefits to be gained by physical exercise undertaken in a noble cause and it is clear that he held no cause more noble than that of 'killing trout'. It would be rough going but manly. Again to Hughes,

> An ordnance map, a compass, fishing tackle, socks and slippers
> are all you want … we could live for 12 hours, a day at the
> outside … kill an amount of fish perfectly frightful, and all the
> big ones, by the simple expedient of sleeping by day, walking
> evening and morning and fishing during the short hot nights.

Kingsley thought John Jones, the parish clerk at Beddgelert, 'the king of
fishermen'. Jones had told him all the right flies and the best places but,
for this trip, they 'must depend on their own legs and on stomachs which
can face braxy mutton, young tatters, Welsh porter, which is the identical
drainings of Noah's flood turned sour, and brandy of more strength than
legality.' They were not going to frequent the classy and thus expensive
'show inns', 'save a night at Capel Curig', they were headed for 'Pen-y-
Gwyrrryynnwwdddelld … the divinest pig-sty beneath the canopy'. (It
should probably be noted here that the PyG was significantly expanded
and refurbished some years after Kingsley's visit!)

Kingsley and Hughes were the very best of friends and, for a third,
they had originally planned on Froude. However, when he backed out
on account of having too much work, it looked as if the whole thing
might fall through; Kingsley appealed to Hughes to find a suitable
replacement, 'Of all men on earth I should like to have Tom Taylor for a
third', he wrote. Hughes should tell him he would see such sights as no
'mortal cockney knows because, though the whole earth is given to the
children of men, none but we jolly fishers get the plums and the raisins
of it.' With Taylor on board as 'salvidge man', they could think of little
else.

Even before they set off, Kingsley's poetic muse was in full force:

> There is no inn in Snowdon which is not awful dear,
> Excepting Pen-y-gwrydd (you can't pronounce it, dear),
> Which standeth in the meeting of noble valleys three.
> One is the vale of Gwynant, so well beloved by me,
> One goes to Capel-Curig, and I can't mind its name,
> And one it is Llanberis pass, which all men knows the same.
> Between which radiations vast mountains does arise.
> As full of tarns as sieves of holes, in which big fish will rise,

That is, just one day in the year, if you be there, my boy,
About ten o'clock at night, and then I wish you joy.
Now to this Pen-y-gwrydd inn I purposeth to write,
(Axing the post town out of Froude, for I can't mind it quite),
And to engage a room or two, for let us say a week,
For fear of gents, and Manichees, and reading parties meek,
And there to live like fighting-cocks at almost a bob a day,
And afterwards towards the sea make tracks and cut away,
All for to catch the salmon bold in Aberglaslyn pool,
And work the flats in Traeth-Mawr and will, or I'm a fool.
And that's my game, which, if you like, respond to me by post;
But I fear it will not last, my son, a thirteen days at most.
Flies is no object; I can tell some three or four will do,
And John Jones, Clerk, he knows the rest, and ties and sells 'em too.
Besides of which I have no more to say, leastwise just now,
And so, goes to my children's school and 'umbly makes a bow.

With the departure date set, Kingsley found he did have more to say and could not but write Hughes a second and longer poem: this one, entitled 'The Invitation', was subsequently published and has been republished in the many collected editions of Kingsley's poetry, so I include only an excerpt here.

Come away with me, Tom;
Term and Talk are done;
My poor lads are reaping,
Busy every one.
Curates mind the parish,
Sweepers mind the court;
We'll away to Snowdon
For our ten days' sport
Fish the August evening till the eve is past,
Whoop like boys, at pounders
Fairly played and grassed.
When they cease to dimple,
Lunge, and swerve, and leap,
Then up over Siabod,

Choose our nest, and sleep.
Up a thousand feet, Tom,
Round the lion's head,
Find soft stones to leeward
And make up our bed...

They set out from Eversley on 11 August, arriving at Bangor by train early the next morning. Fishing rods in hand, as per their plan, they set out on foot at 5am, fishing their way to Pen y Gwryd. Not quite according to plan, however, they did so in the rain. Worse, though, even amidst the more than 20 showers that Kingsley recorded, 'The fish, always sulky and capricious, would not stir', he wrote to Fanny that evening.

This was to be the story for the whole of their visit; rain and ghastly weather frustrated most of their fishing and climbing ambitions and they resorted, on occasion, to botany, another of Kingsley's favourite pursuits and one he recognised as more useful and properly scientific than casting a line. They did scale a number of peaks though, despite the weather, including Glyder Fawr. Among his plans, Kingsley had hopes of writing enough to put together a short book to be called *Letters from Snowdon* for his children and, although the book never materialised, we do still have at least one of the letters he sent to his son Maurice about his climb.

> We had such a climb yesterday, up the Glydyr Vawr, 3300 feet high. First we went up a mile and a half over bogs by a lake, to the foot of the mountain, which is as steep as this.

Here he inserted a quick sketch of three stick figures scaling a near vertical incline,

> & I got into a gully where a torrent ran down, & so scrambled up, over shoes in water, stepping from stone to stone, & often climbing with our hands; & very often sitting down to take breath. When we had gone up about 1000 feet, we came to a down, all over rocks & one of them was just like one of the antediluvian sea monsters at the Crystal Palace, with a horn on his nose looking around at us through the mist...

The 'Dinosaur Court' of immense models of extinct creatures, had been unveiled at the Crystal Palace only two years earlier in 1854.

For the most part though, and aside from such heroic excursions into the rain, the three friends were confined to the comfort of the Pen y Gwryd fireside. The weather did not let up for the whole week and, although they were initially not to be put off, the poor fishing and the rain drove them indoors more often than not. Fortunately, their hosts, Ann and Henry Owen who had acquired the inn in 1847, ran a tight ship and a bounteous kitchen. As Kingsley later described it in his novel *Two Years Ago*, which includes scenes in the area: it was a 'low room, ceiled with dark beams, from which hung bacon and fishing rods, harness and drying stockings, and all the miscellanea of a fishing inn.'

The Pen y Gwryd visitors' book has, or has had, many entries from men and women now famous, and Kingsley and his companions added to it on their last evening as they sat by the fireside, quite possibly under the inspiration of a glass or two of the Welsh brandy renowned for its great strength and questionable legality! Taking turns, they attempted to out-rhyme each other:

T.T.
I came to Pen-y-Gwryd with colours armed and pencils,
But found no use whatever for any such utensils;
So in default of them I took to using knives and forks,
And made successful drawings … of Mrs Owen's corks.

C.K.
I came to Pen-y-Gwryd in frantic hopes of slaying
Grilse, Salmon, 3lb. red-fleshed Trout, and what else there's no saying;
But bitter cold and lashing rain, and black nor' eastern skies, sir,
Drove me from fish to botany, a sadder man and wiser.

T.H.
I came to Pen-y-Gwryd a larking with my betters,
A mad wag and a mad poet, both of them men of letters;
Which two ungrateful parties after all the care I've took
Of them, make me write verses in Henry Owen's book.

T.T.

We've been mist-soak'd on Snowdon, mist soak'd on Glyder Vawr,
We've been wet through on an average every day three times an hour;
We've walked the upper leathers from the soles of our balmorals;
And as sketchers and as fishers with the weather have had our quarrels.

C.K.

But think just of the plants which stuff'd our box, (old Yarrel's gift),
And of those which might have stuff'd it if the clouds had given a lift;
Of tramping bogs, and climbing cliffs, and shoving down stone fences
For Spiderwort, Saussurea and Woodsia Ilvensis.

T.H.

Oh my dear namesake's breeches, you never see the like,
He bust them all so shameful a crossing of a dyke,
But Mrs Owen patch'd them as careful as a mother,
With flannel of three colours … she hadn't got no other.

T.T.

But can we say enough of those legs of mountain muttons?
And that onion sauce lies on our souls, for it made of us three gluttons?
And the Dublin stout is genuine, and so's the Burton beer;
And the apple tarts they've won our hearts, and think of soufflets here!

C.K.

Resembling that old woman that never could be quiet,
Though victuals (says the child's song) and drink formed all their diet;
My love for plants and scrambling shared empire with my dinner;
And who says it wasn't good must be a most fastidious sinner.

T.H.

Now, all I've got to say is, you can't be better treated;
Order pancakes, and you'll find they're the best you've ever eated.
If you scramble o'er the mountains you should bring an ordnance map;
I endorse all the previous gents have said about the tap.

T.T.

Pen-y-gwryd, when wet and worn, has kept a warm fireside for us,
Socks, boots, and never-mention-'ems, Mrs Owen has dried for us;
With host and hostess, fare and bill, so pleased we are that, going,
We feel, for all their kindness, 'tis we not they are Owen!.

T.H., T.T., C.K.
Nostres in uno juncti hos fecimus versiculous;
Tomas piscator pisces qui non cepi sed pisciculos,
Tomas sciagraphus, sketches qui non fecimus ridiculus,
Herbarius Carolus montes qui lustravi perpendiculos.

T.H.
There's big trout, I hear, in Edno, likewise in Gwynant Lake,
And the governor and black alder are the flies that they will take,
Also the cockabundy, but I can only say,
If you think to catch big fishes I only Hope you may.

T.T.
I have come in for more of mountain gloom than mountain glory,
But I've seen old Snowdon rear his head with storm-tossed mist wreaths hoary;
I stood in the fight of mountain winds upon Bwlch-Cwm-y-Llan,
And I go back, an unsketching but better-minded man.

C.K.
And I too have another debt to pay another way,
For kindness shown by these good souls to one who's far away,
Even to this old colly dog who tracked the mountains o'er
For one who seeks strange birds and flowers on far Australia's shore.

The three men then signed their creation and took their leave the next morning. Some years later, Harry Owen refused ten pounds for the pages. The craze of collecting the autographs of the famous has its origins, and was at its height, in the late Victorian period and, subsequently, the pages went missing some days later. (Incidentally, the Victorians were also crazy about collecting ferns, so much so that the practice was mocked as 'pteridomani', or 'fern-fever', and *Woodsia Ilvensis*, the Rusty Cliff Fern which Kingsley mentions in his poem, is now an endangered species.)

Kingsley stayed at the Pen y Gwryd at least once more, in the early 1870s and, hearing of the theft, once more took pen to paper in Harry Owen's book.

> Fifteen years ago, Thomas Hughes M.P., Tom Taylor and myself
> wrote some verses in this book for these dear good people and
> they were cut out and stolen by some snob after ten pounds had

been offered for them. Now, such snobs are unfortunately of the human race and will wed and are, therefore, likely to produce little snobkins. Some such Snobkins may visit Pen y Gwryd, and be still too uncivilised to be weaned from their parent's proclivities. Any such I warn that he cannot well steal this bit of writing and show it again, unless he wish to expose his own shame. And yet, I am not sure that this plan will be successful, for snobs, being half of them fools likewise, he may steal this for the mere pleasure of boasting that he stole it.

Kingsley, Hughes and Taylor were well known at the time of their visit, but went on to become nationally renowned figures. Kingsley was Chaplain to the Queen, as well as one of Britain's most well-known authors. Hughes became a Member of Parliament but was always best known, in his own time as in ours, as the author of *Tom Brown's School Days*. Tom Taylor, editor of *Punch*, was also a professor of English and a playwright of some note. Today, though, he is mostly remembered as the author of the play, *Our American Cousin*, at a performance of which Abraham Lincoln was assassinated in 1865.

Their visit to the Pen y Gwryd did a lot to put the inn on the map for many of the Oxbridge climbing set, just as their other works did so much to promote outdoor pursuits and climbing, as suitable sports for young Victorian gentlemen.

Piers J. Hale is Associate Professor in the History of Modern Science in the Department of the History of Science at the University of Oklahoma in the United States of America. He teaches and researches the history of evolutionary biology, with a particular focus upon the popularisation and reception of evolution in Victorian Britain. His first book, published in 2014, was *Political Descent: Malthus, Mutualism and the Politics of Evolution in Victorian England*, in which he argued that, although evolution has long been associated with the competitive individualism inherent to the Malthusian theory which inspired Darwin, there was also a long counter-tradition of anti-Malthusian evolutionism in England. Hale is Director of the Charles Kingsley Correspondence Project and is currently working on a book on the 19th-century author, science populariser, and social reformer Charles Kingsley, and his evolutionary fairy tale, *The Water-Babies*. Kingsley did more than perhaps any other man to popularise and promote Darwin's Theory of Evolution and Natural Selection in England. Born in England, Hale studied at the University of Glamorgan in Treforest, Wales, and later at Lancaster University before moving to North America in 2000. He now lives in Norman, Oklahoma, with his partner, Jana, and at least three-and-a-half cats.

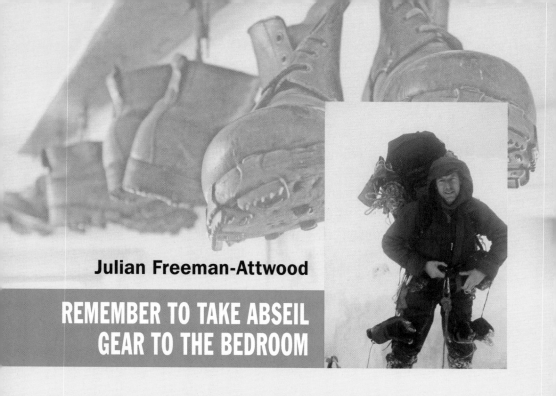

Julian Freeman-Attwood

REMEMBER TO TAKE ABSEIL GEAR TO THE BEDROOM

I FIRST READ ABOUT the Pen y Gwryd in one of Bill Tilman's essays, having become the part owner of his last vessel, the baroque *Bristol Channel Pilot Cutter*, which he sold to a colleague of mine in 1976. The first time I actually stayed in the Pen y Gwryd must have been in the early 1980s, having just come off a rather incompetent climb of Tryfan's East Face.

I say incompetent because I had only then just learnt to place rock gear on lead. In those days, you taught yourself with a bit of advice from friends and then got on with it. None of that passing tests and getting bits of paper in today's hideous health and safety culture. That first time through the hallowed doors of the hotel, I remember only glimpsing into the inner Smoke Room with its paraphernalia on the walls and that wonderful sense of history and adventure – British and understated.

I got to know Jane Pullee very well after my return from Shishapangma in 1987 where I had been on a trip with Stephen Venables, Luke Hughes, Henry Day and John Blashford-Snell. I think it was probably Stephen who obtained my ticket into the inner sanctum. I don't remember having anything but a raucous time in there and blame Jane for 'pulling' too

191

many beers (perhaps that's where her name comes from) and goading us to drink too much.

After Stephen's success on Everest's Kangshung face, his name was added to the ceiling signatures. Although I was not there on that occasion, we met up again at the Pen y Gwryd, when his frostbitten toes were better, to plan our 1989 trip to the Antarctic island of South Georgia – loading barrels with food and supplies at my house near Oswestry for shipping to Portsmouth on to *HMS Endurance*. Rock climbs in the Pass, at that time, were what brought us back to the smoky Everest sanctuary; mostly notably the climb of Cemetery Gates comes to mind. There was no having to go outside the hotel to have a fag in those days.

I often used to go climbing with Paul Rushton, a relation of the comic Willie Rushton. I called him 'Ballast', since he was always happy to second, and his portly frame meant I had a good weighty belayer. We stayed at the Pen y Gwryd one night and got severely drunk with Jane and others in the great room, so much so that, even if I did find the bedroom and even the bed itself, I remember finding it almost impossible to actually get into it, its being a rather high up bed of the Victorian variety. I kept falling back out. It would have been an appalling spectacle if there had been anyone there to see it. I did well to remember it myself.

Ballast occupied the room next door. We were to get up three hours later at 4am, it being summer, and climb Main Wall on Cyrn Las. With foul headaches we got our things together at the appointed hour and went downstairs but found the front door locked from the outside. No way out at all. Retreating back upstairs, and with great good luck that we had the climbing gear with us, I took a turn with the rope around both legs of the bed and threw the double rope out of the window. Ballast went first so that, with his greater weight, I could be sure the bed would not follow him out. It stayed put. I followed and, once out myself (it was the first floor) closed the window almost shut behind but with enough gap to retrieve the rope on landing. We climbed Main Wall, a superb route, and got back late morning. Jane, I remember, found it all highly amusing but only after I assured her that I had not ruined the bed.

The only other signatories of the famous ceiling that I have climbed with many times in the greater ranges are Crag Jones, the first Welshman up the mountain in 1995, and Doug Scott. I went out to climb Everest that time with Crag on a Henry Todd expedition but got a terrible chest infection having climbed Imja Tse (Island peak) first to acclimatise, so I aborted that one in the knowledge that an infection and Everest don't mix.

With Doug I have climbed in Nepal, Sikkim, Tibet and Tierra del Fuego. Except for scaling Shishpangma, Masagang in Bhutan and Ultar in Pakistan, I have stuck to climbing virgin 6,000 metre peaks in obscure areas, not of course worthy of a ceiling signature. Nevertheless, it is always good to get a pint at the great Pen y Gwryd and reminisce about the past, or plan for the future.

Julian Freeman-Attwood is a British forester and mountaineer who has been most interested in first ascents of unclimbed mountains in remote areas and has led or participated in some 30 expeditions to the greater ranges. In terms of exploratory climbing, the most notable trips have been to Tibet (largely less than legal trips), as well as Nepal, Sikkim, Bhutan, Arunachal Pradesh, the Karakoram and Mongolia. Down in the far south, expeditions to Tierra del Fuego, South Georgia and the Antarctic Peninsula with Skip Novak on his sailing vessel, *Pelagic Australis*. Freeman-Attwood lives in the Berwyn Mountains, on the southern edge of Snowdonia. He is a member of the Alpine Club and, at time of writing, sits as a member of the screening committee of the Mount Everest Foundation for the Royal Geographical Society. He continues expedition climbing when opportunities for escape allow.

Christine Birch

THE EVEREST ROOM

W HAT BECAME KNOWN as the 'Everest Room' at the Pen y Gwryd Hotel was first established during the time of Henry Owen as 'The Boot Room'. According to Ken Jones, such a room for drying boots was common in Victorian times. Much later, when Betty Humphreys started work at the PyG in 1937, guests would leave their boots outside their bedrooms every night to be cleaned and polished by a 'Boot Man'. The Boot Man would also lay and light the fires and carry out all sorts of odd jobs. It was common at the time to refer to him as 'Boots'. Betty can remember that during the time of Arthur Lockwood the PyG's Boot Man was one Robin Boots. (And I can remember, during my time at the PyG, guests leaving their boots outside their rooms for Blodwen to clean.)

In 1952, the Boot Room was converted by Chris Briggs into a Tyrolean-style *Stüberl* addition to the PyG's public bar. In turn, the Everest Room assumed its title, recording the names of the entire 1953 Everest and 1955 Kangchenjunga British Expedition teams. Later, the signatures of many notable climbers were added and expanded to include famous men and women from all walks of life who had either visited or stayed at the Pen y Gwryd Hotel. (To complement the signatures, it is likely that Chris Briggs got the idea of the hotel's unique tradition of individual tankards for each of the 1953 Everest and 1955 Kangchenjunga climbers from the photographer and mountaineer Peter Spencer Coppock, who left his personally engraved beer mug behind the PyG bar (for future use) after his first visit in 1951.

The first list of Everest Room signatures was compiled by Vernon Hall in 1982 and was included as an appendix to his book *A Scrapbook of Snowdonia*. What follows is an updated list based on my 2015 survey of the 12 ceiling panels – now protected by perspex. A grid key is included to assist in locating individual signatures. Abridged descriptions have been confined to individuals for whom a public biography is available.

Christine Birch was born in Liverpool and worked at the Pen y Gwryd in the early 1970s whilst Blodwen Griffiths was still working there. After leaving the PyG, she worked at Pen y Pass Youth Hostel as their first assistant warden. Christine has always maintained an interest in Snowdonia and its mountaineering history whilst continuing to live in the Conwy Valley.

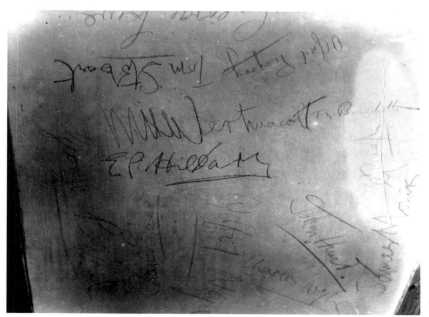

The section from panel 5 of the famous ceiling that features Sir Edmund Hillary's signature.

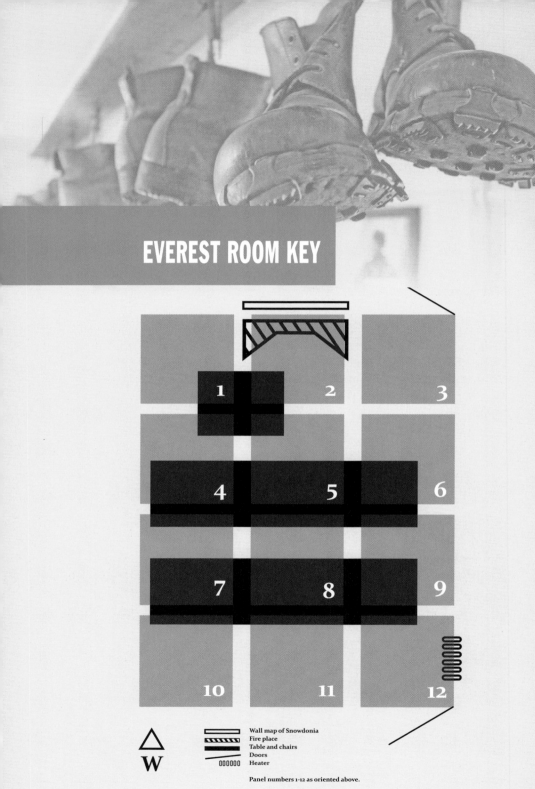

EVEREST ROOM KEY

1 2 3

4 5 6

7 8 9

10 11 12

W

Wall map of Snowdonia
Fire place
Table and chairs
Doors
000000 Heater

Panel numbers 1-12 as oriented above.

Everest Room Signatories, Panel by Panel

PANEL 1

Lionel Terray (1921–1965) was a French climber who made many first ascents, including Makalu in the Himalayas (with Jean Couzy in 1955) and Cerro Fitzroy in the Patagonian Andes (with Guido Magnone in 1952).

Terray was active in mountain combat during the Second World War. He later became known as one of the best Chamonix climbers and guides, noted for his speedy ascents of some of the most notorious climbs in the French, Italian and Swiss Alps.

Terray was a member of Maurice Herzog's 1950 expedition to Annapurna, the highest peak climbed at the time. Terray was also one of the main participants in the attempt to rescue four climbers trapped on the North Face of the Eiger in 1957. This formed the subject of Jack Olsen's book *The Climb Up To Hell*, in which Terray's skill and bravery receive special mention. Terray died on a rock climb in the Vercors, south of Grenoble, in 1965, several years after the publication of his climbing memoir, *Conquistadors of the Useless*.

Robert Paragot is a French alpinist. In September 1963, the BBC broadcast a live programme of an ascent of Snowdon's Clogwyn Du'r Arddu. Climbers were Robert Paragot, Joe Brown, Don Whillans and Ian McNaught Davis. The programme was titled *4 Men, 1 Face* with commentary by Olympic gold medallist Chris Brasher. In 1971 Paragot led a French expedition to climb Makalu in Nepal. Paragot was a 2012 Piolet d'Or Lifetime Achievement winner.

Ernst Reiss (1920–2010) was a Swiss mountaineer who, in May 1956, together with Fritz Luchsinger, climbed Lhotse, the fourth highest mountain on earth. Lhotse is connected to Everest via the South Col on the border of Tibet and Nepal. Their colleagues Ernst Schmied and Jürg Marmet were successful on 23 May, 1956, and one day later Dölf Reist and Hansruedi von Gunten made the second and third successful climbs.

Dennis Davis (1927–2015) was a British mountaineer. In 1955, along with Alf Gregory, Ted Courtney and Peter Boultbee, Davis explored the Rolwaling sub-range and, between the four of them, they climbed 19 peaks of which 16 were first ascents of between 19,000 and 22,000 feet.

In 1957, Davis and Charles Evans, as a two-man team without supplementary oxygen, climbed Annapurna IV before making an ambitious but unsuccessful attempt on Annapurna II. Dennis, along with Sherpa Tashi, completed the first ascent of Nuptse in May 1961.

PANEL 2

Christopher 'Chris' William Brasher (1928–2003) was a British athlete, sports journalist and co-founder of the London Marathon with John Disley in 1981. Brasher acted as pacemaker for Roger Bannister when the latter ran the first sub-four-minute mile at Iffley Road Stadium in Oxford in 1954. Brasher paced Bannister for the first two laps, while his friend Chris Chataway paced the third. Two years later, at the 1956 Summer Olympics in Melbourne, Brasher finished first in the 3000 metres steeplechase with a time of 8 minutes 41.2 seconds but was disqualified for allegedly interfering with another runner. The same evening, after an investigation, he was reinstated as gold medallist.

Brasher was one of the pioneers of Orienteering in Britain and can claim the first public mention of the sport in an article in *The Observer* in 1957. In 1983, he became the second president of the Association of International Marathons and Distance Races, an office which he held until 1987.

Sylvia Disley (née Cheeseman) is a former British athlete. She was winner of a record seven Women's AAA sprint titles in the 1950s. Competing as Sylvia Cheeseman, Disley won the Bronze Medal in the 1952 Olympics in the 4 x 100 metre relay. A journalistic career took her all over the world to cover fashion shows. Sylvia Cheeseman married fellow-athlete and mountaineer John Disley in 1958.

Roger Gilbert Bannister is a former British middle-distance athlete, physician and academic who ran the first sub-four-minute mile.

Bannister achieved this feat, on 6 May, 1954, at Iffley Road track in Oxford, with Chris Chataway and Chris Brasher providing the pacing. Bannister's record lasted for just 46 days. He had reached this record while practising as a junior doctor.

On the 50th anniversary of running the sub-four-minute mile, Bannister was interviewed by the BBC's sports correspondent Rob Bonnet. At the conclusion of the interview, Bannister was asked whether he looked back on the sub-four-minute mile as the most important achievement of his life. Bannister replied to the effect that no, he rather saw his subsequent 40 years of practising as a neurologist and some of the new procedures he introduced as being more significant. In a UK poll conducted by Channel 4 in 2002, the British public voted Bannister's historic sub-four-minute mile as number 13 in the list of the 100 Greatest Sporting Moments of all time.

John Ivor Disley (1928–2016) was born in Corris, a Merionethshire village (now in Gwynedd.) He competed for Great Britain in the 1952 Summer Olympics held in Helsinki in the 3000 metre steeplechase where he won the bronze medal. Disley was responsible for setting five British records in the steeplechase and four at two miles. He also set Welsh records at six different distances. He also broke the record for the traverse of the Welsh 3000 foot peaks. In 1958 he married Sylvia Cheeseman who had also won Olympic Bronze in 1952.

Disley was appointed as the first Chief Instructor and acting Warden of Plas y Brenin, the Central Council for Physical Recreation's new Centre for Mountain Activities. He then served as Inspector of Education for Surrey Education Authority for 13 years (1958-71). During this time, he was appointed Vice Chairman of the National Sports Council (1965-71) and, later, Vice Chairman of the UK Sports Council (1974-82).

However, he is perhaps best known as the co-founder of the London Marathon, launched in 1981, which now attracts over 35,000 runners, raising significant sums of money for charity. He was also a leading pioneer of Orienteering in the UK, organising the World Championships in Scotland in 1976. John Disley became Vice Chairman of the UK Sports Council in 1974, a post he held until 1982. He was a former president of the Snowdonia Society and a member of the Welsh Sports Hall of Fame. Disley passed away in February 2016.

PANEL 3

The 1953 Everest British Expedition 30th reunion 1983

George Band (see Panel 5)

Charles Evans (see Panel 5)

Alfred Gregory (see Panel 5)

Griffith Pugh (see Panel 5)

Mike Westmacott (see Panel 5)

Charles Wylie (see Panel 5)

John Angelo Jackson (see Panel 8)

John Hubert 'Emlyn' Jones (1915–2014) was Welsh climber who served throughout the Second World War as a bomb disposal officer. Jones was selected as one of four reserves for the 1953 British Everest Expedition.

Jones spent much of the war defusing unexploded ordnances in London but, after D-Day, he was posted to northern Europe where he was involved in the destruction of the V3 'super-gun' – which was potentially much more lethal than the V1 and V2 rockets. Initially Jones was selected for the 1953 British Everest Expedition, only to remain a home-based reserve climber for a second, post-monsoon assault should the first attempt fail.

Hamish Gordon Nicol (1929–1997) was a British doctor and mountaineer and a reserve member of the 1953 British Everest Expedition. Linking up with Tom Bourdillon in 1950, both men were determined to re-establish the reputation of British climbers on hard routes in the Western Alps. They practised artificial climbing techniques with pitons and rope ladders used by the top continental climbers on a tree in Bourdillon's garden in Buckinghamshire.

Their success established them as the foremost British alpinists of their generation. Bourdillon went on to reach the South Summit of

Everest in 1953 but Nicol was not so fortunate. In 1952, his climbing partner tripped on steep ice, pulling off Hamish who broke his jaw while his partner escaped injury.

Anthony Keith Rawlinson (1926–1986) was a senior British civil servant, distinguished mountaineer and 44th president of the Alpine Club. Rawlinson was the first president of the Alpine Club to die in office and the first to be killed in the mountains after a fall from Crib Goch in snow and ice.

Rawlinson was also an Editor of the *Climbers' Club Journal* and on the committee of the management of the Mount Everest Foundation of which he was chairman in 1970–71. In 1951, he took part in the first guideless British ascent of the North West Ridge of Aiguille de Blaitière. Rawlinson was one of four reserve climbers on the 1953 British Everest Expedition.

PANEL 4

John Edmond Hugh Boustead (1895–1980) was a British military officer, modern pentathlete and diplomat. Boustead began his career with the Royal Navy but later joined the British Army during the First World War, where he earned the first of two Military Crosses. Boustead spent several years as a mountaineer and explorer prior to being appointed commander of the Sudan Camel Corps (the 'Hajana') with whom he served through the Second World War.

Boustead participated in both the 1926 British Kangchenjunga Expedition and the 1933 British Everest Expedition, organising his own mountaineering expedition in Sikkim. He also explored the Libyan Desert with Ralph Alger Bagnold in 1932, as well as traversing Greenland.

Percy Wyn-Harris (born Percy Wynne) (1903–1979) was a British mountaineer, political administrator and yachtsman. In 1925, Wyn-Harris made the first ascent without guides of the Brouillard Ridge on Mont Blanc. In 1929, while serving with the Colonial Service in Kenya, he met mountaineer Eric Shipton and together they climbed the twin peaks of Mount Kenya, making the first ascent of Nelion, the secondary summit.

A member of Hugh Ruttledge's 1933 British Everest Expedition, Wyn-Harris reached Edward Norton's record height of 28,126 feet. At 27,920 feet he discovered an ice axe that was almost certainly a remnant of Mallory and Irvine's ill-fated attempt at a first ascent in 1924. Wyn-Harris returned to Everest in 1936 in an expedition again led by Hugh Ruttledge.

Harold William 'Bill' Tilman (1898–1977) was a British mountaineer and explorer, renowned for his Himalayan climbs and sailing voyages. At the age of 18, Tilman was commissioned into the Royal Field Artillery and fought in the First World War, including the Battle of the Somme, and was twice awarded the Military Cross for bravery.

Tilman was involved in two of the 1930s Everest expeditions, participating in the 1935 Reconnaissance Expedition, reaching 27,200 feet without oxygen, and as the expedition leader in 1938. He penetrated the Nanda Devi sanctuary with Eric Shipton in 1934 and, in 1936, he went on to lead an Anglo-American expedition to the peak of Nanda Devi itself. With the support of a team that included Peter Lloyd and H. Adams Carter, Tilman and Noel Odell succeeded in making the first ascent of the 25,643 foot mountain, which remained the highest summit climbed until 1950.

In 1939, Tilman was the first man to attempt climbing in the remote and unexplored Assam Himalaya, exploring the southern approaches of Gori Chen, before his team succumbed to malaria. In 1947, he attempted Rakaposhi and then made his way to Kashgar to join up with Eric Shipton in a lightweight attempt on Muztagh Ata, which nearly succeeded. On his way back to India, he detoured through Afghanistan's Wakhan Corridor to see the source of the river Oxus. During his extensive exploration of the areas of Langtang, Ganesh and Manang in Nepal in 1949, Tilman was the first to ascend Paldor and found the pass named after him beyond Gangchempo. In 1952, he was awarded the Royal Geographical Society's Founder's Gold Medal for his achievements.

Following his military career, Tilman voyaged to Arctic and Antarctic waters in search of new and uncharted mountains to climb. In 1977, Tilman was invited to crew on the ship *En Avant* with mountaineers sailing to the South Atlantic to climb Smith Island. The boat was skippered by the youthful Simon Richardson. He and his crew aboard the converted steel tug made it successfully and without incident to Rio de Janeiro. Thereafter, en route to the Falkland Islands, they disappeared without trace – it was presumed the ship had foundered with all hands.

Noel Ewart Odell (1890–1987) was a British geologist and mountaineer. In 1924, he was an oxygen officer on the Everest expedition in which George Mallory and Andrew Irvine famously perished during their summit attempt. Odell was the last person to see the pair alive. Odell spent two weeks living above 23,000 feet and twice climbed to 26,800 feet and higher, all without supplementary oxygen.

In 1936, Noel Odell and Bill Tilman successfully reached the summit of Nanda Devi which, at the time and until 1950, was the highest mountain climbed. Odell returned to Everest with the expedition led by Tilman in 1938. Odell Gully, in the Huntington Ravine of New Hampshire's Mount Washington, is named after Odell who was the first to demonstrate its ascent in winter.

Charles Snead Houston (1913–2009) was an American physician, mountaineer, high-altitude investigator, inventor, author, film-maker and former Peace Corps administrator. He made two important and celebrated attempts to climb K2 in the Karakoram Range.

Houston made the first ascent of Mount Foraker in 1934 with T. Graham Brown and Chychele Waterston. In 1936, Houston was a member of a celebrated expedition led by the British climber H.W. Tilman to the top of Nanda Devi in India. In 1938, he was the leader of the first American Karakoram expedition to K2. Although he did not reach the summit, his party mapped a route to the top that was later used by the Italian team that first summited the mountain in 1954.

He attempted K2 again in 1953. A member of the team, Art Gilkey, became ill as they approached the summit. The team reversed direction and tried to carry Gilkey down. However, he was lost in a disastrous cascade of events precipitated by a fall whereupon multiple ropes became entangled, resulting in most of the team sliding out of control roped together down the mountain. When the last roped man, Pete Schoening, was about to be plucked off by the accelerating climbers, he was remarkably able to arrest the fall of all six climbers using an ice axe belay. 'The Belay' was one of the most famous events in mountaineering history. After the 1953 K2 Expedition, Houston (then aged 40) never participated in any further technical climbs.

Peter Lloyd (1907–2003) was a mountaineer, engineer and a former president of Trinity College Cambridge Mountaineering Club. In 1936, he was chosen for an Anglo-American expedition to India's highest mountain, Nanda Devi, led by Bill Tilman who called Lloyd, 'First-rate on rock and ice'.

In 1938, Tilman assembled a team for an attempt on Everest and, again, he chose Lloyd. This expedition reached a height of 27,200 feet. Lloyd used his engineering skills to work on oxygen equipment for high-altitude climbing, favouring a system that used ordinary air as well as cylinder oxygen. He thus contributed greatly to the successful ascent of Everest in 1953. Lloyd was also a member of the Joint Himalayan Committee that organised and financed the 1953 British Everest Expedition. Lloyd was President of the Alpine Club from 1977 to 1980 and delivered a moving oration at the memorial service of Bill Tilman in 1978.

John 'Jack' Laurence Longland (see panel 10)

Thomas 'Tom' Brocklebank (1908–1984) was a climbing member of the 1933 Everest Expedition for which he provided creditable support up to Camp V. Brocklebank was also stroke for Cambridge in three victories over Oxford in the the Boat Race. From 1934 to 1961 he was a teacher at Eton College where he taught modern languages. Tom Brocklebank's granddaughter Serena, inspired by his efforts, reached the summit of Everest in 2006.

Eric Earle Shipton (1907–1977) was a British mountaineer. In 1929, he made the first ascent of Nelion, the harder of the two peaks of Mount Kenya. In Kenya, Shipton met his future climbing partners Bill Tilman and Percy Wyn-Harris. In 1931, with Frank Smythe, Shipton was amongst the first climbers to stand on the summit of Kamet, the highest peak climbed at that time.

Shipton was involved with most of the Everest expeditions during the 1930s including Hugh Ruttledge's 1933 expedition and the follow-up in 1936. The 1935 British Everest Expedition was Shipton's first as leader and the first for Tenzing. The pioneering 1951 expedition chalked out the now famous route over the Khumbu Glacier. Shipton and Tilman also discovered the access route to the Nanda Devi sanctuary through the Rishi Ganga gorge in 1934. Their shoestring budget expedition operated in the Kumaon-Garhwal Mountains continuously from pre-monsoon to post-monsoon and set a record for single-expedition achievement that has never been equalled.

George Wood Johnson (1905–1956) joined the 1933 British Everest Expedition as an experienced Himalayan climber. However, a gastric ulcer robbed him of his chance to join the final assault on Everest. Wood Johnson grew up in the Lake District but left England at the age of 25 to become a tea planter near Darjeeling. In 1930 he joined Professor Dyhrenfurth's international expedition to Kangchenjunga as transport officer. Then, with Smythe, he attempted the summit of Jongsong Peak despite never having worn crampons.

PANEL 5

Wallace 'George' Lowe (1924–2013) was a New Zealand-born mountaineer, explorer, film director and educator. In 1951, along with Edmund Hillary, Lowe was a member of the first New Zealand expedition to the Himalayas, including a first ascent of Mukut Parbat in Garhwal, India. The following year, he went to Nepal as a member of an expedition to Cho Oyu aiming to explore physiology and oxygen flow rates. Together with Eric Shipton, Lowe and Hillary explored the region around Everest.

In 1953, Lowe was a member of the 1953 British Everest Expedition led by John Hunt. During the expedition, Lowe helped prepare the route from the head of the Western Cwm up the Lhotse Face towards the South Col. On 28 May, Lowe, Alfred Gregory and Sherpa Ang Nyima, all carrying heavy loads, set out with Hillary and Tenzing as the support party for their summit attempt. Camp IX was established and then Lowe, Gregory and Ang Nyima descended to the South Col. The following day, 29 May, 1953, Hillary and Tenzing successfully reached the summit of Everest.

During their descent to the South Col, the two men were met by Lowe. It was then that Hillary delivered his immortal summary of their achievement, 'Well, George, we knocked the bastard off'. Lowe also directed a documentary film during the expedition entitled *The Conquest of Everest* that was nominated for an Academy Award for Best Documentary Feature.

In 1954, he again joined Hillary on an unsuccessful New Zealand expedition to Makalu. However, during this trip, Lowe met Vivian Fuchs who invited him to become a New Zealand representative on the Commonwealth Trans-Antarctic Expedition which, between 1955 and 1958, not only traversed Antarctica becoming the first to reach the South Pole by land since Amundsen in 1911 and Scott in 1912, but also carried out extensive surveying of the continent. At the Pole, he was met by Hillary who had led a route-finding party from the other direction. Lowe worked on the film of the expedition, *The Crossing Of Antarctica.*

Edmund 'Ed' Percival Hillary (1919–2008) was a New Zealand beekeeper, mountaineer, explorer and philanthropist. Hillary was named by *Time Magazine* as one of the 100 most influential people of the 20th century.

Hillary became interested in mountaineering while in secondary school, making his first major climb in 1939, reaching the summit of Mount Ollivier. He served in the Royal New Zealand Air Force as a navigator during the Second World War. Prior to the 1953 British Everest Expedition, Hillary had been part of the 1951 British Reconnaissance

Expedition, as well as an attempt to climb Cho Oyu in 1952. After that attempt failed due to the lack of a route from the Nepal side, Hillary and Lowe crossed the Nup La into Tibet and reached the old Camp II, on the northern side, where all the pre-war expeditions camped.

The route to Everest was closed from Chinese-controlled Tibet, and Nepal only allowed one expedition per year. A Swiss expedition (in which Tenzing took part) had attempted to reach the summit in 1952 but was turned back by bad weather and exhaustion 800 feet from the summit. During a 1952 trip in the Alps, Hillary discovered that he and George Lowe had been invited by the Joint Himalayan Committee for the approved British 1953 attempt and immediately accepted.

Shipton was named as leader but was later replaced by John Hunt. Hillary considered pulling out, but both Hunt and Shipton talked him into remaining. Hillary was intending to climb with Lowe but Hunt named two teams for the assault: Tom Bourdillon and Charles Evans, and Hillary and Tenzing. Hillary, therefore, made a concerted effort to forge a working friendship with Tenzing.

The Hunt expedition totalled over 400 people, including 362 porters, 20 Sherpa guides and 10,000 pounds of baggage and, like many such expeditions, was a team effort. Lowe supervised the preparation of the Lhotse Face, a huge and steep ice face. Hillary forged a route through the treacherous Khumbu Icefall.

The expedition set up base camp in March 1953. Working slowly, it set up its final camp at the South Col at 25,900 feet. On 26 May Bourdillon and Evans attempted the climb but turned back when Evans's oxygen system failed. The pair had reached the South Summit, coming within 300 vertical feet of the actual summit. Hunt then directed Hillary and Tenzing to go for the summit.

Snow and wind held the pair up at the South Col for two days. They set out on 28 May with a support trio of Lowe, Alfred Gregory and Ang Nyima. The two pitched a tent at 27,900 feet on 28 May, while their support group returned down the mountain.

On the following morning, Hillary discovered that his boots had frozen solid outside the tent. He spent two hours warming them before he and Tenzing attempted the final ascent wearing 30-pound packs.

The crucial move of the last part of the ascent was the 40-foot rock face later named the Hillary Step. Hillary saw a means to wedge his way up a crack in the face between the rock wall and the ice and Tenzing followed. Tenzing stated in his narration *The Dream Comes True* that Hillary had indeed taken the first step atop Mount Everest, despite Hillary quoting that both had reached the summit at the same time. They reached the highest point on earth at 11.30am.

The pair spent only about 15 minutes on the summit. Hillary took the famous photo of Tenzing posing with his ice axe but, since Tenzing had never used a camera, Hillary's ascent went unrecorded. Tenzing left chocolates in the snow as an offering and Hillary left a cross that he had been given by John Hunt. Additional photos were taken looking down the mountain in order to confirm that they had made it to the top.

The two had to take care on the descent after discovering that drifting snow had covered their tracks, complicating the task of retracing their steps. The first person they met was Lowe, who had climbed up to meet them with hot soup.

News of the expedition reached Britain on the day of the coronation of Queen Elizabeth II and the press called the successful ascent 'a Coronation gift'. In return, the 37 members of the party received the Queen Elizabeth II Coronation Medal with 'Mount Everest Expedition' engraved on the rim. The group was surprised by the international acclaim that they received upon arriving in Kathmandu. Hillary and Hunt were knighted by the young Queen, while Tenzing received the George Medal from the British Government.

As part of the Commonwealth Trans-Antarctic Expedition, Hillary reached the South Pole overland in 1958. He subsequently reached the North Pole, making him the first person to reach both poles and summit Everest.

Following his ascent of Everest, Hillary devoted much of his life to helping the Sherpa people of Nepal through the Himalayan Trust, which he founded in 1960 and led until his death in 2008. Through his efforts, many schools and hospitals were built in this remote region of the Himalayas. He was the honorary president of the American Himalayan Foundation, a United States non-profit body that helps improve the ecology and living conditions in the Himalayas. He was also the honorary president of Mountain Wilderness, an international NGO dedicated to the worldwide protection of mountains.

In 1985, Hillary and the American astronaut Neil Armstrong, the first man on the moon, flew to the North Pole together in a small twin-engine plane.

Thomas 'Tom' Ralph Stobart (1914–1980) was a zoologist and photographer. He was the official cameraman of the 1953 British Everest Expedition film *Conquest of Everest*. Stobart took part in the International Expedition to Antarctica in 1949-50. He was leader of the 'Abominable Snowman Expedition' in 1954. After Everest, Stobart pursued a career of travel and adventure and used his expertise in film-making to achieve it. In 1941, he had set up the first army film unit in India. In 1956, he was shot while filming in Ethiopia and, in spite of being crippled, he continued with his filming career. He also wrote five books, two of them on cookery.

Henry Cecil John Hunt (1910–1998) was a British Army officer who is best known as the leader of the successful 1953 British Expedition to Mount Everest.

Hunt was born in Simla, British India, the son of Captain Cecil Edwin Hunt MC of the Indian Army, and a great-great-nephew of the explorer Richard Burton. His father was killed in action during the First World War. From the age of ten, Hunt spent much holiday time in the Alps, learning some of the mountaineering skills he would later use while taking part in several expeditions in the Himalayas while serving in India. He made a guided ascent of Piz Palü at age 14. In 1934 he became a Military Intelligence officer in the Indian Army with the local rank of captain and was seconded to the Indian Police.

In 1935, with James Waller's group, Hunt attempted Saltoro Kangri, reaching 24,500 feet. This exploit led to his election to both the Alpine Club and the Royal Geographical Society. Hunt applied to join the 1936 Everest Expedition but was turned down when a Royal Air Force medical discovered a minor heart problem. He married Joy Mowbray-Green in 1936 and she also took part (along with Reggie Cooke) in

Hunt's 1937 Himalayan trip, which included the reconnaissance of Kangchenjunga, the South Western Summit of Nepal Peak and only the third ascent of the Zemu Gap, between Kangchenjunga and Simvo. Here they saw tracks that one of the party's Sherpas told them were those of the Yeti.

Hunt was employed on the staff at Supreme Headquarters Allied Expeditionary Force when he received the surprise invitation to lead the 1953 British Everest Expedition. It had been expected that Eric Shipton would lead the expedition, as he had led the (unsuccessful) British attempt on Cho Oyu the previous year from which the majority of the climbers were drawn. However, the Joint Himalayan Committee of the Alpine Club and Royal Geographical Society that oversaw British attempts on Everest decided that Hunt's military leadership experience and undoubted climbing credentials would provide the best hope for success.

Base Camp was established on 12 April, 1953. The next few days were taken up with establishing a route through the Khumbu Icefall and, once opened, teams of Sherpas moved tons of supplies up the mountain. A succession of advanced camps were created, slowly forging higher up the mountain. By 21 May, Wilfrid Noyce and Annullu had reached the psychological milestone of the South Col. Hunt had selected two climbing pairs to attempt the summit. The first pair (Tom Bourdillon and Charles Evans) set out on 26 May but were forced to turn back.

On the same day, Hunt himself climbed to 27,395 feet with Da Namgyal Sherpa to leave a cache of equipment on the South East Ridge for the second summit party. On 28 May, after spending that night at Camp IX, the expedition began its second and final assault on the summit with the second climbing pair.

Hunt received a knighthood on his return to London in July 1953. Further honours were showered on Hunt and the expedition team including the Hubbard Medal of the National Geographic Society (the first time the medal was awarded on a collective basis, though individual bronze replicas were made for Hunt, Hillary and Tenzing); the Founder's Medal of the Royal Geographical Society and the Lawrence Medal of the Royal Central Asian Society.

Hunt returned to active duty in the Army being posted as Assistant Commandant of Sandhurst. Following his retirement from the British Army in 1956, when he was granted the honorary rank of Brigadier, Hunt became the first Director of The Duke of Edinburgh's Award, a post he held for ten years. In 1966, he was made a life peer for his work with young people.

Charles Geoffrey Wylie (1919–2007) was a Nepali-speaking British Gurkha officer and mountaineer. Wylie had hopes of making the third assault, if Hillary and Tenzing had failed in their attempt, but he also had the satisfaction of being closely involved in the planning from the start. Wylie was in charge of the party of six that travelled by sea from Tilbury to Bombay (now Mumbai) with the bulk of the equipment. He went to Calcutta to ensure the expedition could receive weather reports via India Radio and, on reaching the Nepal border, took responsibility for the 350 porters.

Wylie's greatest achievement was 'the great lift', when he led a small party of Sherpas with stores up the Lhotse Face, on a trail broken by Hillary and Tenzing, to establish a camp on the inhospitable South Col at about 26,000 feet. This was almost as high as Annapurna, the only 8,000-metre peak yet to have been climbed.

As a prisoner of war of the Japanese, Wylie said little of his experience on the Burma 'death railway' beyond writing that, 'hope had kept him going'. He recalled his bemusement two days after the Armistice was signed when prisoners laid out their clothes in red, white and blue to make a Union flag that attracted an allied aircraft; instead of food, it dropped leaflets advising prisoners, 'to boil the water, avoid over-ripe fruit and always to wear a hat', something none of them had possessed for years.

Jan Morris (born James Morris) is a Welsh historian, author and travel writer. She is known particularly for the *Pax Britannica Trilogy* (1968–78), *A History of the British Empire*, and for portraits of cities, notably Oxford, Venice, Trieste, Hong Kong, and New York City.

In the closing stages of the Second World War, Morris served in the 9th Queen's Royal Lancers and, in 1945, was posted to the Free Territory of Trieste during the joint Anglo-American occupation.

After the war, Morris wrote for *The Times* and, in 1953, was its embedded correspondent accompanying the 1953 British Everest Expedition. Morris reported the success of Hillary and Tenzing in a coded telegram message to the newspaper: SNOW CONDITIONS BAD STOP ADVANCED BASE ABANDONED YESTERDAY STOP AWAITING IMPROVEMENT STOP ALL WELL STOP. The news was released on the morning of Queen Elizabeth II's Coronation on 2 June, 1953.

In January 2008, *The Times* named Morris the 15th greatest British writer since the Second World War.

Cuthbert Wilfrid Francis Noyce (1917–1962) was a British mountaineer and author. He was a member of the 1953 British Everest Expedition. Noyce was educated at Charterhouse, where he became head boy, and King's College, Cambridge, taking a first in Modern Languages. In the Second World War, he was initially a conscientious objector, joining the Friends' Ambulance Unit. However, Noyce later chose to serve as a private in the Welsh Guards, before being commissioned as a Second Lieutenant in the King's Royal Rifle Corps. He later attained the rank of Captain in the Intelligence Corps where he was employed as a code-breaker.

Together with George Lowe, Noyce established Camp VII on the South Face of Everest as a climbing member of the 1953 British Everest Expedition. On 21 May, Noyce and the Sherpa Annullu were the first members of the expedition to reach Everest's South Col.

Noyce died in a mountaineering accident together with the 23-year-old Scot Robin Smith in 1962, after a successful ascent of Mount Garmo in the Pamirs. On the descent, either Smith or Noyce slipped on a layer of soft snow over ice, pulling the other, and they both fell 4,000 feet to their deaths.

Lewis 'Griffith' Cresswell Evans Pugh (1909–1994) was a British physiologist and mountaineer. He was the expedition physiologist on the 1953 British Everest Expedition and a noted researcher into the effects of cold and altitude on human physiology.

After the Second World War, Pugh worked in clinical research. An eccentric, Pugh attached electrodes to his body and submerged himself in an ice bath from which he had to be rescued as the cold had paralysed him. In 1950, Pugh moved to the Medical Research Council laboratories in Hampstead to work under Professor Otto Edholm in the Department of Human Physiology as Head of the Laboratory of Field Physiology. He stayed there for the rest of his career.

Expedition leader Eric Shipton invited Pugh, now on the High Altitude Committee of the Medical Research Council, to accompany the British 1952 Cho Oyo Expedition to perform research on oxygen equipment that would be useful on the following year's expedition to Everest. Pugh realised that the best way to do this was to study climbers in the field at altitude and he analysed rates of breathing and food and fluid intake. His findings were, according to George Band, of fundamental value to that expedition.

In *Everest – The First Ascent: The Untold Story of Griffith Pugh, the Man Who Made It Possible* (2013) by Pugh's daughter Harriet Tuckey, Tuckey argues that her father was given insufficient credit in the official accounts of the first ascent – *The Ascent of Everest* by expedition leader John Hunt and in the film *The Conquest of Everest*. These accounts stressed the 'grit and determination' of the expedition team, while simultaneously downplaying the important role that science had played.

Michael Phelps Ward (1925–2005) was the medical officer responsible for the successful 1953 ascent of Everest. He also organised the 1951 Reconnaissance Expedition that explored the possibility of tackling Everest from the south, rather than the north, starting in Nepal, then a closed country.

Ward's discovery of a potential route to the summit from the south happened during his national service with the Royal Army Medical Corps when he unearthed aerial photographs taken by a Royal Air Force Mosquito fighter-bomber of this unexplored side of Everest. Ward also came across a forgotten 1930s map, compiled from photographs and a photogrammetric survey. Convinced this was the key to the problem of climbing Everest from Nepal, he approached the Joint Himalayan Committee of the Alpine Club and the Royal Geographical Society, faced down scepticism about a route into the Western Cwm through the perilous complexities of the Khumbu icefall and persuaded committee members to approve the 1951 exploratory expedition. This project, led by Eric Shipton and which included Edmund Hillary, laid the groundwork for the latter's successful ascent two years later.

In 1983, he was awarded the Founder's Medal of the Royal Geographical Society for medical research, exploration and mountaineering in the Himalayas.

Alfred Gregory (1913–2010) was a mountaineer, explorer and professional photographer. A member of the 1953 British Everest Expedition, he was in charge of stills photography and, as a climbing member of the team, reached 28,000 feet in support of the successful Hillary-Tenzing assault on the summit.

Michael 'Mike' Horatio Westmacott (1925-2012) was a British mountaineer and member of the 1953 British Everest Expedition. During the Second World War, Westmacott served as an officer with the British Indian Army Corps of Engineers in Burma.

Westmacott's role on Everest was overlooked in the years after 1953, partly because of his intense modesty. He told the BBC that his selection was, 'a bit of luck. I was at the right age at the right time and people like Joe Brown, Don Whillans and Chris Bonington were much too young'.

Westmacott embodied all that the public came to admire about the first successful ascent of Everest, a selfless team-player who was genuinely pleased for those who reached the summit. Yet his self-deprecation hid the fact that he was a capable and resourceful mountaineer and a leading figure in the post-war resurgence in British mountaineering – driven largely by university clubs.

Early in his climbing career, Westmacott made an ascent of the East Ridge of the Dent d'Hérens in the Pennine Alps, a route with a difficult descent undertaken late in the day. It was just the kind of substantial challenge that spoke of deep reserves of tenacity; Westmacott himself assumed it was this ascent that secured his place on the 1953 British Everest team. He was president of both the Alpine Club and the Climbers' Club and oversaw the management of the Alpine Club's library.

George Christopher Band (1929–2011) was a British mountaineer and the youngest climber on the 1953 British Everest Expedition. Two years later he and Joe Brown became the first climbers to ascend Kangchenjunga, the third highest mountain in the world. Out of respect for the religious feelings of the people of Nepal and Sikkim, Band and Brown stopped about ten feet below the actual summit.

In 2005, aged 76, Band made the trek to the South West Base Camp of Kangchenjunga in Nepal. He was President of the Alpine Club and the British Mountaineering Council. He wrote the books *Road to Rakaposhi* and in 2003 *Everest 50 Years on Top of the World* (the official history of Mount Everest climbs, for the Mount Everest Foundation, the Royal Geographical Society and the Alpine Club). In 2007, he wrote *Summit*, a book celebrating 150 years of the Alpine Club.

Band was Chairman of the Himalayan Trust (UK) and an Appeal Patron for BSES Expeditions, a youth development charity that operates challenging scientific research expeditions to remote wilderness environments.

Thomas 'Tom' Duncan Bourdillon (1924–1956) was a British mountaineer and a member of the 1953 British Everest Expedition. He made a career as a physicist in rocket research.

Bourdillon was the elder son of Robert Benedict Bourdillon (1889–1971), a scientist who had been a founder member of the Oxford University Mountaineering Club in 1909. In turn, Tom Bourdillon was also President of the Oxford University Mountaineering Club.

Bourdillon had been with Eric Shipton on the 1951 reconnaissance of Everest and on Cho Oyu in 1952 and he was put in charge of oxygen equipment on the 1952 and 1953 British Everest Expeditions. With his father, Robert Bourdillon, he developed the closed-circuit oxygen apparatus used by Charles Evans and himself on their pioneering climb to the South Summit of Everest on 26 May, 1953.

Bourdillon died with another climber, Richard Viney, in a climbing accident in 1956 while ascending the East Buttress of the Jägihorn in the Bernese Oberland.

Robert Charles Evans (1918–1995) was a British mountaineer, surgeon and educator. He qualified as a doctor in 1942 and joined the Royal Army Medical Corps. Evans served in the Burma Campaign and was mentioned in dispatches. He was John Hunt's deputy leader on the 1953 British Everest Expedition. With Tom Bourdillon, he made the first ascent of the South Summit, coming within 300 feet of the main summit of Everest on 26 May, 1953.

Evans was the leader of the expedition that first climbed Kangchenjunga, the world's third highest peak, in 1955. He was awarded the Royal Geographical Society's Patron's Gold Medal. Evans served as the Principal of the University College of North Wales (now called Bangor University) from 1958 to 1984. He was President of the Alpine Club from 1967 to 1970.

Tenzing Norgay (1914–1986) (often referred to as 'Sherpa Tenzing' or 'Tenzing') was a Nepali Sherpa mountaineer. Among the most famous mountain climbers in history, Tenzing was one of the first of two individuals known to reach the summit of Everest, which he accomplished with Edmund Hillary on 29 May, 1953. *Time Magazine* named him one of the 100 most influential people of the 20th century.

Tenzing was originally called 'Namgyal Wangdi' but, as a child, his name was changed on the advice of the Head Lama and founder of the famous Rongbuk Monastery, Ngawang Tenzing Norbu. 'Tenzing Norgay' translates as 'wealthy-fortunate-follower-of-religion'. Tenzing got his first opportunity to join an Everest expedition when he was employed by Eric Shipton, leader of the 1935 British Mount Everest Reconnaissance Expedition.

Tenzing participated as a high-altitude porter in three official

British attempts to climb Everest from the northern Tibetan side in the 1930s. He also took part in other climbs in various parts of the Indian subcontinent. For a time in the early 1940s, Tenzing lived in the Princely State of Chitral (that later became a part of Pakistan on partition of India) as batman to a Major Chapman.

In 1947, Tenzing participated in an unsuccessful summit attempt of Everest. Canadian-born Earl Denman, Ange Dawa Sherpa and Tenzing entered Tibet illegally to attempt the mountain which ended with a storm at 22,000 feet; all three turned around and safely returned. In 1947, Tenzing became a *sirdar* of a Swiss expedition for the first time, following the rescue of Sirdar Wangdi Norbu who had been seriously injured in a fall. The expedition reached the main summit of Kedarnath at 22,769 feet in the Garhwal Himalaya with Tenzing being one of the summit party.

In 1952, Tenzing took part in the two Swiss expeditions led by Edouard Wyss-Dunant (spring) and Gabriel Chevalley (autumn), the first serious attempts to climb Everest from the southern (Nepali) side, after two previous US and British reconnaissance expeditions in 1950 and 1951. Raymond Lambert and Tenzing were able to reach a height of about 28,200 feet on the South East Ridge, setting a new climbing altitude record.

In 1953, Tenzing took part in John Hunt's expedition; the latter's seventh expedition to Everest. Edmund Hillary, who had a near-miss following a fall into a crevasse, was saved from hitting the bottom by Tenzing's prompt action in securing the rope using his ice axe. This led Hillary to consider him as his climbing partner of choice for any future summit attempt.

The expedition set up base camp in March 1953. Working slowly, they set up their penultimate camp at the South Col at about 26,000 feet. On 26 May, Tom Bourdillon and Charles Evans attempted the climb but turned back when Evans' oxygen system failed. Hunt then directed Hillary and Tenzing to go for the summit.

Snow and wind held the pair up at the South Col for two days. They set out on 28 May with a support trio comprising Ang Nyima, Alfred Gregory and George Lowe. Hillary and Tenzing pitched a tent at 27,900 feet on 28 May while their support group returned down the mountain. They reached Everest's summit, the highest point on earth, at 11.30am on the 29th.

They spent only about 15 minutes at the summit. Hillary took the famous photo of Tenzing posing with his ice axe but, since Tenzing had never used a camera, Hillary's ascent went unrecorded. However, according to Tenzing's autobiography *Man of Everest*, when he offered to take Hillary's photograph Hillary declined. 'I motioned to Hillary that I would now take his picture. But for some reason he shook his head; he did not want it'. Additional photos were taken looking down the mountain, in order to re-assure the world that they had made it to the top and to document that the ascent was not faked. The two had to take care on the descent after discovering that drifting snow had covered their tracks, complicating the task of retracing their steps. The first person they met was Lowe, who had climbed up to meet them with hot soup.

Afterwards, Tenzing was met with great adulation in Nepal and India. Hillary and Hunt were knighted by Queen Elizabeth II, while Tenzing received the George Medal for his efforts on the expedition. It has been suggested that the Indian Prime Minister Jawaharlal Nehru refused permission for Tenzing to be knighted.

Tenzing became the first Director of Field Training of the Himalayan Mountaineering Institute in Darjeeling, when it was set up in 1954. In 1978, Tenzing founded *Tenzing Norgay Adventures*, a company providing trekking adventures in the Himalayas. As of 2003, the company was run by his son Jamling Tenzing Norgay who himself reached the summit of Everest in 1996.

PANEL 6

Bertram Clough Williams-Ellis (1883–1978) was a Welsh architect known chiefly as the creator of the Italianate village of Portmeirion in North Wales.

A fashionable architect in the inter-war years, Williams-Ellis's other works include buildings at Stowe in Buckinghamshire; groups of cottages at Cornwell, Oxfordshire; Tattenhall in Cheshire; and Cushendun, County Antrim, Northern Ireland. Williams-Ellis is also known for his design (in the 1930s) of the former summit building on Snowdon, which, after unsympathetic alteration in the 1960s and a long-term lack of maintenance, was described by Prince Charles as, 'The highest slum in Wales'. The Welsh-language novelist Robin Llywelyn is his grandson.

Graham Arthur Chapman (1941–1989) was an English comedian, writer, actor and one of the six members of the comedy group Monty Python (as well as being a Medical Practitioner). Chapman played authority figures such as the Colonel and the lead role in two Python films, *Holy Grail* and *Life of Brian*. Chapman was a keen climber and a regular patron of the Pen y Gwryd Hotel. A section of his book, *A Liar's Autobiography,* is given over to his experiences of mountaineering in Snowdonia and staying at the hotel.

Chapman established a writing partnership with John Cleese, which reached its critical peak with Monty Python during the 1970s. Chapman left Britain for Los Angeles in the late 1970s where he appeared on American television, speaking on the college circuit and producing the pirate film *Yellowbeard*, before returning to Britain in the early 1980s.

Teddie (born Hazel P. Chinery) is one of the Beverley Sisters (and twin of Babs), a British female vocal and light entertainment trio who were popular during the 1950s and 1960s. Their style was loosely modelled on that of their American counterparts, the Andrews Sisters. Their notable successes have included *Sisters, I Saw Mommy Kissing Santa Claus* and *Little Drummer Boy.*

The sisters are widely credited as having been the highest paid female entertainers in the UK for more than 20 years. They entered the *Guinness World Records* in 2002 as the world's longest surviving vocal group without a change in the original line-up. As late as 2009, the Beverley Sisters appeared in concerts and shows across Britain.

Lewis John Wynford Vaughan-Thomas (1908–1987) was a Welsh newspaper journalist, radio and television broadcaster, author and public figure. In the mid-1930s, Vaughan-Thomas joined the BBC and, in 1937, gave the Welsh language commentary on the Coronation of King George VI and Queen Elizabeth. This was the precursor to several commentaries on state occasions he was to give after the Second World War. During the war, he established his name and reputation as one of the BBC's most distinguished war correspondents. His most memorable report was from a Lancaster bomber during a real Royal Air Force bombing raid over Nazi Berlin. Other notable reports were from Anzio, the Burgundy vineyards, Lord Haw-Haw's broadcasting studio and the Belsen concentration camp. He was a great enthusiast for Wales and its history and landscape, and especially for Snowdonia despite its distance from his home in south west Wales.

Bertrand Arthur William Russell (3rd Earl Russell) (1872–1970) was a Welsh philosopher, logician, mathematician, historian, writer, social critic and political activist. Russell was a prominent anti-war activist; he championed anti-imperialism and went to prison for his pacifism during the First World War. Later he campaigned against Adolf Hitler and then criticised Stalinist totalitarianism, attacked the involvement of the United States in the Vietnam War, and was an outspoken proponent of nuclear disarmament. In 1950, Russell was awarded the Nobel Prize in Literature, 'In recognition of his varied and significant writings in which he champions humanitarian ideals and freedom of thought'.

John Stratton (1925–1991) was a British actor. He is best known for his early film roles during the 1950s where he played the young apprentice parts of Ferraby and Ward opposite Jack Hawkins in both *The Cruel Sea* (1953) and *The Long Arm* (1956) respectively. He played a similar role on television in the third *Quatermass* serial.

Janet Quigley (1902–1987) was co-creator of the BBC's *Woman's Hour*. Quigley oversaw the launch of the BBC's *Today* programme. She was married to Kevin FitzGerald, the writer and mountaineer who was a frequent guest at PyG.

Petula Sally Olwen Clark is a British singer, actress and composer whose career has spanned over seven decades. Clark's professional career began as an entertainer on BBC Radio during the Second World War. During the 1950s, she started recording in French and having international success in both French and English, with such songs as *The Little Shoemaker*, *Baby Lover*, *With All My Heart* and *Prends Mon Cœur*.

During the 1960s, she became known globally for her popular upbeat hits, including *Downtown*, *I Know a Place*, *My Love*, *A Sign of the Times*, *I Couldn't Live Without Your Love*, *Colour My World*, *This Is My Song* and *Don't Sleep in the Subway*. The timing and popularity of these songs caused Clark to be dubbed 'the First Lady of the British Invasion'. She has sold more than 68 million records throughout her career.

William Russell Flint (1880-1969) was a Scottish artist and illustrator who was known for his watercolour paintings of women. He also worked in oils, tempera and printmaking. Flint was elected president of Britain's Royal Society of Painters in Water Colours (now the Royal Watercolour Society) from 1936 to 1956.

During visits to Spain, Flint was impressed by Spanish dancers and he depicted them frequently throughout his career. He enjoyed considerable commercial success but little respect from art critics who were disturbed by a perceived crassness in his eroticised treatment of the female figure.

Alan Rowlands (1929-2012) was a British pianist (born in Swansea, Wales) who made notable contributions to British musical life both as a teacher and as a performer.

Al Koran (1914–1972) was the stage name of Edward Doe, who was a former hairdresser turned professional magician and mentalist. Koran invented the Ring Flite and popularised a version of the 'Bagshawe deck' which became known as the 'Koran deck'. Koran appeared many times on *The Ed Sullivan Show*. Al Koran is considered by most mentalists to be one of the best to have ever performed.

Huw Pyrs Wheldon (1916–1986) was a BBC broadcaster and executive. He was awarded the Military Cross for an act of bravery on D-Day + 1. After the War, Wheldon joined the Arts Council of Wales and then, in 1951, became the Arts Council's administrator for the Festival of Britain.

John Edward 'Jack' Hawkins (1910–1973) was a British actor who worked on stage and in film from the 1930s until the 1970s. Hawkins appeared on Broadway in *Journey's End* at the age of 18. He appeared in several films during the 1930s.

After France capitulated in 1940, Hawkins joined up, volunteering for service with the Royal Welch Fusiliers. He was eventually posted to India, attaining the rank of Captain and where he was put in charge of troop entertainment. By July 1944, he had risen to the rank of Colonel and was commanding the administration of the Entertainments National Service Association (ENSA) for India and Southeast Asia. At one point, after he had decided to end the run of the play *Company Love in a Mist,* he received a note from the Officer Commanding – Southeast Asia, General William Slim, asking him to immediately reverse his decision. It was during his time in the sub-continent that he met Doreen Lawrence, a young actress who went out to India to serve with ENSA, under Hawkins. They later married in 1947.

Hawkins became a star with the release of three successful films in which he played stern but sympathetic authority figures, *Angels One Five* (1951), *The Planter's Wife* (1952), and *Mandy* (1952). He consolidated this status with *The Cruel Sea*, which saw Hawkins voted the most popular actor in Britain.

From the late 1950s, Hawkins mostly appeared in character roles, often in epic films like *The Bridge on the River Kwai*, *Lawrence of Arabia* (playing General Edmund Allenby), *Lord Jim*, and *Oh! What a Lovely War*. For *The Bridge on the River Kwai* he had to persuade Alec Guinness to take the lead role, which would ultimately win Guinness an Oscar. One of his films, *The League of Gentlemen*, was considered ground-breaking for its time in its references to sex.

Clifford 'Cliff' Isaac Morgan (1930–2013) was a Welsh rugby union player who played for Cardiff and earned 29 caps for Wales between 1951 and 1958. After his playing career ended, Morgan made a successful transition to broadcasting, both as a commentator and presenter and also as a programme-maker and BBC executive. When the International Rugby Hall of Fame was created in 1997, Morgan was among the inaugural inductees.

Robert Day is an English film director. He directed more than 40 films between 1956 and 1991. Day worked his way up from clapper boy to camera operator to fully-fledged lensman in his native England before directing in the mid-1950s. His first film as director, the black comedy *The Green Man* (1956), garnered fine reviews and a classic notoriety. Using this as a starting point, Day went on to become one of the industry's busiest directors. He relocated to Hollywood in the 1960s and began directing television programmes and made-for-television movies.

Donald Alfred Sinden (1923–2014) was a British actor in theatre, film, television and radio, as well as an author. Achieving early fame as a Rank Organisation film star in the 1950s, Sinden then became highly regarded as an award-winning Shakespearean and West End theatre actor and television sitcom star. He befriended an ageing Lord Alfred Douglas (Bosie), Oscar Wilde's lover. Sinden was one of only two people to attend Lord Douglas's funeral.

Philip Anthony Hopkins is a Welsh actor of film, stage and television, as well as a composer and painter. After graduating from the Royal Welsh College of Music and Drama in 1957, Hopkins trained at the Royal Academy of Dramatic Art in London and was then spotted by Laurence Olivier who invited him to join the Royal National Theatre. In 1968, he got his break in film in *The Lion in Winter* playing Richard I.

Considered to be one of the greatest living actors, Hopkins is well known for his portrayal of Hannibal Lecter in *The Silence of the Lambs*, for which he won the Academy Award for Best Actor, and its sequel *Hannibal* and prequel *Red Dragon*. Other notable films include *The Mask of Zorro*, *The Bounty*, *Meet Joe Black*, *The Elephant Man*, *Magic*, *84 Charing Cross Road*, *Bram Stoker's Dracula*, *Legends of the Fall*, *Thor*, *The Remains of the Day*, *Amistad*, *Nixon*, *The World's Fastest Indian*, *Instinct*, and *Fracture*.

Along with his Academy Award, Hopkins has won three BAFTA Awards, two Emmys, and the Cecil B. DeMille Award. In 1993, he was knighted by Queen Elizabeth II for services to the arts. He received a star on the Hollywood Walk of Fame in 2003 and was made a Fellow of the British Academy of Film and Television Arts in 2008.

Richard Adrian William Sharp is a former Cornish rugby player with 14 caps for England as fly-half and captain. Sharp led England to the Five Nations title in 1963. He played cricket for Cornwall in the Minor Counties Championship between 1957 and 1970. Bernard Cornwell's fictional character Richard Sharpe was named after him.

Geraldine McEwan (1932–2015) was an English actress who had a long career in theatre, television and film. McEwan was nominated for the Tony Award for Best Actress in a Play in 1998 for her performance in *The Chairs*. She won a BAFTA Award for her performance in the television serial *Oranges Are Not the Only Fruit* (1990). From 2004 to 2009, she appeared as Miss Marple, the Agatha Christie sleuth, in the series *Marple*.

Thomas Llyfnwy Thomas (1911–1983) was a Welsh-American baritone concert singer who achieved fame for his performances both in concert halls and on television and radio, most notably on *The Voice of Firestone*, where he was a featured singer. His concert repertoire included lieder, opera arias, ballads, spirituals and songs from musical theatre and operetta. He kept up his connection with his native Wales throughout his life, returning there to sing in 1955, 1956 and 1958, always including a Welsh song in his recitals.

Henry 'HV' Canova Vollam Morton (1892–1979) was a British journalist and pioneering travel writer. He was best known for his prolific and popular books on London, Great Britain and the Holy Land. He first achieved fame in 1923 when, while working for the *Daily Express*, he scooped the official *Times* correspondent during the coverage of the opening of the tomb of Tutankhamun by Howard Carter in Egypt.

Robert Beatty (1909–1992) was a Canadian actor who worked in film, television and radio for most of his career and was especially known in the UK. During the Second World War, Beatty achieved international fame for his eyewitness radio reports of the nightly bombing of London for the BBC Overseas News Service.

Richard Cawston (1923–1986) was a British director and producer of television newsreel. Cawston produced the film, *Royal Family* (1968–9) that documented a year in the private and public life of Queen Elizabeth II.

John Innes Mackintosh Stewart (1906–1994) was a Scottish novelist and academic. He is equally well known for the works of literary criticism and contemporary novels published under his real name and for the crime fiction published under the pseudonym of Michael Innes. Many devotees of the Innes books were unaware of his other 'identity', and vice versa. Stewart wrote several critical studies, including full-length studies of James Joyce, Joseph Conrad, Thomas Love Peacock and Thomas Hardy, as well as many novels and short stories. His last publication was his autobiography *Myself and Michael Innes* (1987).

Gwilym Meredith Edwards (1917–1999) was a Welsh character actor and writer. A Welsh nationalist and Welsh speaker, Edwards stood as the Plaid Cymru candidate for Denbigh in the 1966 General Election.

Edwards also worked with Amnesty International, CND Cymru, Cymdeithas yr Iaith Gymraeg (The Welsh Language Society) and Equity, the actors union, of which he was a Life President. In 1996, as part of the celebrations marking the centenary of cinema, he unveiled the plaque at Rhyd-y-main, where Emlyn Williams's film *The Last Days of Dolwyn* had been made in 1949. This was an acknowledgement of his contribution to the theatre, cinema and television of Wales over more than half a century.

PANEL 7

M. W. Henry Day is a retired British Army officer and mountaineer. He climbed the highest mountain in the Hindu Kush, Tirich Mir in Pakistan, with the Army Mountaineering Association Expedition of 1969. As climbing leader of the British-Nepali Army Joint Expedition, he also reached the summit of Annapurna I by the French route in 1970. In 1976 Henry was a member of the joint British-Nepali Army Expedition to Everest, led by Tony Streather, when 'Brummy' Stokes and 'Bronco' Lane reached the summit but had to return in extremely bad conditions.

In retirement, Henry has made many lengthy road trips by Land Rover across several continents, climbing any peaks that take his fancy along the way, notably including a journey between Nova Scotia and Tierra del Fuego via Alaska in 2004–5. In this vein, Day organised an expedition to the Georgian Caucasus, as part of the Alpine Club's 150th anniversary in 2007. He has been Vice President of the Alpine Club and, most recently, Chairman of the Mount Everest Foundation at the time of the Her Majesty the Queen's attendance at the celebration of the 60th anniversary of the ascent of the first ascent of Everest, at the Royal Geographical Society in 2013.

Caradoc 'Crag' Jones is a Welsh mountaineer and fisheries consultant. In 1995, at the age of 33, Jones was the first Welshman to climb Everest. In October 1996, together with Mick Fowler and Julian Freeman-Attwood, Jones made the first ascent of Yes, Please, a very hard route on the sea cliff at Yesnaby on the Mainland of Orkney. In 2001, Jones made the first solo ascent of the highest of the Three Brothers Peaks at the north-west end of the Allardyce Range on South Georgia.

Vivian Ernest 'Bunny' Fuchs (1908–1999) was a prominent geologist and polar explorer. In 1931, Fuchs joined Louis Leakey on a paleoanthropologist-archaeological expedition to Tanzania (Olduvai Gorge). Fuchs is, however, best known as the leader of the Commonwealth Trans-Antarctic Expedition, a Commonwealth-sponsored expedition that completed the first overland crossing of Antarctica. Planning for the expedition began in 1953 and envisioned the use of Sno-Cat tractors to cross the continent in 100 days, starting at the Weddell Sea, ending at the Ross Sea and crossing the South Pole.

Alan Hinkes is the first British mountaineer to have claimed all 14 mountains with elevations greater than 8,000 metres.

George Lowe (see panel 5)

PANEL 8

John Neil Mather (1927–2005) was a British textile worker, mountaineer and long-distance walker. Unlike many climbers of his generation, Mather was an enthusiastic walker and was well known for 70-mile winter-weekend walks over the Pennine Fells. Mather took part in the Rucksack Club's Tan Hill to Cat and Fiddle Walk in 1952, a distance of 120 miles covered in 54 hours.

Mather was a member of the 1955 British Kangchenjunga Expedition led by Charles Evans. Team members Joe Brown and George Band made the first ascent of Kangchenjunga on 25 May, followed by Norman Hardie and Tony Streather on 26 May. In addition to Mather, the full team also included, John Clegg (team doctor), Charles Evans (team leader), John Angelo Jackson and Tom MacKinnon.

Harry Reginald Anthony 'Tony' Streather (1926–1998) was a British Army officer and mountaineer. In 1955, Streather participated in the first ascent of Kangchenjunga, the third highest mountain in the world. With Norman Hardie, he reached the summit the day after the first summit party of Joe Brown and George Band.

In 1957, Streather, John Emery, Bernard Jillot and Rae Culbert, a team from Oxford University, experienced repeated falls and misfortunes during a failed attempt to climb Haramosh in the Karakoram, leading to the deaths of Jillot and Culbert. Streather and Emery survived. The latter suffered severe frostbite and lost all of his fingers and toes. The epic tale of this expedition is told in Ralph Barker's *The Last Blue Mountain*. In 1959, Streather led a successful expedition that included an ascent of Malubiting South East. He was also leader of the joint British-Nepali Army Expedition to Everest in 1976, when 'Brummy' Stokes and 'Bronco' Lane reached the summit but had to return in extremely bad conditions.

John Angelo Jackson (1921–2005) was a British mountaineer, explorer and educationalist who wrote extensively for many magazines and journals, including *Climber and Rambler, The Great Outdoors, The Himalayan Club Journal, The Fell and Rock Journal* and the *Alpine Journal.*

During the Second World War, Jackson flew with the Royal Air Force in India and Burma, delivering supplies to the 14th Army who were stranded behind Japanese lines (for which he was mentioned in dispatches).

In 1944, Jackson became Chief Instructor at the Royal Air Force Mountain Training Centre, Kashmir. He was also a member of the 1952 British Garhwal Expedition and was first reserve on the 1953 British Everest Expedition (pre-monsoon), as well as being involved with all initial training, including climbing in North Wales with oxygen tanks. Jackson was a full member of the post-monsoon expedition; however, as the first expedition summited, the post-monsoon expedition was cancelled. In 1954, he was mountaineering leader of the *Daily Mail* Abominable Snowman Expedition (Yeti) when the first trek from Everest to Kangchenjunga was completed.

In 1955 he was a member of the team to successfully climb Kangchenjunga. He reached and set up Camp V with Tom MacKinnon. The entire group might have summited except for the encroaching monsoon.

In 1957, Jackson commenced a two-year appointment as Chief Instructor at Plas y Brenin, following John Disley. In 1960, he was a senior member of John Hunt's expedition to the Staunings Alps, north-east Greenland, with a mixed group of mountaineers and scientists including 18 Duke of Edinburgh's Gold Award winners. (Jackson was an enthusiastic proponent of the Award Scheme.)

In 1960, Jackson again became the Director and Warden of Plas y Brenin, this time for a further 16 years until 1976. Along with Jack Longland, he was an instigator of the Mountain Leadership Training Board as well as the MLT Certificate and the Mountain Instructor Certificate. In 1963, he was a member of Trans-Pindus Expedition, Greece, again with John Hunt.

Charles Evans (see Panel 5)

George Band (see Panel 5)

Norman Hardie is a New Zealand civil engineer and mountaineer. In 1955 he participated in the first ascent of Kangchenjunga, the third highest mountain in the world. With Tony Streather, he reached the summit the day after the first summit party of Joe Brown and George Band. In 1948 Hardie had assisted in the epic Mount La Perouse rescue, an eight-day operation involving many of the top guides and climbers of that time. It was on that occasion he first met Edmund Hillary, beginning a lifelong friendship with the fellow adventurer five years before Hillary's historic ascent of Everest.

Hardie played an important part in three Everest expeditions with Hillary and, for 22 years, he was on the board of the Himalayan Trust, Hillary's aid project for constructing schools and hospitals in Nepal. He went to Antarctica three times, as an instructor, surveyor and as the leader of Scott Base.

Thomas 'Tom' D. MacKinnon (1914–1981) was a British pharmacist and mountaineer. In 1950, after two seasons in Norway (1935 and 1936) and five Alpine seasons, he accompanied Douglas Scott, Tom Weir and W.H. Murray on a series of exploratory expeditions through Garhwal and Almora where they climbed Uja Tirche (20,350 feet).

In 1952, he went with Scott, Weir and George Roger to the Rolwaling

Khola of Nepal, where he climbed three mountains of between 19,000 and 22,000 feet. MacKinnon was elected president of the Scottish Mountaineering Club 1958-60 and was a long-standing member of the Alpine Club.

Joseph 'Joe' Brown is a British climber regarded as the outstanding pioneering rock climber of the 1950s and early 1960s. He established an unprecedented number of classic new routes in Snowdonia and the Peak District that were at the leading edge of the hardest grades of their day. Examples on Dinas Cromlech in the Llanberis Pass include Cenotaph Corner (1952, nowadays graded E1, with Doug Belshaw) and Cemetery Gates (1951, E1, with Don Whillans).

As well as creating pioneering routes, Brown helped create new types of 'protection' to improve safety on climbs, and is acknowledged as having created some of the first 'nuts' by drilling the thread out of nuts and threading the centre with a sling. Brown was so well known that the Post Office would often deliver letters simply addressed to 'The Human Fly, UK'.

Brown's mountaineering achievements in the Alps and Himalayas have often been overlooked. He made many significant ascents in both ranges in the 1950s with Whillans and other members of the Rock and Ice Climbing Club. He is remembered for bringing British gritstone climbing techniques to alpine rock climbing, in the eponymous Fissure Brown, 'off-width' crux of the now classic British Route on the West Face of the Aiguille de Blaitière above Chamonix. On 25th May, 1955, Brown made the first ascent of the world's third highest mountain, Kangchenjunga in the Nepalese Himalayas, with George Band. They were followed on the 26th by Norman Hardie and Tony Streather. The following year, Brown made the first ascent of the West Summit of the Muztagh Tower in the Karakoram with Ian McNaught-Davis. The other members of the team, John Hartog and Tom Patey, reached the main summit the next day.

Apart from numerous classic rock climbs in Britain and mountaineering achievements abroad, Brown is remembered for televised rock climbs in the 1960s, three in Snowdonia, and in 1967, a spectacular new route on the Old Man of Hoy, a Scottish sea stack, with

Ian McNaught-Davis and Chris Bonington. Fifteen years later, Brown repeated the climb on the Old Man on a television documentary with his second daughter Zoë.

John Clegg (1925–2015) was a British medical officer and mountaineer. Clegg was the doctor on the 1955 British Kangchenjunga Expedition, the year he was elected to Alpine Club membership. Clegg was a former front-row forward for Liverpool Saint Helens Rugby Union Football Club and was in demand as crew for sailing in northern waters.

PANEL 9

Thomas Joseph Firbank (1910–2000) was a Canadian/Welsh author, farmer, soldier and engineer. His first book, an autobiography entitled *I Bought a Mountain*, was published in 1940 and became a major international bestseller. It describes how, aged 21, he bought Dyffryn Mymbyr, a 2,400-acre sheep farm between the PyG and Capel Curig.

Firbank was a keen mountain walker and the book includes a hair-raising account of how in 1938 he and his two companions were possibly the first to ascend all of the Welsh 3000s in less than nine hours. Firbank's first wife, Esme Cummins, a Surrey-born actress whom he met in 1933 (and who later became Esme Kirby, founder of the Snowdonia National Park Society, now the Snowdonia Society), features prominently.

A list of visiting Nepali Sherpa's names in Nepali script.

PANEL 10

Tony Bennett (1931–1996) was a Flight Sergeant with Royal Air Force (RAF) Valley and RAF Valley Rescue team leader from 1961 to 1967. Bennett was also Warden for Nature Conservancy, Llanddwyn Island and Newborough, Anglesey.

Simon Clark is a British mountaineer who organised and led the 1957 Cambridge 'Puma's Claw' Andean Expedition which made the first ascent of Pumasillo in the Cordillera Vilcabamba of Peru. At the time, Pumasillo was the highest unclimbed peak in the Americas. The expedition named their base camp and advanced camp PyG and PyP respectively, after the Pen y Gwryd and Pen y Pass.

John 'Jack' Laurence Longland (1905–1993) was a mountaineer, climber, athlete, educationalist and broadcaster. As a climber, he was part of a group that opened up a number of the harder grades, for instance with his 1928 ascent of Longland's Climb on Clogwyn Du'r Arddu and in 1930 Javelin Blade on the Holly Tree Wall, Cwm Idwal. Several of these first ascents were made with Ivan Waller.

Jack Longland was a member of the 1933 British Everest Expedition which established a camp at 27,400 feet. As a mountaineer he is remembered for his heroic actions in safely bringing down eight Sherpas from Camp VI above 27,000 feet in a whiteout. In 1935 Longland climbed in East Greenland with (amongst others) Lawrence Wager who had been on the 1930 British Arctic Air Route Expedition under their contemporary at Cambridge University, Gino Watkins.

Longland was President of the Cambridge University Mountaineering Club in the 1920s, and was later President of the British Mountaineering Council from 1962 to 1965.

PANEL 11

Dorothy Pilley Richards (1894–1986) was a prominent British female mountaineer. She began climbing in Wales and joined the Fell and Rock Climbing Club. In the 1920s, she climbed extensively in the Alps, Britain and North America. In 1928, she made the celebrated first ascent of the North Ridge of the Dent Blanche with Joseph Georges, Antoine Georges and her husband Ivor Armstrong Richards, which she described in her well-regarded memoir, *Climbing Days* (1935).

Arnold Henry Moore Lunn (1888–1974) was a skier, mountaineer and writer. Lunn founded and was President of the Oxford University Mountaineering Club and Editor of *Oxford Mountaineering Essays*. In 1909, he traversed the Bernese Alps, one of the first major ski-mountaineering journeys on record. Lunn wrote over 60 books; his classic *Mountains of Youth* was written in 1925. Lunn was the founder of the Alpine Ski Club (1908) and the Kandahar Ski Club (1924).

Geoffrey Winthrop Young (1876–1958) was a British climber, poet, educator and author of several notable books on mountaineering. Winthrop Young began rock climbing shortly before his first term at Trinity College, Cambridge, where he studied Classics and won the Chancellor's Medal for English Verse two years running. While there, Winthrop Young wrote a humorous college climbing guide called *The Roof-Climber's Guide to Trinity*, in part a parody of early alpine guidebooks, in part a useful reference work for those, like him, who were keen to clamber up Cambridge's highest spires.

Winthrop Young also put up new routes on the crags of the Lake District and Wales. He was elected President of the Climbers' Club in 1913 and organised the Pen y Pass gatherings that propelled the advancement of rock climbing and included such technical luminaries as J. M. Archer Thompson, George Leigh Mallory, Siegfried Herford, John Percy Farrar and Oscar Eckenstein. These parties, beginning in earnest about 1907 and sometimes reaching 60 men, women and children, overflowed into Eckenstein's miners' cabin and various tents. They came to an end with the First World War in 1914.

During the war, Winthrop Young was, at first, a correspondent for the liberal *Daily News* but, later, as a conscientious objector, was active in the Friends' Ambulance Unit. He received several decorations but, on 31 August, 1917, an explosion caused injuries requiring the amputation of one of his legs. After the amputation, Winthrop Young walked 16 miles in two days to avoid being captured by the Austrians. He continued alpine climbing for a number of years using a specially designed artificial leg that accepted a number of attachments for snow and rock work, eventually climbing the Matterhorn again in 1928.

At the conclusion of the war in 1918, he married Eleanor Slingsby, who herself was one of the founder members of the woman-only Pinnacle Club (also founded at the Pen y Gwryd). Eleanor Winthrop Young helped him return to climbing after his amputation and often accompanied him on expeditions. (Eleanor's fried Emily Kelly was one of the main founders. She was tragically killed on Tryfan. Married to Harry Kelly, another notable mountaineer, the Pinnacle Club Hut in Cwm Dyli is named after her.)

In 1920, Winthrop Young published the 300-page manual of mountaineering instruction entitled *Mountain Craft*, to which Eckenstein and J. Norman Collie also contributed. The Editor of the *Alpine Club Journal*, John Percy Farrar, wrote to Winthrop Young on the book's publication, saying, 'The book is magnificent ... it will be standard for so long as mankind is interested in mountaineering. The profound amount of work put into it staggers me'.

Robert Lock Graham Irving (1877–1969) was an English schoolmaster, writer and mountaineer. As an author, he used the name R. L. G. Irving while, to his friends, he was Graham Irving.

Irving became a member of the Alpine Club in 1902 and was an advocate of climbing without a mountain guide, which in those days was thought by many to be reckless. Much of Irving's fame derives from his being the person who introduced Mallory to mountaineering.

According to Irving's address to the Alpine Club, entitled *Five Years with Recruits*, the Ice Club's series of controversial expeditions to climb some of the highest mountains in the Alps began in 1904, and peaks such as the Grand Combin, Dent Blanche, Aiguille de Blaitière, Bietschhorn, Aiguille de Bionnassay, Gross Grünhorn, Mittaghorn, Aletschhorn, Monte Rosa and Mont Blanc were successfully ascended. Rock climbing trips were also undertaken to Snowdonia, using the Pen y Gwryd Hotel as a base, with snow craft being practised in the Scottish Highlands in winter.

In 1911, Irving led Mallory and another of his ex-pupils, Harry Tyndale, on the third ascent of the Kuffner Arête on Mont Maudit. According to Helmut Dumler, Mallory was 'apparently prompted by the death of friends on the Western Front in 1916 to write a highly emotional article of his ascent of this great climb'.

René Dittert (1911–1983) was a Swiss alpinist. Dittert joined the Himalayan Club in 1949 and, in the same year, he made first ascents of the Sphinx and the North East Summit of Pyramid Peak in Sikkim. In 1947, Dittert had been a member of the Swiss expedition to Garhwal, organised by the Swiss Foundation in Zurich, and first summiteer of Satopanth, Kedarnath and Balba-la, as well as of Nanda Ghunti. He was also a member of the Swiss expedition on Everest in 1952.

Arthur Lockwood (1885–1973) was a British engineer, mountaineer and hotelier. He made the first ascent of Lockwood's Chimney in 1909 on Clogwyn y Bustach, between the Pen y Gwryd and Llyn Gwynant. Who his companions were (if any) and other details are lost, but if he did not solo the climb it is possible that he climbed with unnamed guests from the hotel. (Part of the mythology of Snowdonia is that this climb should be attended naked and by moonlight.) Lockwood was the Commissioning Superintendent at Cwm Dyli Power Station which opened in 1906. In 1919, he resigned from Cwm Dyli and went to Burma, as well as being appointed the supervisor of the building of a hydroelectric plant at Simla, India.

When former Pen y Gwryd owners Harry Owen and his wife Ann passed away in 1891 and 1896 respectively, ownership of the hotel passed through various hands until 1906 when William Hampson took over. The hotel was extended and managed by Florence Bloomfield, who married a guest in 1909, one Arthur Lockwood. Lockwood eventually bought the hotel in 1921 and was responsible for extending it even further, and for the construction of the trout lake opposite (Llyn Lockwood).

Lockwood was a parish councillor in Beddgelert and Chairman of the Conway River Board. His great passion was fishing; his fish hatchery was the only one in that part of Wales. He was appointed Major for his services to the Territorial Army.

Thomas Graham Brown (1882–1965) (usually known as T. Graham Brown) was a Scottish mountaineer and physiologist. Brown served in the Royal Army Medical Corps during the First World War. After the war, he continued his work on the physiology of the nervous system, particularly reflex movements and posture and, in 1920, he accepted the Chair in Physiology at the University of Wales in Cardiff. In 1927, he was elected a Fellow of the Royal Society.

Brown was the Editor of the *Alpine Journal* from 1949 to 1953. In 1935, he made the first ascent of Alaska's Mount Foraker with Charles Houston and Chychele Waterston. In 1936, Brown was part of the joint British–American team that made the first ascent of Nanda Devi in the Indian Himalaya, though only two of the party, Bill Tilman and Noel Odell, made the summit.

Harry Morton Llewellyn (3rd Baronet) (1911–1999) was a British equestrian champion. Llewellyn achieved success as a showjumping champion during the 1930s and competed in the Grand National Steeplechase, coming second in 1936.

After the Second World War, he concentrated on showjumping, buying the horse Foxhunter in 1947. The duo were part of the British team that won a bronze medal in the team event at the 1948 Summer Olympics. They captured the public imagination for their role in winning Great Britain's only gold medal at the 1952 Summer Olympics in the team jumping equestrian event.

Eustace Thomas (1869–1960) was a British climber and inventor who, at the age of 63, was the first Briton to climb all the 4000-metre peaks in the Alps. Thomas was a long-standing member of the Rucksack Club who, together with a team of members, designed the Thomas Stretcher in the 1930s, which was the most widely used mountain rescue stretcher in the UK, until the early 1970s when it was superseded by the Bell Stretcher. In 1924, Thomas was also the first to complete the Scottish 4000-foot peaks in 24 hours (using a car between Fort William and the Cairngorms). To celebrate his 90th birthday, he was flown over the North Pole.

PANEL 12

George Macaulay Trevelyan (1876–1962) was a British historian and academic. He was a Fellow of Trinity College, Cambridge from 1898 to 1903. He then spent more than 20 years as a full-time author. He returned to the University of Cambridge and was Regius Professor of History from 1927 to 1943. He served as Master of Trinity College from 1940 to 1951. In retirement, he was Chancellor of Durham University.

Once called 'The most widely read historian in the world; perhaps in the history of the world', Trevelyan lived through two world wars, seeing his belief in progress shaken. He was noted for being a strenuous cross-country walker.

Douglas 'Doug' Keith Scott is a British mountaineer. Scott's mountaineering career includes over 30 expeditions to inner Asia and he is regarded as one of the world's leading high altitude and big wall climbers. He is best known for his first ascent of the South West Face of Everest with Dougal Haston on an expedition led by Chris Bonington. (Scott and Haston were the first Britons to climb Everest (discounting Mallory and Irving.) All of his other climbs have been in the lightweight alpine style.

Scott has climbed the Seven Summits, the highest peak on each of all seven continents. He is a past President of the Alpine Club. In 1999, he was awarded the Patron's Medal of the Royal Geographical Society. He was presented with the Golden Eagle Award by the Outdoor Writers' and Photographers' Guild in 2005 and received the Lifetime Contribution Award at the 2011 Piolet d'Or awards in Chamonix.

During Scott's climbing career, his understanding of the culture and the people in the regions where he climbed grew as he formed strong bonds and relationships. Scott founded the charity Community Action Nepal and spends much of his time fundraising for this cause, especially from giving public lectures. Scott is also an advocate of Responsible Tourism. Scott set up his own trekking agency in 1989, which is noted for excellent treatment of porters.

Rebecca Stephens is a British journalist, mountaineer and television presenter. She was the first British woman to reach the summit of Everest. Stephens originally trained as a journalist and pursued that career for some ten years, becoming Deputy Editor of the *Financial Times* magazine *Resident Abroad*.

In addition to her mountaineering exploits, Stephens has sailed the Southern Seas to the South Magnetic Pole and Antarctica and crossed the South Atlantic island of South Georgia. With the polar explorers Ranulph Fiennes and Mike Stroud, she competed in an eight-day Eco-

Challenge, which consisted of running, biking and canoeing across the Canadian Rockies.

Dave Potts is a British mountaineer who was a member of the Trango Tower Expedition in 1975. The Trango Towers are a group of rock peaks situated in Gilgit-Baltistan, an autonomous territory in the north of Pakistan. The Towers offer some of the largest cliffs and most challenging rock climbing in the world.

Donald 'Don' Desbrow Whillans (1933–1985) was a British mountaineer and inventor of climbing equipment who climbed with Joe Brown and Chris Bonington on many new routes and was considered the technical equal of both. Whillans was attributed with safety and mountain awareness, as evidenced by his retreat from the Eiger North Face on several occasions because of bad weather or rock fall. He had few climbing accidents although there were several near misses, such as when a fixed rope on the Torre Central del Paine (in Chilean Patagonia) snapped and he managed to put his weight on the holds with split-second timing before retying the rope.

Whillans designed mountaineering equipment, including the 'Whillans Harness' and the 'Whillans Box' expedition tent. Whillans was the subject of a biography titled *The Villain* by the author–climber Jim Perrin in 2005. The British Mountaineering Council maintains a climbing hut near the Roaches in his memory.

Stephen Venables is a British mountaineer and writer and is a past President of the South Georgia Association and of the Alpine Club. In 1988, Venables became the first Briton to ascend the summit of Everest without bottled oxygen. His ascent, as far as the South Col, was by a new route up the Kangshung Face from Tibet, with just three other climbers, Americans Robert Anderson and Ed Webster and Canadian Paul Teare. All four reached the South Col but Teare decided to descend from here, concerned about incipient altitude sickness. The other three continued up the final section of the 1953 route but Anderson and Webster were forced to turn back at the South Summit. Meanwhile, Venables reached the summit alone.

Christian 'Chris' John Storey Bonington is a British mountaineer, writer and photographer. He is one of Britain's best-known mountaineers and explorers. His career has included 19 expeditions to the Himalayas, including four to Everest and the first ascent of the South Face of Annapurna.

Bonington was part of the party that made the first British ascent of the South West (Bonatti) Pillar of the Aiguille du Dru in 1958 and the first ascent of the Central Pillar of Freney on the south side of Mont Blanc in 1961 with Don Whillans, Ian Clough and Jan Długosz. In 1960, he was part of the successful joint British-Indian-Nepalese forces expedition to Annapurna II. Bonington was President of the Council for National Parks for eight years.

Ian McNaught-Davis (1929–2014) was a British television presenter mainly known for presenting the 1980s BBC TV series *The Computer Programme, Making the Most of the Micro* and *Micro Live*. He was also a well-known mountaineer and alpinist.

McNaught-Davis was President of the International Mountaineering and Climbing Federation between the years of 1995 and 2004 and a keen hill walker and hiker. In the 1960s, he was a climbing partner of Joe Brown, both in the UK and in the greater ranges. He took part with Brown in the televised climb of the Old Man of Hoy. He also took part in a climb of the Eiffel Tower, which was televised on the ABC network's Wide World of Sports. McNaught-Davis was also one of the first to climb the 'unclimbable' Muztagh Tower in 1956. He was Honorary Librarian of the Climber' Club in 1961 and a Patron of the British Mountaineering Council.

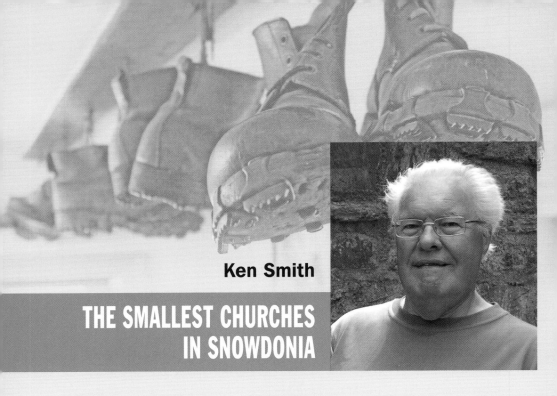

Ken Smith

THE SMALLEST CHURCHES IN SNOWDONIA

O N A PLEASANTLY WARM sunny autumn day in 2007, a group of
some 20 or so persons met in the shadow of the west wall of the
medieval church of St Julitta's, Capel Curig, generally known as 'the
smallest church in Snowdonia'. Though many present were not known
to each other, there were warm pleasantries and smiles exchanged over
glasses of champagne, for all shared a fondness for either St Julitta's,
the Pen y Gwryd Hotel or Peter and Esme Kirby – and in most cases, for
all four.

The gathering's specific purpose was to dedicate a heavy eisteddfod-
type oak chair – handcrafted by Brian Pullee, joint proprietor of the Pen
y Gwryd – to the memory of Peter and Esme. A service was conducted
by Canon Michael Irving, trustee of the Esme Kirby Trust, and the
Reverend Clive Hillman, Vicar of the Parish of Capel Curig and Betws y
Coed, Esme having been the Founder of the Snowdonia Society as well as
lifelong friends of the Briggs family and a singular supporter of the Pen
y Gwryd.

The Friends of St Julitta's Church, a registered charity and a local
history and conservation group, brought together to restore and preserve
the old church, played host. The Esme Kirby Trust and Peter Kirby had

both given considerable financial and practical support to restoration work.

Following the Church in Wales' declaration of St Julitta's redundancy and out of concern for the future of the ancient building, two local residents, Jill Tunstall and Harvey Lloyd, established a support group. St Julitta's was advertised for sale and, following extended negotiations with headquarters of the governing body in Cardiff, The Friends of St Julitta's Church took responsibility for the church and churchyard and, in 1998, entered into a 99-year lease subject to a peppercorn rent.

An architect was employed to report on the state of the Grade II* listed building, the smallest of the vernacular churches of Snowdonia. Little maintenance of the building had taken place since the 1960s. The church had been closed for about 30 years. A plan was drawn up for repairs, commencing with the exterior, to ensure that St Julitta's was kept watertight from the considerable amount of rain that falls on Capel Curig. (Capel Curig has the highest annual rainfall in the British Isles.) New windows and rainwater downpipes were fitted, stone work repointed and the bell cote rebuilt. Attention then moved to the inside of the building. The oak roof timbers were repaired, a new door lintel fitted and, in 2012, the interior plasterwork removed and replaced with lime plaster – work all carried out by our stonemason builder, Will Pierce, from Betws y Coed.

During this time, volunteers were busy too; the derelict bier house was rebuilt and re-roofed to provide a store, and disabled access to the church and churchyard was constructed. Rebuilding and repairing the drystone-built boundary walls provided a serious challenge to our volunteers who needed to learn this new skill. Extensive work was then undertaken within the churchyard, both in repairing individual memorials and establishing a wildlife sanctuary.

Though various small grants have been obtained, the project has largely been financed by voluntary donations, with the Pen y Gwryd having made a significant contribution. Brian and Jane Pullee both encouraged donations and recruited membership to The Friends of St Julitta's from amongst their regular patrons. Two decades on, many of these early members continue to provide support and contribute financially.

Whilst The Friends of St Julitta's Church hold tenancy of St Julitta's, the Gwryd has perhaps gone one better – Brian Pullee designed and built the Pen y Gwryd's own private chapel within the hotel complex itself – a little church that can honestly call itself 'the smallest in Snowdonia' – consecrated in 2000 to commemorate the Millennium. Brian cleverly designed this within the original 19th-century mill for grinding cattle feed and churning butter, later converted into public conveniences. The recycling of a public toilet into a chapel must indeed be a unique conversion. Interestingly, the Pen y Gwryd chapel provided services for the local congregation from Nant Peris church when their church had to close for renovation.

Over the past 15 years, The Friends of St Julitta's Church have organised an annual programme of events for local residents and visitors alike to ensure that it continues to provide an amenity for the local community as it had done for nearly 500 years. The principal event has been a summer exhibition illustrating aspects of local culture, history and the environment. The Friends of St Julitta's Church have two websites, namely www.stjulittas.org and www.ww1insnowdonia. org, and are eager to encourage further interest and participation in this important project – as there is much work yet to be done.

Ken Smith lives in north Staffordshire and enjoyed his early hillwalking in the Peak District. However, on first staying at the Pen y Gwryd and walking the Snowdonia hills, he became enthralled by the landscape and history of Snowdonia. He joined the Friends of St. Julitta's Church in 2000 and now oversees the restoration and maintenance of the ancient building. As the programme of restoration continues, the principal future challenge is to replace the existing concrete paving stone floor with locally-milled slate slabs, more in keeping with the character and importance of this ancient building.

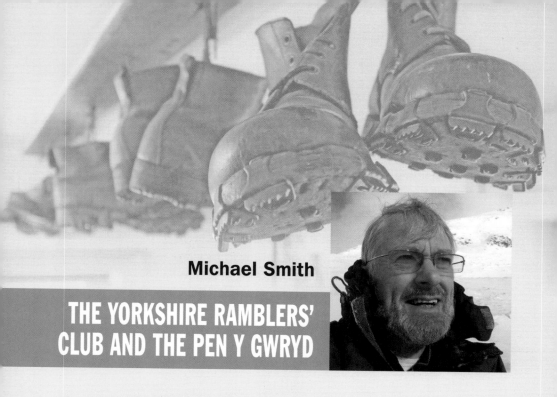

Michael Smith

THE YORKSHIRE RAMBLERS' CLUB AND THE PEN Y GWRYD

IN 1892, the Yorkshire Ramblers' Club was formed, as might be expected, in Yorkshire but was named with tongue firmly in cheek. Nowadays, it still has little to do with pleasant strolls through fields and has members nationwide who are more likely to be found mountaineering or caving.

In the second half of the 20th century, the Yorkshire Ramblers' Club created its own 'special places' in the Lake District and the Yorkshire Dales by building and developing huts: Low Hall Garth and Lowstern. But, from the outset, there were other special places that developed through repeated visits over the decades, places which held memories and featured in those oft-told tales of the club's bonding shared memory.

Founding member H.H. Bellhouse, recalling the early years, noted that besides increasingly visiting Switzerland and Norway on meets, informal groups would go off to 'gatherings at Wasdale, Pen y Gwryd, and elsewhere'. Member and expert mountaineer Frank Payne often visited the Pen y Gwryd in his brief breaks prior to the First World War, after spending his formative years close to the Alps and climbing its most prominent peaks as a youth. (Tragically, he died during the Spanish Influenza epidemic five days after the war ended.)

In the early part of the last century, the reputation of the Pen y Gwryd Hotel as a climbers' mecca had temporarily taken a knock, at least in some quarters. Fred Botterill, he of the eponymous VS climb high on Scafell (Yorkshire Ramblers' Club member 1902-1914), wrote of a 1903 cycle-mountaineering tour of North Wales.

> We had heard a report of the deplumation of Pen y Gwryd Hotel as a climber's resort and decided to seek accommodation elsewhere. We found a very comfortable berth at the house of John Owen, Bron y Graig, in the little village of Glanaber, Nant Gwynant and, failing Pen y Gwryd or Gorphwysfa, would recommend this village as a temporary climbing centre.

Fred and his brother Matthew (Yorkshire Ramblers' Club 1907–1937), late on the afternoon of Saturday 20 June, climbed Lliwedd's Slanting Gully 'with 80 feet of rope, a light English axe, a hand camera and a rucksack containing cooking outfit and eatables'. Fred reported that

> Reaching the little grass ledge where the crack overhangs the cave I put down my impedimenta and mounting on M.'s shoulders tried the crack. It would not go, and after fumbling about for a time my companion politely asked to be allowed to let me down as the extra big nails in my boots were making serious impressions on his shoulders. I then invited him to mount on my shoulders or on my head if he found that necessary, and try and discover a way. He tried bravely for some time but without success, and after a short rest I turned my attention to the slabs on our left.

Moving left on those slabs gave an easier variation, which they likened to Eagle's Nest on Great Gable.

Lieutenant Colonel Wingfield, twice Mayor of Shrewsbury (visiting flood-bound cottages in a coracle), thrice High Sheriff of Shropshire and prominent potholer with the Yorkshire Ramblers' Club prior to the First World War, called in at the Pen y Gwryd on 7 October, 1911. Having earlier in the year skated and skied at Finse, Norway, he explored caves in Symonds Yat, hill-walked around Alston and the Welsh Marches, ballooned over Shrewsbury getting a view of the Berwyns but unfortunately not Snowdon, sailed his 60-ton yacht *Gwynfa* to Ostend, Antwerp and back, then motored 'from Shrewsbury by way of Llangynog, Bala, Festiniog, Beddgelert, Pen y Gwryd, Capel Curig, Bettws y Coed, Corwen, Llangollen and back to Shrewsbury', some 150 miles with 5,600 feet of ascent – quite a feat in those days.

In 1929, the stalwart Pen y Gwryd was again the fallback venue when the Easter Meet 'had to be transferred from Ogwen' and the meet leader '(Lockwood) saw to it that men enjoyed themselves'. While Snowdonia is familiar ground to Yorkshire Ramblers' Club members, in 1922, Ernest Edward (E.E.) Roberts (Yorkshire Ramblers' Club 1908–1960), the then *Journal* Editor and Vice President, admitted that he had never seen the magnificent crags of Clogwyn Du'r Arddu but 'strongly recommends every climber not to miss them. They can be seen on days when Snowdon top is reached from Pen y Gwryd, by descending the Llanberis Path and the return made by Cwm Glas, without adding much to the day'.

On the last day in September 1955, an ageing E.E. Roberts wrote from his home, 12 Southway, Harrogate, to relatively new member Geoff Scovell (Yorkshire Ramblers' Club 1950–1995), a caver, rock climber and alpinist who was his devoted follower. Bemoaning his lumbago-induced lack of mountaineering, Roberts writes:

> I thought Pen y Gwryd would cure me, but the most I managed in a day was five miles in three goes. The Hotel is very good, expensive, and frequented by many motorists, passengers. The road is a maelstrom of motors, driven by cads and hooligans with a few lorries driven by gentlemen.

Perhaps back pain coloured his perceptions as he continued,

> I should think next summer the Llanberis Pass may be a complete deadlock as the parking space is hopelessly insufficient and the crowd will be larger still.

Inactivity must have frustrated Roberts – who had climbed all the standard Alpine peaks with the likes of Frank Smythe and J.H.B. Bell – was proposed for the Alpine Club by Geoffrey Winthrop Young, made many first descents of Yorkshire and some Irish caves, and was the first chairman of the Cave Rescue Organisation.

In the 1960s, member Eddie Edkins was working and climbing in the Llanberis area. He had a couple of anecdotes arising from his time working at the Pen y Gwryd when Chris and Joe Briggs were running the place. Part of a refurbishment involved relaying drains towards the rear of the property. Eddie was working in a yard overlooked by staff quarters, skimming an open manhole surround and taking a break for a smoke and a cuppa from his Thermos. He looked up to notice one of the long-standing female employees looking down at him from a window, with a mischievous grin on her face, who then shot away. Immediately, there was the sound of a flush and along the sewer pipe, past Eddie's feet, slithered one of the largest 'Turkish gunboats' he had ever seen. (The expression is from the antipodes and originates from the Australian and New Zealand experience at Gallipoli in the First World War.)

Yorkshire Ramblers' Club members from Manchester, Harvey Lomas and Glyn Edwards, with others including Audrey Lamb, would pile into the Mini Traveller, drive to Snowdonia and mark the start of their regular 1970s weekend visits by stopping off at the Pen y Gwryd's bar on Friday evening for a pint and pork pie. Later, they would camp and climb, often in the Llanberis Pass, Harvey once returning to find his sleeping bag had been stolen. Saturday, they would progress to Cobdens and Sunday, with the Welsh licensing restrictions, required a return to England. Forty years on, Harvey is still caving and mountaineering. Yorkshire Ramblers don't quit readily.

I have often supped in the hotel's bar myself and deciphered the eminent mountaineers' signatures. I recall stopping there on another occasion for a pint after finishing a particularly wet Welsh 3000s. Despite the place being crowded that June evening in the 1980s, my mud-splattered legs and dripping jacket provided a cleared circle, ensuring my drinking arm remained unjostled. There had to be one advantage to such awful conditions.

The Pen y Gwryd's refreshments came in handy again in February 2013. Two Yorkshire Ramblers' Club members staying at the Pinnacle Club's Cwm Dyli Hut ascended directly up an ice-encrusted Snowdon and descended via Crib Goch, taking great care with their footing. At the eastern end of the ridge, in heavy snowfall, in the absence of tracks and adequate attention, they kept on the ridge north towards Dinas Mot. Realising their error, they made an interesting traverse of Cwm Beudy Mawr and descended in failing light to the upper Llanberis Pass. A kindly motorist gave them a lift to the Pen y Gwryd where a swift half (as they say) refreshed them for the last mile or so down the old road to the hut and an awaiting meal.

The Archivist of the Rucksack Club, Mike Dent, was recently a guest at the Yorkshire Ramblers' Club's 101st Annual Dinner in 2014 (international hostilities put paid to some Yorkshire Ramblers' Club Dinners). When signing the Dinner Guest book, he took the opportunity to look back to the 1901 page and among the guest signatures was Dr Joe Collier's. Collier from Manchester commented on the civil war rivalry of 'Yorks' and 'Lancs' when proposing the toast to the Yorkshire Ramblers' Club, stating that he regretted that no similar club had arisen in Lancashire. This was reported in Club's Journal and, quite by chance, during the next summer in the Pen y Gwryd Hotel two Manchester chaps on a walking tour, Arthur Burns and John Entwistle, happened upon a copy, read this report and, that autumn, they called a meeting of those interested, resulting in the Rucksack Club being formed in October 1902.

The Pen y Gwryd has a long tradition of being the meeting place of mountaineers, the starting place for great days out, and nights in when those great days are transformed into even greater tales. Beyond the rhetoric, plans and friendships are forged – long may it remain so.

Michael Smith is a Harrogate teacher of Physics who 'morphed into a researcher of dental education in Sheffield'. This past-president of the Yorkshire Ramblers' Club, board member of the Slingsby Trust and member of the Alpine Club is equally at home caving in the Dales, mountaineering in the greater ranges, squelching through Peak District bogs, trekking and climbing in Africa, investigating archaeological sites in Peru or pulking over Arctic ice caps. He prefers less-visited mountain areas and, through careful selection of both these and competent partners, has forged a number of first ascents and new routes in the Bolivian Apolobamba, Cocapata and Greenland's Liverpool Land.

Material cited from Yorkshire Ramblers' Club Journals was reproduced with permission.

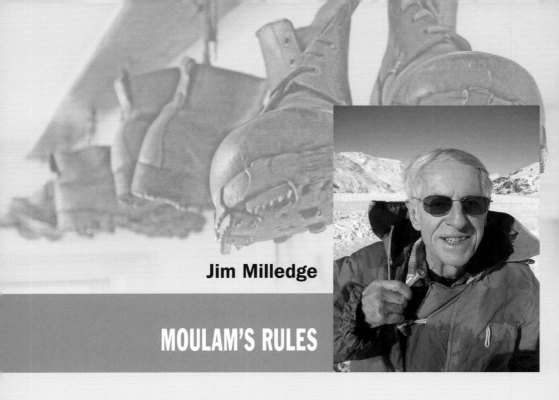

Jim Milledge

MOULAM'S RULES

IN 1953 I was in my fifth year of medical school at Birmingham University and had been well and truly bitten with the mountaineering bug. I got up to Snowdonia as often as I could, to walk and climb. I had attempted the 'Welsh 3000s' on a couple of occasions but had been defeated.

At the end of the summer vacation, I spent three weeks acting as a handyman at the Pen y Gwryd. My hours were 9am to 6pm Monday to Friday with Saturdays and Sundays off and my pay was 50 shillings plus 'all found'. The food was wonderful hotel fare prepared by Jo Briggs herself and two very attractive hotel trainees. On one weekend, the Saturday was wet and I went for a hill walk with a friend, John Neill, a well-known Climbers' Club member and Editor of the Club's Journal.

In the evening, we got to discussing our next day's walk. I had long wanted to scale the 14 Welsh peaks over 3,000 feet, but to Moulam's rules. (Tony Moulam was a well-known climber of that era). These stated that you had to do the walk by including all of these peaks and that you started and finished at the same place. The usual way to do this walk was to have someone take you to the start and pick you up at the other end. Often people would have friends to bring them food and drink at the points where the route crossed roads in the valleys. I suggested that we have a go the next day. Chris Briggs and everyone in the hotel derided our presumption. It was still pouring with rain outside but that, and the Worthington 'E', only made us more determined. Jo Briggs said there was no question of any support for our crackpot idea; they were fed up with helping various walkers who had then given up. Indeed, Chris was prepared to wager the PyG against our doing it! I took him on and put up Ynys Ettws [1] as my wager.

John and I retired to the bunk house behind the hotel and set our alarm clock. At 3am it went off. I woke up, stopped it and listened. The rain was pattering on the roof of the bunk house. John seemed to be still asleep. It looked hopeless and I thought if I just went to sleep again we could say we had overslept and not lose face. But then I thought I had better give John a chance to agree and, so, woke him up. 'All right', he said, 'Let's go'. Our first problem was that we found we had left our walking clothes and boots in the hotel drying room so had to burgle our way in to retrieve them. At least they were dry; but before we had reached Pen y Pass, short of a mile up the road, we were wet through.

I was grateful to have John lead up the Pyg Track and from there to the Col, Bwlch y Moch. There we left the track for the broad ridge up to Crib Goch and it began to get a little less dark. By the time we reached the first of 14 summits, the rain had stopped but we were only just below the heavy mist. Along the knife-sharp ridge we went carefully on the wet rocks to Crib y Ddysgl and on quickly to the Snowdon summit. There we encountered a huddle of miserable walkers who had come up to see the sunrise! (The only view was the inside of a wet cloud.) As we strode down the broad path towards Llanberis we came below the cloud. At Clogwyn station, we dived over the edge to the right, steeply down with no path into Cwm Glas Bach and made our own route down to the road in the Llanberis valley.

---

[1] Located in the heart of the Llanberis Pass and surrounded on all sides by mountains, Ynys Ettws is probably the best-situated hut in Britain. It is within easy walking distance of all the major climbing areas of the Pass, and is found west of the Cromlech Boulders, and accessed by the bridge beside the road. There is a large carved stone at the entrance with 'Climbers' Club' carved on it.

Now, it was down the road, past Beudy Mawr, a climbing hut belonging to the Wayfarers Club. We were short of food and hoped we might beg a cup of tea and perhaps a snack but no one was in residence. So we ate our only sandwiches there on the door step in our wet clothes. As we went up the long pull up to Elidir Fawr, the first of the next range of peaks, the weather improved and, beyond its long summit ridge, the sun came out.

Our spirits rose as we hurried along over Foel Goch and Y Garn to the Glyderau, both Fawr and Fach. Down beside the Bristly Ridge, we pushed on to Bwlch Tryfan and up the rocky ridge to Tryfan summit. It was now 1pm, the sun was out and I felt great. John had been very good to come with me because he knew he could not complete the walk as he had to be back at the Gwryd to get his lift back to London at 5pm. So we said goodbye, he went south whilst I ran down north towards Llyn Ogwen, which I reached in about 15 minutes.

Halfway up the long pull up to Pen yr Ole Wen, I assessed my provisions. I had part of a Cadbury's milk chocolate bar with centimetre blocks. I calculated that I could have one small block on alternate summits. But the sun was out and I felt strong, so on over Pen Yr Ole Wen to Carnedd Dafydd, a detour to take in Yr Elen, back up to Carnedd Llewelyn. There my luck changed and I met a couple of Liverpool men out for the day. Each of their wives had given them food for both and they generously shared it with me. I remember devouring a Penguin bar and it never tasted so good.

With Snowdon, the Glyderau and four of the six summits of the Carneddau under my belt, I completed the last two summits, Foel Grach and Foel Fras by 5pm. Then back past Llewelyn and Craig Yr Ysfa to the A5 road, as it was getting dark. The final seven miles along the road to Capel Curig and up to Pen y Gwryd were a slog but, knowing I had done it against the odds and that I had won the wager, kept my spirits up. I arrived to a hero's welcome and a fry-up supper just before 10pm, secure in the knowledge that I was now the titular owner of the Gwryd.

Jim Milledge started hill walking as a boy in North Wales in the 1940s and rock climbing in the 1950s as a student. He has been involved in High Altitude Medicine and Physiology since 1960 when he was a member of the 'Silver Hut' scientific and mountaineering expedition. With other scientists, he spent nine months in the Everest region carrying out research on the physiology of acclimatisation, mainly in the Silver Hut at 5,800 metres. Since then, he has been on numerous expeditions to many of the great ranges. These include science expeditions to Kongur (1981), Everest (1981), Mount Kenya (1987), Bolivia (1989), Kangchenjunga (1998), Chamlang (2003), Everest BC (2007), Monte Rosa (2010), as well as field studies in Wales, the Lake District and Switzerland (1977–84).

His career has been as a General and Respiratory Physician. After house jobs, he had three years in the Royal Air Force as a medical officer, mostly in Hong Kong. There followed three years in Southampton in general medicine and training in respiratory medicine. After the Silver Hut Expedition, he joined the staff of Christian Medical College at Vellore in South India where he worked from 1962–72, with a year as research fellow in San Francisco in the middle. On return from India, he was appointed to the staff of Northwick Park Hospital, Harrow, as consultant in Chest Medicine and as a Scientific Member, MRC.

Milledge retired from the MRC and NHS in 1995 and now is able to devote most of his time to Mountain Medicine, writing, lecturing and some researching. His published work is mainly in this field and he has written, with others, the standard textbook on this subject now in its 5th edition (West, Schoene, Luks and Milledge 2013). He was appointed Hon. Professor at UCL in 2006.

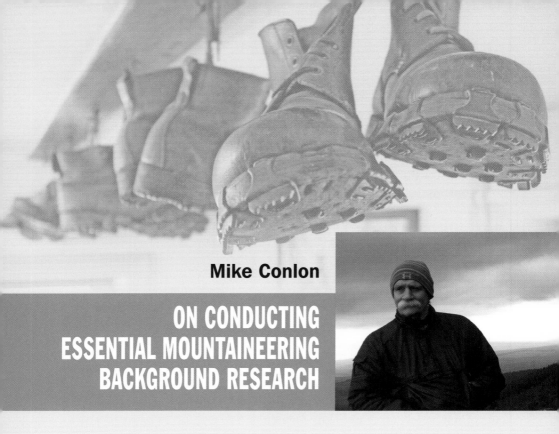

Mike Conlon

ON CONDUCTING ESSENTIAL MOUNTAINEERING BACKGROUND RESEARCH

M<small>Y MODEST INTRODUCTION</small> to the Pen y Gwryd was in the summer of 1984. I was an assistant housemaster at a Benedictine school and had organised the Scout summer camp. We were based on the shore of Llyn Gwynant and ten days of uncharacteristically fine weather contributed to a wonderful stay. In appreciation of my efforts, I was treated to supper at the Gwryd by one of the mountaineering monks. We had, that day, completed the Snowdon Horseshoe and, so, had a healthy thirst and appetite. Whether it was my host's climbing reputation or monastic credentials, I know that we received wonderful hospitality and, like many before and after me, the place left a lasting impression.

It was not until 1998 that I next encountered the Pen y Gwryd Hotel. I had booked a course down the road at Plas y Brenin and was determined to give it my full attention. As it turned out, quite out of the blue, some old friends from 'across the pond' announced they would be visiting Europe and a reunion was a vital part of their itinerary.

These friends were American north-west backwoods folk and great horse people. By coincidence, they had arranged to ride the Ring of

Kerry just prior to my course and a ferry from Dublin to Holyhead was an acceptable means of returning to the UK mainland. Plas y Brenin was, as always, accommodating and allowed me to book a couple of fine guest rooms for my visitors. We met in the bar and, being a beautiful evening, set off for a drive down Ogwen and back up the Pass. Knowing my American friends' thirst for history, I felt that rounding off our tour at the Pen y Gwryd would be a fitting conclusion to our day in the mountains.

Unfortunately, we were too late to eat but we were made very welcome in the public bar all the same. We had lots to catch up on but patriarch Barry was more interested in his surroundings. I did my best to retell what I had learned years before and subsequently read. The lady of the house heard my inadequate effort and, sensing Barry's enthusiasm, removed her apron and took charge. Needless to say my friends received the grand tour, culminating inevitably in the Everest Room where they spent the next two hours being regaled by the redoubtable Mrs Pullee. She concluded by explaining that she was busy organising the 45th Anniversary Dinner for the 1953 team – but was never too busy 'for our American friends'. She pointed to the signatures on the ceiling and did a roll call of the 1953 Everesters, explaining who would and who would not be attending. I seem to remember she hoped for at least one Sherpa representative. She was saddened that it would probably be the last of the dinners due to the dwindling number of surviving members. As a unique memento, Barry was given a copy of the menu to take away with him. It was an unexpectedly special visit.

We returned to Plas y Brenin and down to the bar for a nightcap. Although we found time to reminisce, Barry remained overwhelmed by such privileged insights into the history of the PyG. As the others retired to bed, the young lady behind the bar bade us goodnight and said, 'Would you be good enough to switch off the lights when finished'. A duty-free bottle of Bourbon, of course, appeared and, with the place to ourselves, we talked into the early hours.

I was a little worse for wear the next morning and some minutes late to the Orienteering Room for our course briefing. As I was making my apologies to the two hairy mountaineer types whom I assumed were leading the course, a charming young woman introduced herself as Louise the course leader and explained that I would be spending the next two days with her! What was more, as the two bearded tyros had obviously partnered up, would I mind climbing with the equally amiable Sarah from behind last night's bar. Conscious of American whiskey fumes, I shot down to Capel Curig for some mints. As I was paying for them, my attention was drawn to a climbing magazine in the periodical stand. To my amazement, the cover featured the photogenic Louise who the magazine announced had just completed a first ascent in some magnificent mountain location.

Reconvening with our climbing kit, I explained to the then Louise Thomas that my sorry state was due to conducting 'mountaineering background research' at the Pen y Gwryd the night before. With a knowing smile, she accepted my explanation and, with great grace, went on to provide the best of climbing experiences – finishing our course on Creigiau Llynnau Mymbyr in sight of the legendary establishment itself.

Post Script

I organised a club meet in Snowdonia last year. A pal and I made up an advance party to open up the hut. The weather was typically lousy so we abandoned the severes of Dinas Cromlech and retired to the PyG. As tradition dictated, we had a couple of pints to sustain us for 'Plan B', which was of course Lockwood's Chimney. Someone in the bar offered to accompany us, but still with considerable reluctance we vacated the fire and headed down the road. Our 'guide' took one look at the approaching weather, excused himself but reassured us that it was the best possible conditions for Lockwood's and saw us on our way. I misread the guide book and we jibbered our way up some frightening route on the face in big boots.

We returned to the PyG to dry out, where our expert was back enthroned in front of the fire. He explained our error and we returned the following day. At least we found the chimney on this occasion but only managed to enter it by aiding up some very steep and wet rock away from the V Diff approach. Our group arrived for the weekend and being again rained off on the Sunday we returned with a party for round three and completed it in more text-book manner. I am organising another meet this year and despite our three recent experiences with it, Lockwood's (and the PyG of course) are top of our wish list.

Mike Conlon is an enthusiastic rather than accomplished rock climber and mountaineer. Through Scouting and his professional career, he has had the privilege of introducing many young people to Britain's crags and mountains. After years of playing rugby, Conlon now pursues his outdoor interests with The Cleveland Mountaineering Club. He particularly values the companionship of the hills and the old and new friendships that provides. His nearest claim to fame is having had Joe Tasker as his Patrol Leader in the Scouts and, some years later, Tasker took him up Overhanging Bastion on his first ever day of climbing; according to Conlon, 'It all went pretty downhill from then'.
www.clevelandmc.com

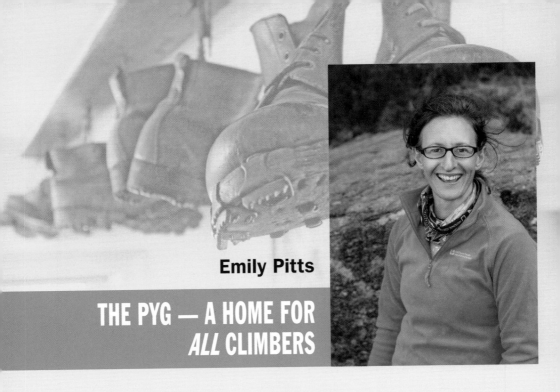

Emily Pitts

THE PYG — A HOME FOR *ALL* CLIMBERS

THE PEN Y GWRYD is the embodiment of climbing: weathered, embedded in its landscape, friendly, nuanced, stimulating and traditional, somewhat like an old friend whom one sees every so often but who extends an encompassing welcome, signifying the comradeship known to few outside the climbing and walking tribes.

The walls of Pen y Gwryd are an ode to a time that is passing from us. It is a place filled with the memories of an era of seemingly exclusive male achievement characterised by the hotel's historic artefacts, set as they are in aspic, like an old curiosity shop; a reminder of another time and another world. Mountaineering has always looked like a man's game, on the face of it at least, but if you scratch the surface you will discover pioneering women who have dissolved gender boundaries by challenging the assumed *status quo* in the most unassuming of ways.

The progress made by women has largely developed subversively, and mountaineering is no exception. While the men of climbing history have generated and perpetuated an exclusive aura about themselves, women have worked at their art inclusively, in conjunction with their complex roles as mothers, wives and workers. Seen in this light, it comes as no surprise that the UK climbers who are at the top of their game today, the ones best known in competition circles for pushing the boundaries, are mostly women. Their forebears, Lucy Walker, Nea Morin, Gwen Moffat, Emily Kelly, Una Cameron, Alison Hargreaves, Barbara James, Mabel Barker, Jill Lawrence, Angela Soper, and countless more, quietly broke new ground in the shadow of the celebrated achievements of men, laying the foundations for today's women to shine, including Shauna Coxsey, Lucy Creamer, Natalie Berry, Michaela Tracy, Leah Crane, Mina Leslie-Wujastyk, Emma Twyford, Hazel Findlay, Katy Whittaker, to name just a sprinkling of our most revered, powerful and accomplished climbers.

In December 1897, the idea of a 'Climbers' Club' was proposed at a dinner at the PyG (the club was actually formed in London at the Monico Restaurant in 1898.) Then, the PyG, with its already esteemed history, saw the inauguration of the women-only Pinnacle Club in March 1921, thereby truly laying the foundations for the hotel's place in climbing history as the inclusive home of British mountaineering. Now, as a new golden age of British climbing begins to flourish, women are at the forefront, taking the lead and inspiring *everyone* to be bold, to aspire, to climb and also to harness the power of the internet, using tweets, posts, blogs, vlogs and apps, the ephemera of the 21st-century climber, to connect with and share the wonders of our world.

PyG's historical position is firmly cemented, but its aspic-set walls are not the end of the story. Like the very best of homes, the PyG and its many dedicated staff have adapted to a changing society, meeting the needs and desires of the diverse and exciting generations of climbers, walkers and other outdoor enthusiasts who have passed over the hotel's threshold since it was established in 1810. Today's PyG is evidence of the enduring power of the mountains, a living and breathing monument, waiting with bated breath for the next chapter of its history.

Emily Pitts is the Founder of Womenclimb UK. Emily saw that there was not enough for and about women in the sport of climbing and decided to do something about it. She is the Chief Editor of this web portal, leading a small team of skilled volunteers to provide information, to share skills and opportunities that inspire women, and to help them define and achieve their goals in climbing, bouldering and mountaineering. For a living, Pitts does a mix-and-match of art, arts education, climbing instruction, gardening, social media training and working with disadvantaged young people. She absolutely adores climbing and being a part of the community of climbers.

www.womenclimb.co.uk

About the Compilers and Editors

Rob Goodfellow (PhD) is a writer, historian, educator and cross-cultural risk management specialist. He is the author, co-author or editor of a number of books on Australia, Indonesia and China, as well as in the broad field of comparative cultural studies. He worked at the bar of the Pen y Gwryd in 1979.

www.culturalconsulting.com.au

Jonathan Copeland (LLB) was a solicitor in the City of London for a quarter of a century and is now a writer and photographer. He has written books on Bali, Bangkok and Rye, East Sussex. When not writing or photographing, he helps his Balinese partner Murni in her hotel in Ubud, Bali.

www.murnis.com

Peter O'Neill OAM (BA Fine Arts) is an arts administrator, writer and educator with over 40 years' experience in the development and management of art museums and representative organisations within the cultural sector. Although not a climber himself, he lives in the Blue Mountains of New South Wales, a World Heritage Site that attracts climbers from all over the world.